WESTFIELD PUBLIC LIBRARY
333 West Hoover Street
Westfield, IN 46074

D1125076

Discarded by
Westfield Washington
Public Library

FINDING YOUR STRONG SUIT

FINDING YOUR STRONG SUIT

HOW TO READ YOUR SPOUSE, BOSS, PARTNER, LOVER,
OPPONENT, & YOURSELF

MIKE WAS, ALLAN COMBS, PH.D., &
JULIE COMBS

RENAISSANCE BOOKS
Los Angeles

WESTFIELD PUBLIC LIBRARY
333 West Hoover Street
Westfield, IN 46074

Copyright © 1999 by Mike Was, Allan Combs, and Julie Combs

All rights reserved. Reproduction without permission in writing from the publisher is prohibited, except for brief passages in connection with a review. For permission, write: Renaissance Books, 5858 Wilshire Boulevard, Suite 200, Los Angeles, California 90036.

Library of Congress Cataloging-in-Publication Data
Was, Mike.
    Finding your strong suit / Mike Was, Allan Combs, and Julie Combs.
        p. cm.
    Includes bibliographical references and index.
    ISBN 1-58063-067-7 (trade pbk. : alk. paper)
        1. Typology (Psychology) 2. Interpersonal relations. 3. Interpersonal
communication. I. Combs, Allan. II. Combs, Julie. III. Title.
    BF698.3.W38   1999
    155.2'64—dc21   99-15914
                                                                CIP

10 9 8 7 6 5 4 3 2 1

Design by Jesus Arellano and Lisa-Theresa Lenthall
Illustrations by Mary Ross

Published by Renaissance Books
Distributed by St. Martin's Press
Manufactured in the United States of America
First Edition

ACKNOWLEDGMENTS

Some relationships are beacons. In these rare instances, another person casts a beam for finding a meaningful part of yourself. Thereafter, your own light is a reflection of these source beacons who aided your growth. My spirited friends Joel Reaser, J. R. Davison, Carolyn and Wilson Taylor, Leslie Sizeland, Sarah Richter, Liz Smith, and Judith Herseth offered their encouragement at just the right times in my journey. So, too, did my cousin Suzi Kallam, my sister Martha Was (who tested this book's ideas in the workplace), my brother Jeff Was (who provided computer tools), and my mom Ruth Was Nicolaysen (who stabilized me, yet supported my quest). Margaret Was gave me thirty years of lessons in free independence, which eventually made complete sense, and for which I am grateful. Our children, Beth and Ben, are now beacons in their own right, and have given me wonderful friendship and unending joy. Synchronicity led me to Allan and Julie Combs, who became superb collaborators and dear friends. Once this book was under way, our agent John White and executive editor Richard O'Connor believed in the project and made it real. And editor Laura Golden Bellotti skillfully added clarity and richness to our work. To all of these people, thanks from my heart.

—*Mike Was*

To our families of origin, Thelma, Les, Rose, Suzanne, Walter, Lynne, John, and Susan, and our daughters Mollie and Monica. We continue to delight in our differences.

—*Allan and Julie Combs*

CONTENTS

UNDERSTANDING THE FOUR PERSONAL STYLES

CHAPTER ONE

DEALING WITH PEOPLE'S DIFFERENCES

Affirming Your Own Style

Why are some people so difficult? Perhaps you are experiencing discord with someone in your family—your spouse, for instance. Or maybe your ideas clash with someone at work. While your own methods suit you, certain people in your life always seem to want things done differently. Almost every discussion leads to a disagreement. Each of you wishes the other would change. Why do we differ with certain types of people? Or take issue with those we love? This book will help answer these questions, and show you ways to reduce conflict so that your relationships will become more agreeable and rewarding.

In the course of this book, you'll develop a keen understanding of how differences in individual styles can result in marital quarrels, antagonism between family members, friction between coworkers, or problems between a boss and a subordinate. On a larger scale, you'll realize how these differences develop into political rivalries and cultural divisions, such as the way that half the people always seem to oppose the other half. All of these forms of disharmony arise from natural variations in the ways that people think.

How does this book differ from others about conflict resolution? Many theories for describing people's temperaments are so academic that it's hard to apply them to your own difficult relationships. For example, you may have taken one of the many personality tests available today, such as the respected Myers-Briggs Type Indicator which is widely used in psychological counseling and business applications. While such comprehensive systems can give you an understanding of yourself, often it takes a trained professional to grasp how such differences in temperament affect relationships. Our system creates four easy-to-spot contrasts in thinking styles, so you'll be able to quickly recognize the differences between yourself and others, and have tools to resolve and avoid the problems that arise as a consequence.

You will learn the four ways people's styles differ. And using this information, you will discover specific skills to improve your relationships with others. Armed with the new awareness of your differences, you will experience a sense of relief. You'll find yourself saying, "That explains what we've been arguing about all this time! Now I understand where he's coming from. I know now why I'm so frustrated and what I can do about it."

All of us experience the unpleasantness of confrontation. An innocent comment ignites a hot argument and suddenly the other person becomes your opponent. You verbally spar like boxers coming at each other from opposing corners. The fight can be about anything from world politics to how to load the dishwasher. No matter what the subject, the debate defines who you are and what you stand for.

For instance, consider two hypothetical married partners, George and Hope, whose arguments often fit the following pattern. One day while they are relaxing together, Hope proposes that they trade in their second car and buy a new one. "I'm tired of driving that old clunker every day," she says. "It's no fun. I want a sportier car, so I feel more alive."

George falls into his regular response: "You know we planned to save for retirement. Buying a new car now wouldn't be responsible. We should stick to our plans."

"You made those plans, George, not me. Life is too short. We could die next week. Then what would be the use of your saving?" Hope pauses, then continues with new resolve. "You know, you really are dense. Can't you see that I'm dying inside? I mean, part of me dies every time I get into that ancient Chevy of yours. And you can't see it!"

"Give it a rest, Hope. There's nothing wrong with the Chevy. It's dependable transportation."

"Then you drive it, George. I want a sportier car. A convertible."

"You'd trade in our reliable Chevy, on some frivolous whim, for a convertible?"

"Yes, George, I need a change. I'm trading in the Chevy, or you. Which is it?"

Hope and George repeat this argument about other shared decisions, large and small. Hope tends to be the impulsive, free-spirited partner who pushes for change. George takes the role of the responsible partner who resists taking risks, and protects their financial security. The purchase of a car is just one of many continually emerging topics that rekindle an ongoing debate about George's prepared, conservative style and Hope's more lighthearted, capricious nature. Depending on your own style you may be inclined to side with one or the other. But objectively, both stances are appropriate at various times. Certainly, both George and Hope believe their own position is the right one. And it is very likely that they chose each other because they admired the qualities the other brought to their romance. Now, however, for this couple's long-term success, they must learn to strike a balance between playing it safe and spending with a sense of freedom. Later in this book we will share with you the steps that George and Hope might take to break their deadlock.

Before you attribute the opposition between George and Hope to basic differences between men and women, consider that the table could easily have been turned, with Hope having the more conservative style and George displaying the capricious nature. He could be the one perennially promoting sporty new cars, with her cautioning, "How can we afford it?" On this and many other grounds for division, gender knows no specific turf. Both men and women are equally as likely to display either of these two styles. The popular belief that "men are like this, and women are like that" is frankly too simplistic.

Our system of personality styles differs from advice books based on two-type gender differences, which presume men operate one way and women another. If that oversimplification were valid, all political battles would reveal this opposition between the sexes. But they do not, for both sexes hold a wide range of views across the political spectrum. The same is true of attitudes and behaviors within a relationship. Many people possess traits and behaviors that are different from, or even counter to, conventional stereotypes that society holds for each sex. For example, some women are tough, hard-driving business executives, while some men are the caring, sensitive nurturers of their families. Couples exhibiting such non-stereotypical styles are confounded by the conventional and limiting two-type remedies. For a theory of people's differences to be truly useful in strengthening relationships, it needs to encompass more than two opposite categories—men versus women. Not all men think alike, nor do all women.

By broadening your understanding of individual differences, you will be able to relax into your own true nature and accept others as well. With the knowledge of your own personal style and those of others, you will gain a new means for appreciating how and why people differ, and acquire skills for solving and avoiding problems in your relationships.

This book explains people's personality styles by using the symbols in a deck of cards—hearts, diamonds, clubs, and spades—as an easy-to-understand system that also reveals the fundamental framework of discord. You'll learn how other people's personal styles are reflected in the particular words they choose, and that when their language contrasts with your own, disputes usually arise. You'll see how opposition is hardwired into our language and thought. You will also learn how to reduce your level of stress and defuse conflicts when people challenge your views and values. By the end of this book, you will feel a much deeper understanding of people whose styles are different and, implies others' are even better, you will have improved your ability to communicate with them. Above all, you will understand your own style as being right for you so that you won't feel pressured to conform to stereotypes or to other people's expectations of the way you must think or behave.

In the following pages special attention is given to many kinds of conflicts—those involving couples, families, and work groups. You'll find practical solutions for dealing with a spouse, in-law, or boss whose style may be very different from your own. But before getting down to specific applications, you will learn about you. You will come to an understanding of your own role in the game plan of human opposition, and along the way develop a vocabulary with which to talk about it. Then you will read about techniques to make life with diversity easier.

To embark on this new understanding, take a few minutes to complete the brief self-test that will identify your thinking style in terms of this new four-way scheme of things. Simply answer the following twenty questions, score your own answers, and keep the results handy as you proceed. The instructions for scoring the self-test and completing your own Personal Style Profile are provided in appendix 1. Those results will take on their full meaning as you progress through the book. Don't worry about right or wrong answers. This is not that sort of test. All answers are valid, depending on your own point of view.

Don't put off taking the test. Answer the test questions now and record your responses before reading additional chapters. That way your answers will be spontaneous and intuitive, without biases you may acquire as you read on. You will find the answer form on the next page, followed by the directions for the self-test, and then the twenty test questions.

As you learn more about your personal style and find out how to better define and validate your own values, your understanding will help you resolve conflicts and deal successfully with others. Now take the test and discover your own strong suit!

Discovering Your Personal Style

Answer Form for the Self-Test

PART 1	PART 2
1. *a.* ____ *b.* ____ *c.* ____ *d.* ____	11. *a.* ____ *b.* ____ *c.* ____ *d.* ____
2. *a.* ____ *b.* ____ *c.* ____ *d.* ____	12. *a.* ____ *b.* ____ *c.* ____ *d.* ____
3. *a.* ____ *b.* ____ *c.* ____ *d.* ____	13. *a.* ____ *b.* ____ *c.* ____ *d.* ____
4. *a.* ____ *b.* ____ *c.* ____ *d.* ____	14. *a.* ____ *b.* ____ *c.* ____ *d.* ____
5. *a.* ____ *b.* ____ *c.* ____ *d.* ____	15. *a.* ____ *b.* ____ *c.* ____ *d.* ____
6. *a.* ____ *b.* ____ *c.* ____ *d.* ____	16. *a.* ____ *b.* ____ *c.* ____ *d.* ____
7. *a.* ____ *b.* ____ *c.* ____ *d.* ____	17. *a.* ____ *b.* ____ *c.* ____ *d.* ____
8. *a.* ____ *b.* ____ *c.* ____ *d.* ____	18. *a.* ____ *b.* ____ *c.* ____ *d.* ____
9. *a.* ____ *b.* ____ *c.* ____ *d.* ____	19. *a.* ____ *b.* ____ *c.* ____ *d.* ____
10. *a.* ____ *b.* ____ *c.* ____ *d.* ____	20. *a.* ____ *b.* ____ *c.* ____ *d.* ____

After answering all twenty questions, turn to appendix 1 for scoring your results.

DIRECTIONS FOR THE SELF-TEST

The test has two parts: ten questions on your typical reactions to a variety of situations, and ten questions on the words that best characterize your perception of yourself. Each question has four replies *(a, b, c, d)* and all are equally valid. Put your rating of each reply on the separate answer form or a sheet of paper. Rate all four replies to the questions by this ranking method:

- 2 points for the reply that is most like the way you feel about the question.

- 1 point for any reply that somewhat applies to your feelings.

- 0 for any reply that is unlike your feelings on the question.

On some questions you may record several 1s. On others you might have several 0s. But for every question, try to determine the trait that is most like you and assign it a 2. As an example:

When I was young, my favorite hobby was to:

a. draw or paint.

b. take things apart and try to fix them.

c. collect things and exhibit them in order.

d. sing or play music.

If *(d)* is most like you, *(a)* and *(c)* somewhat apply, and *(b)* is unlike you, you'd respond:

a. __1__ *b.* __0__ *c.* __1__ *d.* __2__

Relax and be yourself. Give the highest values to your personal thoughts and feelings. This is a self-profile, not an intelligence test. It simply helps you describe your strengths and your natural way of being.

Discovering Your Personal Style
The Self-Test—Part 1

1. I have a good day when I
   a. have meaningful times with friends.
   b. go through my ordinary daily routine.
   c. solve a challenging problem.
   d. do just whatever the spirit moves me to do.

2. I believe most in
   a. freedom of expression.
   b. sound traditional values.
   c. working together for the common good.
   d. individual rights.

3. In my opinion, young people should be
   a. showered with love.
   b. refined into independent, self-sufficient adults.
   c. given the freedom to develop.
   d. taught to be civilized and responsible.

4. I am most likely to be drawn to ideas that are
   a. tried-and-true.
   b. offer potential for change.
   c. popular and satisfy people.
   d. the most logical reasoning.

5. If I were president of this country, I'd probably be a
   a. bold and self-confident decision-maker.
   b. visionary for the future.
   c. peaceful advocate for the common good.
   d. sound-minded defender of time-honored values.

6. I most readily make friends with others who are
   a. caring and supportive.
   b. rational and in the know.
   c. industrious and dependable.
   d. inspiring and perhaps even a bit over the edge.

7. If we were working on a community event, you'd find me
   a. enterprising and laying out clear goals.
   b. careful in following through the organizational details.
   c. easygoing and able to work with others.
   d. eagerly generating innovative concepts.

8. I sometimes cause problems for myself and others by being too
   a. headstrong.
   b. conventional.
   c. permissive.
   d. sentimental.

9. I am most capable at
   a. strategizing and enforcing decisions.
   b. representing the needs of other people.
   c. developing intuitive, creative ideas.
   d. working through the details of a matter.

10. I do best with others who
    a. respect my independence.
    b. I can rely on to be honest and trustworthy.
    c. appreciate and support me.
    d. let me try out new ideas, even if I fail.

Discovering Your Personal Style
The Self-Test—Part 2

For this portion of the test, rate each word as it applies to you. Use the same rating scale as you used for the first part (see page 17). Continue marking your answers on the same form.

11. *a.* harmonious
    b. logical
    c. regular
    d. imaginative

12. *a.* warmhearted
    b. open-minded
    c. cool-headed
    d. orderly-minded

13. *a.* sensible
    b. trusting
    c. candid
    d. objective

14. *a.* dreamer
    b. chief
    c. judge
    d. peacemaker

WESTFIELD PUBLIC LIBRARY
333 West Hoover Street
Westfield, IN 46074

15. *a.* reason
    b. principle
    c. feeling
    d. intuition

16. *a.* picture
    b. account
    c. story
    d. essentials

17. *a.* conscientious
    b. original
    c. amiable
    d. analytical

18. *a.* sympathetic
    b. proper
    c. impulsive
    d. impatient

19. *a.* tough cookie
    b. solid citizen
    c. kind soul
    d. free spirit

20. *a.* organized
    b. creative
    c. decisive
    d. personal

That's the end of the self-test. Take time out here to score the results, using the guide in appendix 1 to form your own personal style profile. Then, as you read on, refer to your profile to identify your own traits among the characteristics of the four basic personal styles that are introduced in the next chapter.

CHAPTER TWO

YOUR PERSONAL STYLE

How the Card Suits Symbolize People's Differences

If you haven't done so already, take the self-test before you read on. If you've completed the self-test and Personal Style Profile, you probably are eager to discover what the results say about you. And if you coaxed someone else into taking the test, then you may be longing to read what all this means to your relationship. You will soon find out how to interpret your test scores, but let's begin with the big picture of how the four styles of thinking fit together into a marvelously interactive system.

To give you some faces for recognizing the four styles, imagine that you have tuned in to watch Oprah Winfrey's blockbuster show of the decade, featuring seven famous guests. But instead of talking as usual, Oprah and the celebrities are playing cards! They've just begun a Great Styles Poker Game, surrounded by TV cameras. The players are laughing and telling jokes while seated at two round tables—one with Oprah and three other women, and a second table with four men. (We're giving you examples of one man and one woman for each personality type—gender doesn't matter in the Strong Suit system.)

The show first highlights the women's game between Oprah, Martha Stewart, Madonna, and Attorney General Janet Reno. Oprah is the first to deal and calls a simple five-card draw, nothing wild. The cameras zoom in on all the players' hands with multiple-screen images. Naturally most attention is focused on the show's star. Let's follow Oprah's hand as she finishes the initial deal: three high hearts, a low club, and a high diamond. Discarding the club and diamond in the next round, Oprah finds she has dealt herself two more hearts! Ace, king, queen, jack, and ten of hearts! A royal flush of hearts in the very first game! She continues dealing then bets the bank. The strange thing is that the others are doing the same. All four are betting with the same passion. Oprah goes to the limit with three raises.

At last, the moment of truth. Players begin to unveil their cards: Janet lays down a royal flush of clubs; Oprah shows her royal flush of hearts; now Madonna reveals her royal flush of diamonds—unbelievable! Then Martha tops everyone with a royal flush of spades! Incredible. Four top hands!

In the excitement of this turn of events, the women stop playing to watch the game at the other table. The men are into their second round: Mike Wallace, Robin Williams, former federal drug czar William Bennett, and Bill Clinton. As luck would have it, all of them are betting with the same intensity as in the women's game. The audience gasps in wonderment as the men reveal their cards. Bennett discloses a straight flush of clubs; Williams displays a straight flush of diamonds; Clinton lays down a straight flush of hearts; and Wallace caps it all with a straight flush of spades! Truly amazing!

In this tale of the astonishing poker match, let's focus on the players, their cards, and their personal styles in order to develop a new vocabulary for talking about individual differences. The card game represents four basic personal styles that are evident in human society, and each of the styles is founded on one of four thinking processes. Virtually all of us possess the capacity for all four types of thinking, but people favor various combinations that give rise to certain opposing biases in attitudes, behavior, speech, and expression that characterize their respective temperaments or styles. Men and women are almost equally likely to display any one of the four styles. To see how this actually works, let's return to the card table. Each of the four personal styles and its favored type of thinking is symbolized by a different card suit. And the players are prime examples of the four styles. We begin at the women's table.

THE PROPER CLUB

In her work life, at least, Janet Reno seems to be an excellent example of the club style—people who are particularly skilled in setting order, organizing, and establishing rules and procedures within their social groups. After a long legal career in public service, Reno was named U.S. Attorney General for the Clinton administration. Her responsibilities as the nation's top law-enforcement official superseded her loyalty to the president, and she appointed an independent prosecutor to investigate Clinton's alleged wrongdoings. Throughout those proceedings, however, she continued to elicit the president's respect. Reno could relate well with others yet be decisive with the tough choices. Her primary role was to set the procedures and routines required for administering the nation's laws, and to close in on, and close down, those who had broken the rules. Reno is conservative in method, dress, and behavior. Not noted for imaginative vision, she tends instead to support law and order and uphold the tried-and-true, thus stabilizing the system.

THE PRISMATIC DIAMOND

Madonna often seems to represent the diamond style—people who are skilled in conceiving new ideas, who possess an open, questing temperament. Madonna began her entertainment career as a singer who seemingly broke all the rules. She championed hedonistic lifestyles and gave us her slant on life in a material world. Both her songs' lyrics and revealing music videos stirred controversy. While inventing new images for herself, her ventures into fashion transformed underwear into outerwear. Indeed, she made openness her art form. And she continues to be experimental. In a recent music video she again stunned her audience by incorporating unusual visual and musical elements from India. As an actress Madonna evolved from a supporting character in the film *Desperately Seeking Susan* to the lead role in the innovative film musical *Evita*. She is multifaceted, gutsy, and imaginative. Continually reinventing herself, she is ever pioneering. Fascinated by what the future offers, the outlook of people with a diamond style might be characterized by the word *change*. They push the envelope, thus expanding our limits.

Before sketching the two remaining styles, consider how the first two examples differ with each other. Janet Reno has been an advocate for setting order and stabilizing our society by concentrating on the rules we follow. Madonna, on the other hand, challenges convention and consistently conceives new ideas for us to consider, thus expanding our awareness and understanding. These two traits are as opposite as the words *close* and *open*. The clubs are primarily devoted to the smooth functioning of the status quo as we know it, and the diamonds urge us to dream of ways to free ourselves from old patterns. Stabilizing versus expanding.

Let's now turn to the two remaining styles and see how the second pair of opposites rounds out the four-way system.

THE INDEPENDENT SPADE

The career of Martha Stewart, home style arbiter and business entrepreneur, gives us an insight into the spade style—people who are skilled in objectively analyzing information and identifying a program or course of action. Martha had the creativity to fashion her own independent approach to home design and accessorizing, which she then translated into techniques for others to follow. She landed a contract with Kmart to produce her name-brand line of home merchandise and served as its advertising spokesperson. Her own company, Martha Stewart Enterprises, developed *Martha Stewart*

Living magazine plus weekly TV and radio shows starring Martha Stewart. All of these media vehicles sell her solutions to a better style of living. Her own corporate publicity accurately stated that "Martha has already figured it out. She will personally take us by the hand and show us how to do it."[1] Martha leads her organization with strong determination and cool decision-making. Essentially, she excels in separating out what won't work and identifying what will. She is both imaginative and procedural, but her warmheartedness doesn't show up in her business dealings. People with a sharp, spade style tend to take charge, to identify goals and agendas.

THE CONSOLING HEART

Though she is, like Martha Stewart, a superlative businesswoman, Oprah Winfrey in her public, on-air incarnation represents the heart style—people who are gifted in relating to other people and empathizing with their interests. Oprah began her TV career as a local news anchor, but she came into her element when she had the opportunity to do a morning talk show. Upon relocating to Chicago, her show was renamed *The Oprah Winfrey Show*. Her success comes from her ability to connect with guests one-to-one and establish warm, informal intimacy. The show's viewers feel such closeness and involvement that they often think of her as a girlfriend. Her own company, the Harpo Entertainment Group, now manages her productions, which includes a video, *Oprah Winfrey: Make the Connection*. In addition to TV, she has been acclaimed as an actress. In the films *The Color Purple* and *Beloved*, she personally related the historical struggles of African-Americans.

While she is an inspiring role model for self-development, she also feels a part of the traditions of her race. Quite spiritual herself, she thinks of her show as a ministry to others. Warmth, sensitivity, and caring are the keys to Oprah's heart-style persona. In a public survey about people deemed most likely to get into heaven, Oprah ranked second only to Mother Teresa.[2] These women shared a connecting, relating interest in the needs of others, which serves to bring people together to care about each other and unify the group.

Note how the spade and the heart styles differ. Martha Stewart is an expert in figuring out techniques. Oprah is gifted in the way she relates with people. We watch Martha's show to get expert strategies for creating a beautiful home, but we tune in to Oprah to learn about people. Martha's analytical skill differs from Oprah's knack for relating and bringing people together. Their traits are as opposite as the concepts of *cut* and *connect*. The spade focuses on solving a particular problem and narrowing down options to identify a program that advances one's success. The heart cares more about people than abstract objectives, and unifies the group for some common good. Identifying versus unifying.

In figure 2.1, the four card players are at the table. (We've represented each player schematically as a head with two arms as seen from above.) They are seated in such a way that natural opposites in style are diagonally across from one another—stabilizing clubs across from expanding diamonds, and unifying hearts across from identifying spades. By this positioning you can see each player's style in relation to other styles. You can also see that a person's most likely secondary traits are the neighboring thinking styles on either side of their primary style. Therefore, a person may share similar attitudes and values with people whose styles are on either side of their own. Yet they may have difficulty getting along with someone of the style which opposes them across the table.

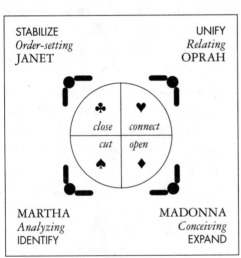

STABILIZE
Order-setting
JANET

UNIFY
Relating
OPRAH

close | connect
cut | open

MARTHA
Analyzing
IDENTIFY

MADONNA
Conceiving
EXPAND

FIGURE 2.1

Think of each of these players as having both arms out toward the secondary characteristics of her style, but she can't very easily reach directly across the table to her opponent's style. For example, Oprah might combine her relating talents with both the imagination of the diamond and the respect for traditions of the club, but she is least likely to display the spade's analytical focus. Across the table, Martha Stewart could supplement her analytical skill with diamond vision and club procedures. But we may not see much evidence of the heart's caring and relating. This is not to say that either woman never shows her least active mode of behavior. Of course, Oprah can be decisive and tough when needed, and at times Martha Stewart can be sensitive in relating to others. But of all four kinds of traits, these least active modes are the ones you would not readily associate with each woman's natural style. The same is true of both Janet Reno and Madonna. From their opposite seats, they combine their respective predominant strengths with a set of secondary skills they hold in common: the analytical directness of the spade as well as the relating abilities of the heart. But neither is known for the predominant trait of her opponent across the table. Each player is most likely to get along with the two players sitting on either side of her, yet find less in common with the player across the table.

Also note that women, in this case, occupy all four seats though the four personal styles are traits of human thinking equally available to both men and women. To find out how men play the same game, let's turn to the second table of poker players.

THE STABILIZING CLUB

William Bennett is our male representative of the club style—people who tend to set order and routine. As Secretary of Education under President Reagan and Director of the Office of National Drug Policy Control under President Bush, Bennett directed policies for educating the nation's youth and reducing drug use. In his advocacy for conservative, family-oriented values, Bennett has authored two books—*The Book of Virtues*, promoting moral education, and *The Death of Outrage*, attacking the misconduct of President Clinton. In the latter, Bennett wrote: "'Judgment' is a word that is out of favor these days, but it remains a cornerstone of democratic self-government. It is what enables us to hold ourselves, and our leaders, to high standards. It is how we distinguish between right and wrong, noble and base, honor and dishonor. We cannot ignore that responsibility."[3] If you compare both Bennett and Reno with other club-styled individuals like former senator Bob Dole, Independent Counsel Kenneth Starr, or the Reverend Jerry Falwell, you'll find a similar emphasis on following procedures and doing what is "right."

THE EXPANDING DIAMOND

Robin Williams is our male example of the diamond style—people who emphasize their imaginative traits. Williams is widely admired as both an ingenious comedian and a versatile actor. His movie roles have included the psychoanalyst in *Good Will Hunting*, the caring father and housekeeper-in-drag in *Mrs. Doubtfire*, a playful Peter Pan in *Hook*, and the voice of the Genie in *Aladdin*. In comedic performances and interviews, he is a master of wide-open, unrehearsed spontaneity. His mind is continuously creating and giving rich expression to delightful humor. While not all diamonds are humorous, they all tend to be free-spirited and open to new ideas, as are Madonna, Steven Spielberg, or Michael Jordan. And like former wrestler-turned-governor of Minnesota, Jesse Ventura, diamonds often reinvent themselves, as well as facets of the world around them.

THE IDENTIFYING SPADE

Though his private life shows other tendencies, on camera Mike Wallace represents the spade style—people who are sharply analytical.

Wallace has been the lead reporter on the TV news show *60 Minutes* since its inception. It is his style to identify problems and wrongdoing in our society and to bring them to our attention. Wallace's method of interviewing is challenging and confrontational. His questions are cutting and tough. Indeed, he doesn't hesitate to call a spade a spade. Wallace can be innovative. And in staying with the show for decades, he has adapted to routine. But his strength is his cool, calculating nature, which cuts to the essence of a problem to suggest a solution. Men such as former Speaker of the House Newt Gingrich, Alan Greenspan, and attorney Johnnie Cochran tend to be willing to unleash their analytical dominance, but and women like Secretary of State Madeleine Albright and Hillary Clinton are equally incisive. The revealing trait of spades is their ability to reduce options, identify solutions and make decisions.

THE UNIFYING HEART

Bill Clinton's popularity is largely based on public appreciation of his heart style—people who are masters at relating to other people. Fundamentally, President Clinton is a peace-loving crusader who is sensitive to the needs of others and works to build harmony among people. During his childhood, Bill Clinton was the family member who consoled his mother when she was in distress. In his political life, he has stood for common causes, fighting against elimination of social programs. Clinton summed up his supportive interests in his first inaugural address: "In serving, we recognize a simple but powerful truth—we need each other, and we must care for one another." President Clinton has been inspiring in his idealistic open-mindedness, yet he also supports orderly traditions such as family values and religious principles. It is his nature to aid peace missions and efforts to unite nations. In this regard Clinton is an extroverted version of the introverted former president Jimmy Carter, a respected elder statesman for missions of the heart. Other heart-styled people such as Oprah Winfrey, the Reverend Billy Graham, and Fred Rogers (of the PBS children's TV show *Mr. Rogers*) all share an interest in people that tends to define their style.

Clinton's intimate interests of the heart caused him great embarrassment and brought pain to his family and the nation. It could be said that in those personal affairs, he let diamond liberties overtake his club limits and responsibilities to his marriage and his office.

STYLE DIFFERENCES PROVOKE DISCORD

At the men's card table (figure 2.2), players are seated in the same pattern of personal styles as at the women's; those located diagonally across the table oppose each other. Quite often, when opposites confront one another, divisiveness and disagreement can occur. For example, while Mike Wallace has tended to stay clear of politics, other news analysts such as Sam Donaldson, Cokie Roberts, and John McLaughlin sharply criticized Clinton's style. And Clinton's arch political rival was

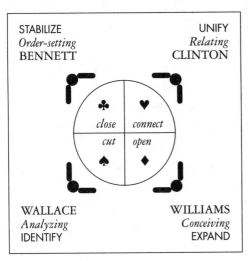

FIGURE 2.2

former Speaker of the House Newt Gingrich, who led the fight to cut taxes and government spending while Clinton was an advocate for the people affected by the cuts. Such opposition arises from basic differences between the spade's cutting, analytical strengths and the heart's connecting, relating concerns.

Similar differences apply to the club-diamond axis. When Clinton's irresponsibility in private affairs and his rule-breaking behavior disclosed a diamond abandon, the clubs, en masse, attacked his desertion of moral standards and his illegal acts. Similarly, when clubs attempt to limit expressive freedoms, diamond artists or filmmakers protest loudly. And in turn, clubs like William Bennett and Bob Dole take issue with the diamond-based entertainment industry for its disregard of wholesome family values and standards of decency. Such discord arises from fundamental opposition between the club's procedural, orderly interests and the diamond's open, imaginative flair.

Instead of being opposing advocates in the Washington-versus-Hollywood battle, try to imagine Bill Bennett and Madonna having once been fascinated by the differences between themselves, and ending up married to each other. In that case, most likely they'd have arguments like George and Hope's—the couple who debated purchase of the convertible in chapter 1. Similarly, Bill might want them to save and make do with the car they have. But with a more open attitude, Madonna would be inclined to push for the sporty convertible to free their spirits. This is conjecture, of course, but it is difficult to picture either one of them taking the opposite position—that is, with Bill as the free spirit pleading for the new convertible, and Madonna saying, "Bill, dear, you don't need it, and we can't afford it." While both might have it in them to take such out-of-character positions, it would be unusual, to say the least.

GENDER STEREOTYPES CORRESPOND
TO SPADE-HEART OPPOSITION

Traditionally, men and women have been stereotyped into opposing spade and heart styles. Until recent decades, our society has expected the sexes to fill customary roles in their thinking and behavior, with a man having the spade characteristics of the dominant, assertive, problem-solving leader, and the woman being the caring, peace-loving, family nurturer associated with the heart. Children were taught to take on these gender roles in preparation for adult responsibilities. Girls were given dolls that fostered nurturing and relationship skills. Boys got game equipment and toy

guns that encouraged mental agility and toughness. This pat-
terning occurred in school as well. Girls were encouraged to be
sensitive, caring nurturers. Boys were disciplined to be single-
minded and decisive in preparation for a competitive life in
business or the military. So indeed, the traditional generalizations about male/female differences seem to fit, in part because
people have been taught to fit stereotypes. And we try to conform
to the stereotypes to avoid being thought of as abnormal. After
all, no man wants to be tagged a wimp, and no woman likes
being called a bitch. We more readily accept a heartless man or a
woman who can't make up her mind. As a result, many people of
both sexes may pretend to have traits that run counter to their
natural style in order to fit in and be accepted.

There will be more discussion about coping with gender
stereotypes later on, but note that individual men may have
personal styles that tend to oppose each other, as in our example of
Mike Wallace and Bill Clinton. Neither is more masculine than
the other. Rather, one tends to be more challenging and the other
more peace-seeking. And the same goes for the other example,
with Martha Stewart and Oprah Winfrey. Neither is more feminine
than the other. They simply have different strengths. Women can
be spades, and men can be hearts. Indeed, this has been Hillary
Clinton's position vis-a-vis Bill in their marriage of opposites.
Hillary played a key role in bolstering her husband's resolve to
stick to his guns and take on his opponents. She has been a cool
and capable advisor, and the indispensable balance for Bill's good-
natured, trusting sensitivities.

THE FOUR STYLES SQUARE OFF AGAINST
EACH OTHER IN NATIONAL DEBATE

The card players are reference personalities for their respective
styles. Each of them can be thought of as an example of the
qualities of their own particular quadrant of the table. In total,

they represent the full circle of styles of thought and behavior. The card-table diagram illuminates the dichotomies of America's political oppositions as well: Republicans cut government spending, while Democrats connect with people; conservatives protect social order and family values, while liberals champion free expression; hawks take a strong stand on military might, while doves rally for peace. New players will take their places at the nation's table and the game will go on along much these same lines, because this is simply human nature. Disagreements continually arise over such differences in temperament and thinking style.

Figure 2.3 makes it easy to recognize the long-running political battle of the right versus the left. The political right is found on the left side of the diagram, and vice versa, because this layout also depicts the tendency for types of thinking to go along with one or the other side of the human

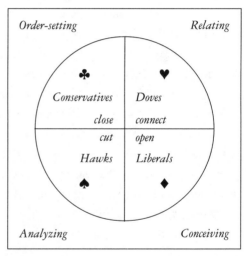

FIGURE 2.3

brain. Language, logical analysis, sequenced operations, and ordered routines are associated with the left-brain hemisphere. Imagination, open-ended conception, and connective feeling are often associated with the right-brain hemisphere. The left hemisphere of the brain controls the right side of the body; the right hemisphere controls the left side. The typical thinking of hawks and conservatives of the political right are specialties of the left-brain hemisphere. And the worldview of doves and liberals of the political left are specialties of the right-brain hemisphere.

33

THE FOUR TYPES OF THOUGHT PROCESSES

Since the four personal styles are founded on combinations of thinking processes, it will be useful for you to have a general knowledge of them. While reading the following summaries, think of each suit as a shorthand description for its many subprocesses of thinking—just as each card suit consists of thirteen individual face cards and number cards. The suit represents all members of a particular group of cards, or in this case, a particular group of mental processes.

The analyzing spade specializes in separating things into parts by logic, making decisions, and identifying objectives. Information is assigned a name, label, or sign. Evaluations are made by narrowing things down, excluding (or cutting out) less workable choices to identify a goal or course of action. This process reduces multiples to a singularity. From many possibilities, a single choice is selected and identified. Moreover, this type of thinking enables each of us to develop our own ego, which is the identity of oneself separate and apart from others. And it allows each individual to make conscious decisions about his or her own life: I set goals; I decide by reason; I control my actions. Subvarieties of the spade group of thought processes include these mental operations: distinguishing, differentiating, setting apart, deducting, naming, and concluding. Without the spade, there is aimlessness (i.e., no direction or sense of self-purpose).

The order-setting club specializes in putting things in sequential steps (such as 1, 2, 3 or *a, b, c*) and functioning through established programs that we call routines. Its procedures are structured and detailed sets of tasks or standards to guide actions. Routines are an experienced way of proceeding that does not require rethinking each new occasion. Once rules are formed, a person applies what is known to work. Following such efficient practices ensures dependability and safety. "If it isn't broke, don't fix it." Subvarieties of the club group of thought processes include these mental operations: scheduling, timing, planning a course, making lists, setting rules, complying with policy, and following ritual. Without the club, there is chaos (i.e., no structure or organization).

34

The conceiving diamond specializes in imagining and generating new ideas. The field of possibilities is widened and expanded on a series of "what if" plateaus. New concepts are envisioned by mind-doodling (or daydreaming). Ideas are often represented in symbols that stand for a complex set of thoughts, such as how a dream might portray one's own need for more freedom with an illustrative vision of a butterfly. (Language is the primary province of the spade and club, but the diamond often thinks in images rather than in words.) This group of mental processes allows us to develop holistic, all-encompassing ideas in the "mind's eye." They help us to form a "big picture" of a situation, or a "mental map" of where we are. Typically we cannot actually see these imagined images, pictures, and maps. Rather than seeing them, we sense them guiding us from a place in the mind that is beyond conscious awareness. Subvarieties of the diamond group of thought processes include these mental operations: imagination, "seeing through the mind's eye," creating, wishing, hoping, fantasizing, and dreaming. Without the diamond, there is stasis (i.e., no change or growth).

The relating heart specializes in connecting, associating, linking, and harmonizing. Ideas are layered and assembled, building meaning—that is, a sense of deep significance that is found in the rich connections between oneself and others, (For example the heart might say: "Caring for you gives meaning to my life"; or "I find meaning in working to help save the whales".) This type of mental experience, produced by connections that resonate in the mind when one person or set of ideas is joined with another, can seem beautiful and make us feel good. Musical harmonies and the rhyming of words and thoughts, as in songs and poetry, are examples of artful connections. Subvarieties of the heart group of thought processes include these mental operations: building, unifying, grouping together, convening, harmonizing, and integrating. Without the heart, there is isolation (i.e., no commonality of interests or interrelationship).

It is easy to see that each of us makes use of all of these categories of thinking and feeling processes to some extent every day. Research indicates that each of the four styles is nearly equally distributed among the population.[4] That is, each of the four kinds of behavior is characteristic of approximately one-quarter of the population. This numerical balance suggests that all four types of thinking—and, accordingly, all four personal styles—are equally necessary to the functioning of life. What's more, because each type opposes and counteracts another, it is natural that personality conflicts arise.

Additionally, within our own inner lives, the strongly opposing characteristics of the spade versus the heart, or the club versus the diamond, generate a lively discord at times. For instance, how do you give yourself to a relationship and also defend your self-interests? Or, how can you change if you remain fixed in safe, tested routines of behavior? Such dilemmas involve a constant interplay of thought processes across polar stances within the mind. This internal division represents the same opposition that occurs in couples or groups when people espouse or attach themselves to contrary points of view.

All of these processes are activities of the brain. But as a culture we are most conscious of the club-and-spade pair, the ones most assisted by language. On the other hand, the diamond-and-heart processes can seem mysterious. Popular expressions for them suggest that they come from somewhere outside of one's own awareness. A person may say, "Have a heart!" to someone who seems out of touch with their own relating process. Yet such thoughts of connection occur in the mind. The same applies when someone asks, "How do you feel deep in your heart?" Likewise, diamond processes often occur outside of one's language-oriented consciousness. This is expressed in statements such as, "It came to me from out of the blue"; or, "God sent me a vision." Often people are unaware of the creative impulses and feelings of the diamond-and-heart processes within their minds.

THE DEEP INSIGHT OF THE CARD SUIT SYMBOLS

Why do the card suits so well portray each of the sets of thinking and feeling processes in this four-way system? Is it simply coincidence? Most likely the card suits represent an intuitive expression of the way the mind is organized. They are a deep reflection of the fundamental ways people think and behave. This surprising set of associations evolved as the card suits were developed and refined over centuries from their antecedent, Tarot cards. Note how the symbols visually represent the four kinds of thinking as shown in figure 2.4.

- The spade has the appearance of a shovel cutting the soil; it also looks like an arrow moving in a straight line. It is actually a descendent of the Sword in the Tarot deck, an instrument for cleaving one part from another.

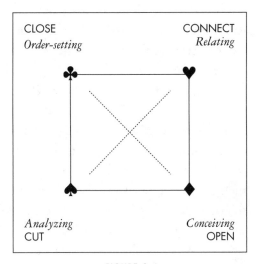

FIGURE 2.4

- The heart has two semicircular mounds that are unified on a single base point. It expresses relationship and connection between separate persons. It is the symbol for love and caring.

- The club is a series of lobed shapes folded into themselves, and looks like a protective enclosure. The word "club" also implies membership and stability.

- The diamond is pointed in all four directions. When polished and cut in facets, diamonds disperse light in divergent rays of color. These multicolored rays are symbolic of creativity.

Interestingly, the spade and club, usually shown in black, sit upon stems and appear to be grounded. The diamond and heart, usually shown in red, have points at the bottom, as if dangling in space. Is this not how we picture conservatives versus liberals? People with spade-and-club styles often think of themselves as solidly grounded in hard reality, judging bleeding-heart liberals to be "in outer space." People with diamond-and-heart styles, on the other hand, often think of themselves as hanging on to their dreams and intuitions, or as being attached to the needs of others, seeing heartless conservatives as fixed "stick-in-the-muds."[5]

It is not yet known how the dispositions in style develop in individuals. But, as in the case of electricity, you don't have to know how something works to make use of it. What is relevant here is that characteristic styles of thinking are part of our nature, and that they play opposing roles in human affairs. With this in mind, it stands to reason that dissent between differing styles is here to stay. Ideally, however, such dissent can lead us to select optimum courses of action. By considering all sides of a problem, we stand the best chance of finding a successful solution. Cooperative disagreement is evolution at work. That's why democracy works. The same principle applies to all groups, from whole societies down to work teams, families, and couples.

By picturing a group's options as a spinning top—with logical and routine choices to one side and caring and imaginative preferences to the other—one senses that life is all about finding the right balance. So when everyone contributes their different views and each is given equal weight, the group dynamically spins along like a balanced top. Each of the diverse styles participates in a four-way game of weighing in, to set the course over some imaginary center pin. And as we do, we make progress—not too fast or too slow, or too hard or too soft, but just right. It is amazingly beautiful to think of life actually working this way.

Of course, the reality is that in working this out, people form camps of like-minded individuals which then proceed to challenge opposing camps in an attempt to get their way as often as possible. But since this give-and-take game is about balance, no camp can always get their way. Indeed, if you can be even half-satisfied in things going your way, you might consider that par for the course. The important thing to remember is that the well-being of the group depends on each of us weighing in—contributing our beliefs in a constructive way.

EVALUATING YOUR PERSONAL STYLE PROFILE

Now that you've taken the self-test in chapter 1 and used appendix 1 to score it, this is an appropriate time to review your profile. Your highest scores are your strongest suits. As noted earlier, your profile is likely to demonstrate a preference for one or two suits or personal styles. It is also likely that you will have a relatively low score in another style; this is your weakest suit. Therefore, the characteristics that have been ascribed to your stronger suits are more accurate in describing you than the characteristics associated with your weaker suits.

The Four Personal Styles

On the following page are more detailed lists of the characteristics of the four personal styles.6 Recall that the styles result from favoring certain sets of thought processes over others, and that most people exhibit secondary traits in combination with their primary style—it is rare for a person to exclusively use one process or style. As you become familiar with the styles, and in later chapters read more about how they typically operate, you will begin to notice distinguishing traits of each personal style in the behavior of the people you know.

Spade Personal Style
♠ The Identifier

Spades tend to be individualistic and self-confident, with an assurance in their ability to form the most logical conclusions and identify both problems and solutions. Often perceptive and resourceful, it is their nature to challenge others in the process of generating ideas. They can be cool in attitude and willing risk-takers, urging others to "be reasonable." Life is a series of new problems to be resolved, mountains to be climbed, or things to be fixed.

Strengths—Their talent is the ability to analyze, solve problems, critique, evaluate, and make decisions. Spades may be highly inventive of better ways to get things done, and able to implement them into systematic policies and procedures. They tend to select a goal, persist without wavering, and get it done— self-reliantly and capably. They are skilled in narrowing down ideas, choosing, and defining a program.

Weaknesses—Spades may be insensitive to the feelings and interests of others, as well as impatient and inflexible, with a cleverness that may border on scheming. They may be seen as coolly egocentric, arrogant, or demanding. They may be blind to others' needs to be cared for and appreciated.

Work—Their ideal work situation involves individual challenges with the freedom to act, control events, and direct results. Spades often get top billing and top jobs, as their qualities can develop into entrepreneurial and managerial skills. Career specialties include . . . policy analysts, managers, attorneys, military leaders, engineers, scientists, pilots, and equipment operators.

Other traits—Spades can be masters of precise language, intellectual thought, engaging debate, or other challenging tactics. If extroverted, they may be resourceful, witty, sophisticated manipulators of their environment, or people of action who gamble in brinkmanship and strive for a one-up position. They may assume that all problems are solvable by technology, a show of force, etc. If introverted, they may be preoccupied with analysis and retreat into books, theories, or designs. They may even be loners, insubordinate to authority, and masters of tools. Spades can feel unloved due to the way that they tend to isolate themselves from others.

Motivations and interests—Spades wish to be independent and respected for their knowledge or control of a situation. Spades seek the next challenge, be it fixing a car or fixing world problems.

Prominent examples of the spade style—Martha Stewart, Mike Wallace, Prince Philip, Newt Gingrich, Johnnie Cochran, Hillary Clinton, Secretary of State Madeleine Albright, Judge Judy, Gloria Steinem, Sam Donaldson, Henry Ford.

Club Personal Style
♣ The Stabilizer

Clubs are responsible, judicious, thorough, want to do right, and try not to let others down. They work to set and preserve a base of orderly methods, codes, and traditional values. Others feel they can count on the loyal, dependable club, who keeps things in their proper place and proceeds step by step. Avoiding risks, clubs ensure a safe predictability and work with others to solidify gains and carry out operations. Life is a myriad of things to do.

Strengths—Their expertise is the determination to follow through with precision. They attend to detail and are consistent, practical, and honest. Clubs are civic-minded protectors of institutions (education, church, family). They are skilled in coordinating and administrating programs.

Weaknesses—Clubs may be cautious, risk-adverse, and near-focused. They can be rigid about procedures for doing things and about being punctual. Some may be viewed as conservative, outmoded, or slow to accept progress. They can be blind to others' longings for freedom and change.

Work—Their ideal environment is a secure one, with steady tasks clearly defined, and enough time to do them correctly. Clubs respect a chain of command, many preferring to have a boss, rather than be one. Career specialties include executives, administrators (religious, educational, governmental, military, business), legal authorities, accountants, auditors, insurance agents, financial and investment managers, tax specialists, librarians, and teachers.

Other traits—Clubs believe in duty. They may judge people by standards and have a difficult time understanding those who would change the system. They may strive to find a good way to do something, stick with it, and want others to do the same. Clubs tend to be self-disciplined and believe in disciplining others for breaches of order. They are what they seem to be—solid, stable, and devotees of sound, straight values. If extroverted, they can be pillars of the community, active in social, political, and religious organizations. If introverted, clubs may be preoccupied with detail and insist on things being neat and orderly. They can feel very wounded if blamed for a problem.

Motivations and interests—Clubs wish to be a part of the solution and recognized for their careful heedfulness in doing the right thing at the right time. Clubs seek to get a job done correctly.

Prominent examples of the club style—Attorney General Janet Reno, William Bennett, Queen Elizabeth II, Independent Counsel Kenneth Starr, Congressman Henry Hyde, General Colin Powell, Bob Dole, the Reverend Jerry Falwell, Gerald Ford, George Washington.

Diamond Personal Style
◆ The Expander

Diamonds are open to new ideas or experiences, and often dream of greener pastures. They can be unpredictable, enigmatic, and creative, often saying, "Look at it another way," or "What if . . . ?" They may undauntedly journey an uncharted course, following their intuition, raising awareness, and broadening perception. Life is a wide world to be experienced and understood.

Strengths—The uniqueness of diamonds is their ability to perceive and imaginatively conceive the new. Diamonds create by envisioning fresh possibilities or ways of looking at things, and are optimistic about the future, often taking the long-term view. They can be flexible, witty, and inspiring. They are skilled in expanding ideas and developing alternatives that push the envelope.

Weaknesses—Diamonds may be loose on procedures, make light of obstacles, and fail to follow through to the finish. They may be nonconformist, idealistic, and willing to jump ship if unable to exercise their talents. They may be blind to others' needs for preparedness and stability.

Work—Their ideal situation is unstructured, with the freedom to deal with people and problems in a playful and intuitive way. Often preferring unrestricted openness, they benefit from positions where they can pass the details on to others once the conceptual work is done. Career specialties include jour nalists, researchers, inventors, marketing/ advertising creators, designers, architects, artists, dancers, entertainers, comedians, playwrights, novelists, and teachers.

Other traits—Diamonds often have a "can-do" attitude in a risk-enabling environment. Generating anew (be it a movie, painting, scientific theory, or business venture) is their focus, and problems are pushed to the side or ignored. If extroverted, diamonds are likely to be charming, exciting, enthusiastic, spontaneous, or adventurous. They may be bubbly, alert, and radiate energy. If introverted, they may quest inwardly, exploring greater awareness and bettering life. They may make the unusual sacrifices associated with the lone artist or questing pioneer.

Motivations and interests—They wish to be free and open to explore—to develop possibilities. Diamonds seek the freedom to experience growth and express their spirit.

Prominent examples of the diamond style—Madonna, Robin Williams, Princess Diana, Steven Speilberg, Jay Leno, Michael Jordan, Picasso, Alanis Morissette, Elizabeth Taylor, Georgia O'Keefe, Albert Einstein, John F. Kennedy, Thomas Jefferson.

Heart Personal Style
♥ The Unifier

Hearts tend to be empathetic, trusting, gentle, and sociable. They value relating with others as their highest priority, and are deeply involved in sharing people's concerns. This harmonizing may also be expressed through music, literature, or artistic endeavors. It is the connections and richness of meaning which energize them. Life is about working together for the common good.

Strengths—People skills make hearts good listeners and communicators, with abilities to deal with emotion and to extend caring. They are very good at face-to-face communication, which they often prefer over writing. Loyal, consistent, and supportive, hearts avoid conflict. They are skilled in building team spirit and togetherness among people, with customers, friends, and family.

Weaknesses—Hearts can be indecisive, unwilling to face controversy, possessive, or expect others to conform to group desires. They may be blind to others' needs for independence.

Work—Their ideal situation involves working with people where they can be accepted and appreciated in the group. If they do not feel connected with others at work, they may develop sideline interests that provide the needed meaningfulness and connection, such as a church group or a community-service association. They tirelessly provide time and energy to group activities, and many serve as charity volunteers. Career specialties include service-business operators, sales-related activities, public relations, nurses, teachers, counselors, religious administrators, ministers, musicians, social workers, environmental advocates, union organizers, and politicians.

Other traits—Hearts place trust in cooperation and harmony. Family and friends are often of paramount importance, ahead of a career, although they might break the rules for a free-spirited fling. Values may be conveyed as feelings that should be expressed. If extroverted, hearts are likely to be warm, amiable, well-meshed into a broad network of lives, and may be outstanding, attentive hosts. If introverted, they may quietly serve and contribute to the welfare of others.

Motivations and interests—They wish to interact with people and be appreciated for the caring services and warmth of compassion they provide. Hearts seek peace, unity, and a harmonious life. Indeed, their concerns may extend to all life on earth, and even universal sanctity.

Prominent examples of the heart style—Oprah Winfrey, Bill Clinton, Prince Charles, Pope John Paul II, the Reverend Billy Graham, Mother Teresa, Betty Ford, Jimmy Carter, Fred Rogers, Alan Alda, Abraham Lincoln, Martin Luther King.

MERGING STYLES

You may actually engage in each of the styles at different times and to varying degrees. Indeed, sometimes you can sense when you shift your thinking between opposing modes. For example in a negotiation, during the initial stage of the talks you may have a relaxed, free-flowing discussion to build a relationship and get to know the other party. Then, in getting down to business, you ease off the heart-style communications and focus on the analytical spade set of your mental operations. Or, you might shift from an initial, club-like interest in procedural standards, toward the diamond's willingness to try something new. In any event, you will most likely have the most trouble when you shift into the attitudes and values of your weakest suit.

The fact that this system of personal styles sees the individual in his or her total life context means that this system encompasses the way we all tend to change a bit depending on different situations. This is a departure from many personality typing systems that rigidly categorize a person into a single way of being.[7] In reality, a woman may be a club-spade at her job as a public-works administrator, but slide over toward the heart corner at home with her family. She may even be a spade with her husband but a heart with her son. In addition, this four-suit system recognizes each individual's capacity for growth. It sees the possibility of shifting one's style as one matures. At midlife, for instance, it is common for men to shift away from the isolated spade corner of the table toward the heart quadrant, softening emotionally and taking an increased interest in their families. At the same time, at midlife women often shift away from the heart corner toward the spade, growing more independent in thought and action. Nonetheless, people usually maintain a marked preference for their favored style throughout their adult lives.

A review of the previous descriptions of the suits should give you a good sense for your own pattern. Most people find themselves strongly identified with one of the four styles, modestly agreeable to one or two others, and indifferent, if not downright hostile, to the last one (which is probably catercornered across the card table from their highest suit). This, however, is not always the case. Some will find themselves drawn almost equally to two, three, or even four of the suits. This seems to be more the case for women, particularly. Research has indicated that women have more flexible and integrated thinking patterns across many regions of their brains than do men, who show more specialized thinking patterns. Facility with multiple styles may also reflect either an unusually high degree of personal development or significant training (through education or parental influence) in styles that are not your own natural style—a condition that will be fully discussed in later chapters. It is also important to note that if the test is given to a young person or a child, and their test results do not reflect a typical pattern, it may simply mean that maturity has not yet shaped the adult pattern that is to come.

You will be returning to the profile of your personal style throughout the book. In the next chapter you will see how different styles generate friction within groups, and particularly in families.

CHAPTER THREE

BOXING IN
THE PALACE

A Royal Example of Personal Styles

Now that you are familiar with the four styles, let's see how their differences can lead to problems at home. The example here will be the world's best-known family—the Windsors. You've read about the British royal family, or seen them on TV. You've watched Queen Elizabeth's children grow up, marry, and divorce. You were saddened by Princess Diana's tragic death in 1997, just a year after her divorce from Prince Charles. So you already know a lot about this family. But if you look beneath the tabloid surface to the root of their conflict, you'll see how varying styles produce a divisiveness that is common to many families.

Diana's gradual estrangement from the Windsor family was witnessed by people worldwide, and millions of them could relate to what she went through. When she ultimately broke free, Diana endeared herself to the public by serving as a beacon of compassion to the sick and the unfortunate. After she died in a car accident in a Paris tunnel, the words from her 1995 BBC-TV interview took on special meaning: "I think the biggest disease this world suffers from in this day and age is the disease of people feeling unloved. And I know that I can give love, for a minute, a half hour, for a day, for a month. . . . I think the British people need someone in public life to give affection, to make them feel important, to support them, to give them light in their dark tunnels."

With such admirable intentions, why would the palace courtiers have distrusted Diana as unfit and unstable? What touched off the family row that reverberated around the globe and prompted critics to call the Windsors "dysfunctional"?

Their rifts are understandable when you take into account the personal styles of key members of the family: Queen Elizabeth II, her husband Prince Philip, their son Charles (the Prince of Wales), and his late ex-wife Princess Diana. As you read about each of them here, consider how they might exemplify traits of members of your own family. You'll notice here also that social situations often bring out characteristics in individuals that seem different from their basic personal styles.

QUEEN ELIZABETH II
(♣ The Stabilizer)

The queen is the family's keystone. She is the rock steadying the entire royal structure. The responsibilities Elizabeth upholds as monarch are all but overwhelming, yet she carries them with sincere humility. Etched in her mind is the motto on the Windsor family crest, "I serve." And serve she does. Quite businesslike as she attends to daily paperwork and events, Elizabeth can be amiable and easygoing in private. This queen seems to have a temperament that is perfectly suited to her duty. One might ask if her eminent suitability is the result of the royal training she received throughout her youth, or whether it is also "in her blood." To watch Queen Elizabeth before the public, however, is to see someone who seems born to her role. There is a quality to her manner that hints of an in-the-blood suitability. She seems made to be a monarch, unlike Edward VIII, for example, who abdicated his throne in 1936 to marry the divorced American woman, Wallis Simpson. The point here is that one's essential temperament seems to play a vital role in making us the people we are—but training helps. Elizabeth is well-suited to her role not only through upbringing, but because that training perfectly fits a natural disposition toward stability and sound, conservative thinking.

Elizabeth's basic steadiness of disposition has allowed her to ride out many storms while keeping her feelings to herself. But in 1992, her "annus horribilis" as she called that horrible year when two sons' marriages erupted in scandal and Windsor Castle burned, the queen's out-of-stripe public admission of discomfort touched the world. At long last, this strong woman allowed herself to be candid for a moment, or as open as the guarded Elizabeth can be.

PRINCESS DIANA
(♦ *The Expander*)

One cannot imagine the queen telling all in a media interview as the late Princess Diana did just that in 1995, when on BBC-TV she revealed secrets of her estrangement from Prince Charles, other romantic affairs, details about her eating disorders and her future plans. Diana knew she would not be Charles's queen. The palace establishment had judged that she didn't have it in her. "I do things differently," Diana said in the defiant interview. "I don't go by a rule book." She could only hope to be the "queen of people's hearts."

The following year, when Diana was the first to announce that she and Charles had agreed to divorce, the palace was infuriated by her "premature disclosure." The public, however, continued to support her, for she had openly dealt with marital problems, depression, infidelity, and divorce as commoners everywhere do. And she maintained her charitable role of visiting with sick and troubled people to offer inspiration.

When Diana died, the public dubbed her queen of their hearts and pressured the Windsors to put aside protocol and show their love for Diana. Diana's funeral revealed a public outpouring of love for the princess that was so effusive as to have been called surreal.

Diana and Elizabeth were opposites in many ways. Elizabeth quietly fulfills her role, all with proper care and attention to detail. She is reserved and gracious. In her world, people know their place in the hierarchy and mind their p's and q's. One does not drop in on the queen. Even friends and family must schedule visits. She likes things well-planned and is not clever at imaginative ventures. Alternating between firm decisiveness and warm compassion, the queen fundamentally believes in order and tradition. She possesses a deep religious faith and would not shirk her responsibilities. By nearly everyone's standards, Elizabeth is right for the office she holds. Even Prince Charles feels his mother carries out the functions of the monarchy better than he could do.

Princess Diana, on the other hand, was distressed by routine protocol. Cloistered in the palace after her marriage to Charles, she suffered years of agony trying to adapt to restraints imposed by the queen's courtiers and privy councils. Contrary to Elizabeth's formality, Diana was bored with meddling details and craved the freedom to be out casually with people. She was lively, fun-loving, irreverent, and open with strangers. She thrived on impulsive flexibility. So is it any wonder that the established royal "club" could not understand her, or that she could not stomach their ways? In these two women we can see the same kind of closed/open opposition as in the club and diamond players at the illustrative card table (figure 2.1).

Diana was warm and caring, as Elizabeth can be, but with a light-heartedness the queen is unable to sustain. Diana was the bright, sweet spirit who enlivened a room with her liberating style. Railing against oppression after fourteen years of her frustration with the royal family, in 1995 Diana made the decision to be interviewed by BBC without palace approval. As she disclosed in the interview, the establishment she had married into thought of her as a "non-starter." She acknowledged that her behavior had cost her the support of the royal household. "They see me as a threat of some kind," Diana said. "But I'm here to do good. I'm not a destructive person." In fact she had taken her children—the heirs to the throne—to shelters for the homeless, to visit people dying of AIDS, to "all sorts of areas where I'm not sure anyone of that age in this family has been before. And they have a knowledge. They may never use it, but the seed is there. . . . I want them to have an understanding of people's emotions, of people's insecurities, of people's distress, of people's hopes and dreams." Speaking of her own situation, Diana said, "I think every strong woman in history has had to walk down a similar path. And I think it's the strength that causes the confusion and the fear. 'Why is she strong? Where did she get it from? Where is she taking it? Where is she going to use it? Why do the public still support her?'"

Think of the late Diana's open spirit as the pivotal point of her fluctuating temperament. Just as Elizabeth can at times be warm and sensitive yet firmly resolute at other times, Diana balanced an endearing, affectionate nature with a cool, strong side to her character. This more strategic, decisive aspect of her personality grew evident as she cut through royal entanglements to extract herself from the marriage. No doubt Diana was sincere in her efforts to expand her sons' mindfulness of the less fortunate. In essence, Diana aimed to open the minds of others to new facets of experience, to an expanded awareness that would arouse change—disregarding traditions. Indeed, even after her death, Diana's spirit symbolized change for a public pleading with the palace to loosen up and adapt the monarchy to addressing people's needs.

Imagine these interactions taking place in a boxing ring (see figure 3.1). This fictional setting shows how the royal opponents were experiencing a state of discord vitally different from the previous players at the round card table (figure 2.1). Squaring the family circle, let's picture the two women facing each other as boxers who invariably return to their corners. In this match, Elizabeth seeks conditions of stabilizing closure, while Diana sought expanding openness. The terms *open, close, cut,* and *connect* (the key words characterizing the divergent styles) should not be thought of as absolute. Rather, Diana preferred more openness in her life than does

Elizabeth, who for her part upholds more closed, fixed traditions. Elizabeth is at the stabilizing club corner. She can reach out to her left toward connective relationships of the heart, and to her right toward the spade's cutting decisiveness. Diana stood against the ropes of the

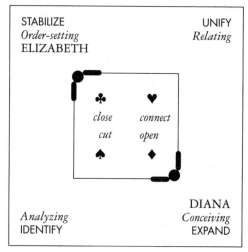

STABILIZE	UNIFY
Order-setting	*Relating*
ELIZABETH	

♣ ♥
close *connect*
cut *open*
♠ ♦

	DIANA
Analyzing	*Conceiving*
IDENTIFY	EXPAND

FIGURE 3.1

two remaining sides of the ring, at the expanding diamond corner. She reached out along the ropes to the same analyzing and relating traits as Elizabeth. But Diana and Elizabeth were at the greatest possible distance from each other. Diana avoided the order expected by the family's matriarch and her palace staff. And Elizabeth could not reach the imaginative openness that Diana exhibited. Each displayed a range within half the boxing ring. It was simply not in each woman's nature to be perfectly well-rounded.

While the queen and Diana respected each other and often affirmed a mutual admiration in public statements, nonetheless their personal styles worked at cross-purposes. They did not literally fight each other as boxers do, nor did they deride each other in public. They were above such expressions of conflict. But their values and methods did clash. The challenges that Diana represented to Elizabeth, and vice versa, were the central bones of contention with which each of these women dealt. The reason they are portrayed here as opponents is that neither woman seemed to fully understand the value of the other's traits.

You probably know who will occupy the two vacant corners of the ring, for Prince Philip and his son Charles have also been embroiled in their own simmering, lifelong struggle.

PRINCE PHILIP
(♠ *The Identifier*)

Since her early teens, Queen Elizabeth has known Prince Philip of Greece, who was then a young British naval officer occasionally charged to escort her. Philip had the handsome looks of a Viking and did everything well. He was the independent, assertive personality that she was not. Elizabeth remained fascinated with Philip, for he was exactly the style of partner she needed. Extroverted, proud, self-reliant, and seemingly determined to contest the old order, he advocated modern improvements in palace operations. Unfortunately, after they married, Philip's only job was being the queen's husband, and it perturbed him to be subservient to anyone. He often secretly ventured to the Soho district in London to lunch with actors, artists, and photographers. Philip enjoyed this freewheeling set, for they were uncomplicated by what he called "fundungus," or meaningless trappings. They stimulated the open, spontaneous side of his bold, sporting nature. Yet he could also comply with the palace regimen and be the orderly, respectful consort. Philip is impatient with indecision and often exhibits an abrasiveness that has caused others to find him cold. He is frequently described as self-contained and a born leader—a man's man. He has a talent for critiquing and evaluating, identifying what needs to be done, and challenging others single-mindedly.

PRINCE CHARLES
(♥ *The Tentative Unifier*)

Prince Charles was born in 1948 to an outspoken, often exacting father, and a reserved, orderly mother. Early on, it became obvious that he was unlike either of his parents. Those near him in the palace said that from an early age he was acutely sensitive. After brushes with his father, he invariably ran to his grandmother, the much-loved queen mother, who possessed the warmth and laughter to make things right again. Philip decided that young Charles needed to be toughened up, and so sent him to the Spartan Gordonstoun private school in Scotland which he himself had attended as a child. At Gordonstoun, Charles stood apart from the other boys because of his gentle nature and interests in drawing, painting, and music. Indeed, music could bring him to tears. Contemplative and quiet, Charles later would characterize himself as an introvert. His inwardness and softhearted concern for others put Charles at odds with his father, who did not cotton to his son's sentimental whims. Philip thought dear Charles was a bit of a wimp.

As an introspective boy in royal training, Charles became an archconformist. He acquired a sense of duty, enjoyed palace ritual, and was politely conservative. Of the two parents, Charles is more like Elizabeth, as both are introverts who combine the traits of caring and orderliness. But Charles is unlike his mother in his depth of feeling and also in his romantic outlook. While Elizabeth can be caring, Charles invariably is caring. His private secretary, Edward Adeane, once commented, "If I hear the word 'caring' again, I'm going to be sick."[1] Any references to Charles being uncaring came well after his marriage to Diana. Charles's nature was to be a heart, though in his childhood and even in his marriage, he often accepted a club role.

As captain of a navy minesweeper, Charles displayed a sensitivity to the problems of his sailors, and sustained high morale onboard. He has excellent rapport with young people and loves his children devotedly. His activities often go off schedule, as he takes time to listen to people. These are all indications of a life that values connective relationships. He yearns for the pleasurable harmony of relating one-to-one with others, yet his introverted nature and his high office are obstacles to achieving the closeness he seeks. He continually tries to get to know people through extended visits and conversations, as opposed to the perfunctory, ceremonial contacts that are common to royalty. He feels a genuine need to connect with people. Staff members in the palace complain that the prince makes snap decisions without adequate thought. His interests often reflect the most recent article or conversation that has captured his attention.[2] Shying away from analysis, Charles prefers to set a course of action by relying on his intuition. Applied to relationships with other people, this mental pattern carries him toward a sympathetic understanding of their feelings.

Unlike Charles, Philip has never claimed to be sensitive or sentimental. He was not very warmhearted to his children, about whom he remarked, "I don't goo over them. I think they're just people."[3] Though periodically critical of all his children, Philip was appalled by Charles's softness and tendency to retreat into himself. When Charles was in one of his soul-searching periods and cut back on public engagements after his son Prince Harry was born, Philip went public with his disgust of Charles's behavior and refused to see his new grandchild for six weeks.

As father and son were, by nature, so different, Philip could not understand Charles, and this strained their relationship. On family business matters Charles kept their contacts to a minimum to avoid rebuke. Yet Charles admired his father, saying he respected Philip's ability "to get to the heart of the matter and analyze things in a practical way."[4]

Here are the primary poles of their opposing styles: Philip is sharply analytical; Charles is deeply relational. One's expertise is the other's blind spot. With this insight into the thought processes that differentiate their temperaments, the gulf between them makes sense. Philip's spade nature, shown in his analytical predisposition, makes him rather indifferent to the feelings of others. Charles, on the other hand, is not tough like his dad, for it is his style to relate sensitively with others. Charles's long journey to becoming his own person was doubly arduous, since not only did his father and male role model have a style opposite to his own, but our culture's stereotypical notions of what a man should be also contradicted his style. Here you have an inkling why Elizabeth, an upholder of traditional order, sided with Philip in pushing their son to be strong and decisive, for after all, Charles was destined to be a king!

In figure 3.2— depicting the styles of mother, father, and son during Charles's youth— Charles is shown as a one-armed boxer. This illustrates how his caring conservatism lacked a diamond balance. No one in the immediate family embodied the openness Charles needed to help him evolve from

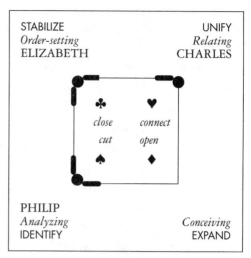

FIGURE 3.2

his childhood conservatism. In this regard Philip's uncle, Lord Mountbatten, was the diamond go-between for father and son. Mountbatten was the lively, charming star of family gatherings who encouraged Charles's free-spirited side. Charles knew that he could confide to his great-uncle and always be accepted. As biographer Jonathan Dimbleby wrote, "only Mountbatten provided the combination of compassion and criticism that no other friend was able to offer."[5] Unfortunately, Mountbatten died in 1979 when his boat was bombed by terrorists. All of England grieved. Eighteen months later, Charles and Diana Spencer announced their intent to wed.

Although the sources of love's allure are rich and mysterious, one aspect of attraction can be a need to cultivate some undeveloped dimension of one's nature. We desire what we lack. What Charles still lacked in his early thirties was the personal freedom to openly challenge the constraints of his parents and the establishment. Might this offer some account for his attraction to the irrepressible Diana? She could, and did, loosen him up. After five years of marriage, Charles took on the medical establishment. Then he struck out at contemporary architects for their plain, brash buildings, which did not blend sensitively into existing communities. In words perhaps meant for his father as well as the architects to whom they were spoken, Charles said, "We've been led . . . by the noses long enough, down a path which totally ignores the principles of harmony and well-calculated relationship of the parts to the whole."[6] Approaching the age of forty, the Prince had found real backbone. In Diana's open, liberating company, Charles had been growing a second arm. That is, she pulled and expanded Charles's thinking in a new direction, which enabled him to challenge the establishment and take on the surprising traits of a crusader. However, as his free-spirited side really took hold, such conduct was inevitably hooted down by the institutions he defied. And both his parents and their courtiers most certainly urged him, as well as Diana, to settle down, play it safe, and rationally assess the ramifications of taking on causes against the establishment. With twenty-twenty hindsight now, you see where the understandable suppression of Charles's and Diana's natural styles unfortunately led.

TRANSFORMING RANCOR INTO RESPECT FOR FAMILY MEMBERS' DIFFERENT SKILLS

The interaction among members of the royal family reveals how differences of personal styles can spark disputes that are bound to recur again and again. When people feel derided, rather than validated, they may identify opponents as personal sources of irritation. Such sentiments can fester into frustration and deep bitterness, sometimes to the extent that the squelched person can no longer live or work in the environment where this friction occurs. Although topics of disagreement can vary widely, core antagonisms often boil down to the disparities between diverse thought processes. The four-suit model not only provides a master key for unlocking persistent conflicts, but also offers an insight into group dynamics—how family members can transform negative attitudes about each other's weaknesses into positive appreciation of the varied skills needed for mutual growth.

This time imagine the royal family sitting around the card table (figure 3.3), with each member symbolizing one of the four styles needed for the group to find its optimal dynamic. Think of Philip and Diana as the perceptual leading edge of this family system, providing input information to the group. Elizabeth and Charles are the output experts, operating on the basis of their mates' perceptions. In an ideal

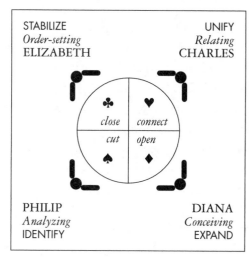

FIGURE 3.3

situation, Philip obtains and breaks down information, separating it out and analyzing ideas to identify important findings. He also keeps the group on course, working mostly with Elizabeth. At the same time, Diana found new ways for the family to function, thus expanding and adjusting its role in the world at large, as well as in its own consciousness. It was often noted that she assumed traditional royal duties—involvement in charities, for example—and gave them a freshness that made it seem she had invented the role. When Diana and Charles were a team, she mostly passed her ideas on to him. Charles's job is to unify the family, attend to social ties, link its members with their environs, and rally them to useful causes. Elizabeth, meanwhile, takes it all in and sets up the routines and procedures for the family to follow. Her role is to stabilize or give structure to the family and limit the speed of change so it will not overwhelm the group's ability to survive.

Not surprisingly, in her last few years outside the family, Diana took on both the diamond and heart roles. As commoners empathized with her struggles, and Diana endeared herself to a public longing for the royals to show compassion, she seemed to be a "queen of hearts." With such deeds as visiting the sick and denouncing the use of land mines, Diana prodded the monarchy to pay more attention to the concerns of common people. In so doing, she paved the way for Charles to continue in her footsteps so that he might ultimately develop the capacity to break from the style of his parents, follow his nature, and be a real "king of hearts." Why did the heart function become such a worthwhile cause? To her credit, Diana recognized that the royals needed someone the public could relate to. What was at stake was the future of the monarchy itself, and the chances for her own son to ascend to the throne.

ACKNOWLEDGING FAMILY MEMBERS' DIFFERENCES IN PERSONAL STYLE

Regrettably, during Diana's life among the Windsors, the royal family did not attain the ideal of the mutually supportive, four-way, functioning group described above. Why? Perhaps the failing is due, at least in part, to the common misconception that all people in a group are of the same nature and therefore operate by common criteria. From that point of view, there is the assumption that there must be something wrong with others who don't think and behave as we do. With this false premise, it is impossible for the members of a group who operate differently to feel validated for their natural gifts. Thus, people are inclined to square off and attack each other personally in a match that one must win and one must lose. What they fail to see is that their respective styles have equal value in a game in which all parties are constantly learning from and balancing each other; and like a never-ending version of a truly democratic card game played around a table, all must win an equal share.

Failures in group cohesiveness, whether in families or other social organizations, can be clarified, healed, or avoided if the people involved have an awareness of the four-way, mutually supportive structure, the kinds of dynamics that support it, and where each person fits into the big picture. In other words, people can help themselves a great deal by knowing that these varying roles—represented allegorically in this chapter by Philip, Elizabeth, Charles, and

Diana—are natural and universal; that they represent normal but differing personal dispositions; and that together, if family members can overcome the normal and inevitable tensions that build up among them, they can get beyond conflict to an effective—indeed optimal—pattern of human interaction.

Consider how this understanding of the four styles applies to your own family. Are differing family members respected for their unique talents? Or are they, instead, treated as "royal pains"? To be sure, it might seem peculiar to appreciate someone who continually challenges you. With family members it can be doubly difficult to transform hostility into positive esteem, for you may have experienced a lifetime of ill feelings. Over time, arguments solidify into grounds for disliking someone for the way they've treated you—and no wonder. Quarrels within families are often highly personal and emotionally charged. Real feelings are unleashed, not kept under wraps as when debating someone at work. Therefore, family conflicts frequently escalate into personal insults aimed at the messenger rather than the message. In order to get beyond the negative feelings about a family member, recognize that the differences in your individual messages may have been provoking the insults all along. If you can accept life's fundamental need for differences in thinking, you can see why disagreement occurs. And you may even come to respect those people who naturally oppose your own thinking.

In some cases, friction between family members may stem from an altogether different set of conditions. If a family tends not to include one of the four types of thinking, then one of its members might feel the need to shift out of his or her own natural style to fill the breach. For example, a heart-style person may step in to fulfill the club role among the family, simply because no one else in the group is inclined to do so. As a result, this person may feel "drafted" into a position that feels unnatural to them in order to be responsible to the family. Under these circumstances, this person may harbor a latent anger for having been cast into a role that he or she no longer wishes to play.

In reality, there are many ways that different personal styles affect family relationships. This chapter's glimpse of the royal family was just an introduction. Chapters 6, 7, and 8 (part 2) deal with the problems of various styles faced by couples, and chapters 9 and 10 (part 3) focus on family differences with parents, in-laws, siblings, and children. Those chapters will expand your awareness of thinking styles, and in them you'll find useful techniques for adjusting attitudes, shifting styles, and rebuilding relationships. But take note that we'll be discussing common differences in people's thinking styles that give rise to arguments and disagreements—normal, everyday give-and-take. More serious family schisms attributable to psychological disorders, criminal acts, incest, physical abuse, substance abuse, and the likes, are not the subject of this book.

THE STANCE OF YOUR PERSONAL STYLE

Let us return to a key point of the self-test exercise. With the benefit of your profile scores, position yourself in the boxing ring in figure 3.4. Go ahead, pencil yourself onto the blank diagram as one of the boxers. Now think of the people in your family with whom you regularly disagree or feel some discord. Based on what you have gathered so far from reading about the personal styles, place these people on the diagram as well. This doesn't mean that they actually belong at a particular corner or side, for you can't know

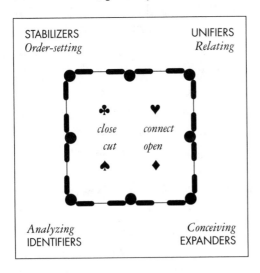

STABILIZERS
Order-setting

UNIFIERS
Relating

♣
close
cut

♥
connect
open

♠

♦

Analyzing
IDENTIFIERS

Conceiving
EXPANDERS

FIGURE 3.4

that unless they also take the same self-test and are willing to share their results. However, this positioning will represent your perception of where you and they stand.

Recognize that there is something about your style, and that of others, that can cause disagreement. As you become more familiar with the attributes of your own strong suit, you will form a clear idea of why your style tends to clash with the style of a particular family member. In the next chapter, you will learn that it isn't just their behavior and silent thoughts that get to you. It is their words, too—perhaps it is their words most of all.

CHAPTER FOUR

LANGUAGE STYLES

How Thinking Styles Are Expressed by Different Sets of Words

With such differing attitudes among the four personal styles, be thankful that people don't know one another's thoughts, or you might be having telepathic arguments with half the human race. Unless you speak with someone, you're usually not aware of whether or not his or her views oppose your own. We're rarely upset merely by the looks of another person, although looks and behavior can reveal meaningful clues about another person's style. Consider how disheveled a young, free-spirited diamond could look to an older, proper-minded club. Usually, though, it takes words to start someone's blood boiling. Words provide the evidence that another person's thinking is different from ours.

How are differences of opinion coded into words that cause us to get mad at each other, to feel angry and upset? How can two loving people be having a wonderful day, until one of them makes an innocent remark and the other says, "There you go again," which starts a new battle of their ongoing war? How do words stir such emotion? It is because categories of words differ in the same way that the personal styles oppose each other. Over the course of human evolution, words have come to articulate and foster each of the four types of thinking processes. So, it turns out that we have four distinct word-sets, each favored by types of people who prefer a certain way of thinking. Each of the four personal styles has its own language style, which is a cluster of words they favor. Such words express the way that people of a particular style like to think. With this insight you can identify what it is about another person's spoken or written words that negatively affects you.

HOW SIGNATURE WORDS REFLECT THINKING STYLES
The prospect of attempting to recognize four distinct language styles might sound complicated since there are so many words. But surprisingly, it is not. To see how this works, let us simply pare down our ordinarily complex language to basic words, then consider how these combine to form the diverse views found in everyday life. Fortunately, this doesn't require memorizing whole dictionaries of words. We already have four key words marking the essence of each of the thinking styles.

Style	Key Word	Thinking Process
♦	Open	Conceiving
♣	Close	Order-setting
♠	Cut	Analyzing
♥	Connect	Relating

Language styles branch out from these elementary root words: *open, close, cut,* and *connect.* Let's give this a try by generating four different sets of word strings. See if you can decipher which one of the following word sets goes with each of the four personal styles.

a. Together, flow, harmony, care, link, embrace, like, mesh, community, peace, love.

b. Evaluate, question, part, separate, choose, pinpoint, problem, inquire, solve, decide.

c. Maintain, require, keep, routine, step, should, save, conserve, limit, locked, safe.

d. Free, view, wish, could, space, wonder, out, fantastic, imagine, vision, new, leap.

The answers are in the notes at the end of the book, if you need them.[1] But you probably won't, for these represent basic divisions in thought. Linking and separating are opposing processes, as are routine steps versus new leaps. Each string is an elaboration on one of the four key words—*open, close, cut, connect*—so you can take almost any word and readily make this determination. Just figure out which of the four key words is closest in meaning to the word you are evaluating and you can quickly determine which type of thinking process the word represents. Decipher several words in a sentence, paragraph, or series of statements, and you get an understanding of the underlying intent, of which the speaker or writer may not even be aware.

This is easiest to do with written statements, because speech passes through perception so quickly that you usually don't have time to stop and analyze individual words. In face-to-face conversations, it's often all you can do just to figure out the speaker's literal meaning, let alone a hidden pattern in the message. With written words, or even videotaped speech, you have more time for reflection. Keep in mind, however, that no one uses a particular language style all the time. In daily activities, people draw on the words of all thinking styles. It's unlikely, for instance, that you would detect someone's language style as they order food from a menu. Language styles are most noticeable when people are called upon to state what they truly believe, or describe the kind of work that is important to them. When it comes to explaining what a person values, out pours a flurry of words that signifies his personal style like a signature.

Such signature words mark the thinking styles individuals favor, and with which they identify themselves.

For example, here are two sets of phrases that were spoken by people you know: Bill and Hillary Clinton.[2] See if you can figure out which set of phrases was spoken by which Clinton.

QUOTATION SET 1

"We need to start rewarding people for making the tough decisions instead of just talking about them. We need to hold people accountable, so that if their rhetoric outpaces results, they know we're watching. We need to solve problems, not just talk about them."

"There are things that I think are wrong or things that I think should be fixed, and I am not at all shy about expressing my opinion. I try to be a direct person—but I don't tell people what to do."

"I don't mind criticism, and I don't mind controversy, as long as people are criticizing what is being done or said instead of personally attacking each other."

QUOTATION SET 2

"Family values mean to me that people make common sacrifices to stay together, to work together, to put primacy on the family unit . . . and to put their children first."

"No one will love this state more, care more about our people's problems, or work harder to see that we become what we ought to be."

"This beautiful Capitol, like every capitol since the dawn of civilization, is often a place of intrigue and calculation. Powerful people maneuver for position and worry endlessly about who is in and who is out, who is up and who is down, forgetting those people whose toil and sweat sends us here and pays our way. America deserves better."

With only a hundred words spoken by each of them, you can quickly identify the first speaker as someone who is direct, analytical, and challenging, while the second speaker empathizes with people's feelings. In this case it is the woman, Hillary, who is direct, and the man, Bill, who is empathetic. Note that their styles are evident by the following signature words.

♠ Hillary
Decisions, results, solve, problems, fixed, criticizing.

♥ Bill
Family, people, common, together, unit, love, care.

Their signature words match the tone of the key words *cut* and *connect*, which stand for the respective ways that Hillary and Bill like to think. Yes, both of them used the other's signature words in their own phrases, but in different contexts and meanings. Thus, when Bill used the word problems, he was referring to difficulties that people often face. When Hillary used the word people, she was pointing out the behavior of individuals, rather than the collective we, as Bill thinks of people. When each of them reinforced their fundamental messages by use of their own signature words, these were indicators of their personal styles.

By the use of just a few words defining their thinking specialties, this husband and wife express divergent approaches to life. Hillary projects the analytical acumen, decisiveness, and executive traits that give rise to strategic calculation and power. Bill, however, stands against those who are calculating and makes a case for relating to the needs of common people. While these attitudes oppose each other, Bill and Hillary have learned to value their partner's strengths, which compensate for their own deficiencies. He is the gifted campaigner, so good with people, and she is the tactical manager and policy mastermind. Together they are a team.

While both Bill and Hillary at times engage in their partner's area of expertise—he making tough decisions and she fostering family values and togetherness—you can read in their words and even their body language that Bill is most comfortable in the heart mode, and Hillary is most confident in the spade style. It is simply their nature to be this way, and you can detect it in the signature words of their individual language styles.

There are a number of other interesting examples of people whose language styles have been similarly noted. In appendix 2, phrases from famous people are categorized into the four styles, each reflecting their own approach to life. Combining those phrases with what you know about these people, you'll find that their words, attitudes, and tones all tend to reinforce their personal style. Typically, words and attitudes align to form a general pattern that identifies the person's thinking process as one of the four basic styles. Recognize the language style and you get a sense of which kind of thinking he or she is trying to express. And if you disagree with what someone is saying, it is likely that what's truly at odds are the styles you individually favor. The issue under dispute is just fodder for the underlying differences in your styles.

For a better understanding of the divergent meanings of signature words representing the four different styles, review tables 4.1.–4.3 As you scan the words listed under each of the styles, think of how they indeed reflect the key words *open, close, cut,* and *connect.* Try reading several lines from one of the styles, then shift to its opposing style (from club to diamond, or spade to heart) and read several more lines. Note how such contrasting sets of words can put you in different states of mind. You may even sense greater comfort as you read the words listed under your favored style than when you read the others.

Signature Words that Convey Club Style Messages

♣ Key Word: Close

TABLE 4.1

abide	fixed	permanent	slow
accepted	ground	persist	solid
account	halt	place	sound
authoritative	hierarchy	position	stable
base	hold	prevent	stand
caution	honorable	procedure	standard
calendar	immutable	recognized	standing
check	inflexible	regular	station
close	insure	reliable	status
code	judge	remain	stay
condition	keep	reputation	steadfast
conserve	lasting	require	step
constant	law	responsible	stick
continue	legal	resolute	still
delay	legitimate	restrain	stock
detail	limit	right	stop
determined	linger	rigid	straight
discipline	lock	rigorous	structured
dogma	maintain	ritual	substantial
durable	method	routine	sure
duty	meticulous	rule	system
earnest	neat	sacrament	tenant
effective	normal	safe	tidy
endure	obligation	sanction	time
ensure	official	save	unbending
established	order	schedule	unwavering
faithful	organize	security	unyielding
firm	patient	settled	values
	period	should	warranted

Signature Words that Convey Spade Style Messages

♠ Key Word: Cut

TABLE 4.2

affect	discern	mark	segregate
analyze	discount	measure	select
answer	discriminate	narrow	self
ascertain	dispose	name	separate
ask	dissect	negotiate	sever
assign	dissimilar	one	sharp
best	distance	part	shortcut
break	distinct	piece	shrink
challenge	diverge	pinpoint	simplify
chop	divide	portion	single
choose	divorce	power	slice
classify	downsize	premier	smart
compete	evaluate	prestige	snub
control	exact	preside	solve
concentrate	fix	problem	sophisticate
correct	focus	question	special
critique	get	rank	strategy
cross	goal	rating	strike
crosshairs	grade	reason	sway
curtail	guide	rebuff	target
debate	identify	reduce	test
decide	identity	refine	thrust
define	independent	refuse	tool
demand	inquire	remove	top
determine	knife	repel	tough
differentiate	lead	restrain	use
direct	leave	restrict	win
disband	logic	screen	weigh
discard	machine	segment	zero in

Signature Words that Convey Heart Style Messages

♥ Key Word: Connect

TABLE 4.3

add	correlate	knot	romantic
affinity	couple	layer	rub
associate	embrace	liaison	same
attach	enfold	like	sensitive
attraction	engage	link	sew
band	fabric	love	share
bind	face-to-face	marry	similar
bond	family	mediate	soft
bridge	fasten	meaning	soul
build	feel	meeting	splice
care	fit	meld	stick
cement	flow	merge	sympathetic
clasp	friendly	mesh	synthesize
cluster	fuse	mix	team
coalesce	give	mutual	tender
cohabitate	grasp	mystical	tie
collect	group	nation	together
combine	harmonize	near	touch
common	hearty	neighbor	trust
commune	include	net	unify
community	integrate	network	union
compassion	intimate	partner	unite
complex	intricate	peace	vicinity
communicate	join	people	warm
connect	juxtapose	poetic	we
concurrent	kin	relate	weave
construct	kind	relations	web
contiguous	kiss	rhyme	weld
converge	knit	rich (multiplicity)	yoke

Signature Words that Convey Diamond Style Messages

♦ Key Word: Open

TABLE 4.4

apparition	germinate	loose	space
art	grow	mind's eye	speculate
assume	guess	multifaceted	spellbound
bare	hint	multiply	spirit
believe	holistic	muse	spontaneous
candid	hope	new	spread
charmed	hunch	next	stretch
clear	hunt	notion	suppose
clever	idea	nude	surmise
conceive	ideal	open	suspect
conjecture	image	original	unclothed
could	imagine	out	unconfined
create	impulse	picture	unconstrained
design	increase	possible	unfettered
develop	informal	potential	unobstructed
divine	incredulous	prefigure	unrestricted
dream	initiate	preview	up in the air
expand	inkling	progressive	vague
explode	inspire	propose	vacillating
explore	instinctive	prospect	view
fancy	intuition	quest	visionary
fantasy	invent	quixotic	visualize
far	launch	reject	whenever
float	lawless	remote	whim
fluctuate	lax	search	whole
fly	leap	see	wild
free	liberal	seek	winged
future	light	sense	wish
generate	look	sky	wonder

Table 4.1 is not an all-inclusive listings of signature words, and certain words can uphold the attitude of a neighboring style as well. But at least this gives you a head start at recognizing the structure of an argument, and may be useful for pinpointing what others are driving at. Of course, you can't realistically carry around a list of signature words for daily reference, but remember, many words can be seen as evolving from the key words: *open, close, cut,* and *connect.* Figure out which key word is closest in meaning to the word you are deciphering and you can determine which style of thinking that it represents.

COMBINING WORDS OF NEIGHBORING STYLES

An individual's signature expressions may exhibit as many as two or even three active styles, but usually there will be a notable weakness in at least one of them. That is, one of the four categories of word sets will rarely be used by that person, and would rarely be used in descriptions of the person, as well. Your own void is illustrated by the lowest score(s) in your profile of self-test results. It represents the thought processes you prefer to avoid. Sometimes it is easier to identify a person's style by this void than by their most used words. For example, President Clinton rarely uses analytical words such as *evaluate, deduce, conclude.* One can spot the obvious absence of spade words in his public messages. Most often a person's strong suit is the opposite of the void, and they will prefer to use their strong suit's words.

Study people's messages and you will find that the configurations of their signature words generally follow either a one-armed or two-armed boxer pattern. That is, their thoughts are expressed using words from their strong suit along with words from one or two neighboring suits. Over the next few pages, this concept will be explored by analyzing the speech of two American politicians. Since you have heard these people speak and know their personalities, they will serve as useful examples here. By studying their speech patterns, you'll have a head start in understanding various language styles.

In order for politicians to garner large followings, they must be able to reach out to neighboring styles (or "camps" as they are often called in politics). The successful ones must be able to convincingly communicate with at least three of the four styles to gain strong support. This is no easy trick since two of any three styles will oppose each other. In the following examples, note how seasoned leaders reconcile two opposing secondary styles from the solid base of their primary style. As revealed by signature words, their thoughts weave among three of the four types of processes.

First, listen to Bob Dole, longtime United States Senator and 1996 Republican candidate for president. (Emphasis is added for key words.) Early in the campaign, upon winning enough primary votes to secure the nomination, Dole said, "I *think* it's *safe* to say I will be the nominee. That's only the first *step*. That's only the first *step*."[3] Later, when asked in an interview what he hoped might be said of a future "Dole era" if he were elected president, he said (emphasis added), "I *think* a *period* of *stability*, a *period* of *downsizing* the government, maybe of *reconnecting* government with (people), *basic* American *values*, you know, sort of regaining our *status* as a world leader—whether we like it or not we are the world leader—and, you know, *reducing* the deficit, balancing the budget."[4]

Dole's italicized signature words, which express his personal style, show that the order-setting club routine prevails, as indicated by the words *step, stability, safe, period, basic values*. Next in quantity are the cut/analyze spade words: *think, downsizing, reducing*. Here, *think* indicates an evaluation, whereas someone else might have said, "I feel," or "I believe," or "I guess." And the word *status* attests to the combination of these two processes, that of evaluating and establishing one's position by measurable standards. Also represented here, but used least of all, is the heart's reconnecting with people (and only a tentative "maybe" at that).

Now, where is the void? What suit is missing? It is the expansive, conceptualizing diamond dimension that is absent. So is it any wonder that Dole was panned for a lack of vision? Sensitive to this criticism, he later began to emphasize his "view" in political comments. All of a sudden it was, "Bob Dole's view is this . . . ," or, "It's my view that. . . . " However, the word *view* sounded hollow, because it did not match his method of operation. In fact it conflicted with other, solidly stabilizing words in the very same statements. A speechwriter can work such opposing themes into political speeches, but you know when the messages don't fit a politician's personal style. One might say that for Dole, club words were his dominant style, spade and heart words were his secondary styles, and diamond words were almost absent from his speech.

Let's turn now to Dole's opponent. As Bill Clinton delivered the State of the Union address early in 1996, he was already campaigning. In that speech he undermined the Republicans' position by adopting, as his own, several of their initiatives toward family values and public safety. Then he finished in classic Democrat fashion with an appeal for Americans to go forward toward their dreams together (key words have been italicized):

> "We can only achieve our destiny *together*—one hand, one generation, one American *connecting* to another. There have always been things we could do *together*—*dreams* which we could make real—which we could never have done on our own. We Americans have forged our identity, our very *union,* from *every point of view,* and *every point on the planet, every different opinion.* But we must be bound *together* by a *faith* more powerful than any doctrine that divides us, by our *belief* in *progress,* our *love* of *liberty,* and our relentless *search* for *common ground.*"

Here, the dominant process is the heart's connective relationships: *together, connecting, union, faith, love, common ground.* And these are opposed to "any doctrine that divides us." Clinton's highest density cluster, in hearts, is marshaled against his implied void of spades. He also features the open, conceptual diamond style: *dreams, belief, progress, liberty, search*. The reiteration of *every point of view, every point on the planet*, and *every different opinion* generates a multifaceted, holistic image. This is a heart-diamond finish to a speech that, earlier, detailed in a heart-club manner, his programs to serve the people's needs, with an emphasis on traditional family values. The overall theme countered the Republicans' spade message of budget-cutting. Clinton's tone was conciliatory, but showed his resolve to stick to his concerns for people. Throughout, Clinton demonstrated his dominant heart style with secondary strengths in clubs and diamonds.

Nearly everyone speaks or writes using signature words of two and sometimes three thought processes, the fourth usually being void or in shadow. Many people favor a pair of processes, of which one is usually dominant. Combine words from any two adjacent suits and you activate those thought processes. With this insight, it is easy to see why people favor certain careers, because career fields develop from sets of neighboring processes. And the specialists in different career fields tend to communicate using various combinations of language styles. Think of fields (such as law, religion, poetry, art, or science) as occupying positions around the card table, much like the card players, or perhaps sitting between them. Thus, over time, people of all styles have found ways to earn their livings in career fields that use their favored thinking processes and allow them to speak and write in the language styles they prefer. It stands to reason, then, that certain fields might be philosophically at odds with certain others. Examples include the age-old debate between science and religion, or the differences between lawmakers and motion-picture artists. If people's personal styles are to some degree genetically influenced, as they may well be, then there could be considerable truth to the adage that a person is born to be a lawyer, poet, preacher, or policy analyst.

In the next few pages, you will move around all sides of the card table as you listen to the four language styles reflected in the speech of people in particular careers. In these examples, you will see why people with certain personality styles become interested in certain vocations. But more importantly, you might find similarities between these speech styles and the tone of someone at work or at home who may be frustrating you. If you are having a problem getting along with someone, identify which of these four examples sounds most like them; then note which thinking styles are represented and compare them with your own personal style profile. As another exercise, determine which of the four examples makes you most comfortable, which makes you least comfortable, and see where they are positioned relative to your own profile.

THE SPADE-CLUB COMBINATION

Let's begin this look into various career fields and their language styles by stringing together some words that characterize both the analyzing spade and the order-setting club processes: *decide, rule, evaluate, judge, responsible, justice, proper, keep, order, code, classify, save.* What have you got? *Law.* With a dozen basic words from two types of thought, a field of specialty emerges. The field of law perpetually refines its classifications and procedures to further specify spade-club thinking, which in turn generates more and more laws and field-specialty words. In the practice of law, these specialty words can become so narrow and exclusive that they form a jargon that only legal specialists understand.

There are, of course, other careers for people who favor spade-club thinking. Here is a statement by Dr. Leslie Gelb, president of the U.S. Council on Foreign Relations. In his address here on policy guidelines, note the tone of the message and his signature words (which have been italicized for emphasis in this and later examples):

> In *order* to have a coherent national *security policy,* you have to come back to the issue of *security.* That's the beginning of it,

because you can't achieve these *goals* unless you find some way of establishing security. . . . I think that the essence of an American security policy has got to be the establishment and the maintenance of a legitimate international *order*. That is the essential condition for the pursuit of our *goals*. And to do that gets us involved in all these incredibly tricky and difficult *problems* about *how to deal* with ethnic and civil conflicts—what I call "wars of national debilitation." I don't pretend to have answers to how you deal with them, but I think I have some sensible *guidelines* about how to *think* about them: that we need to take various kinds of *preventative action* to deal with them, that we ought to be in the business of *institution* building. . . .[5] ♠ ♣

This is conventional reality speaking: handle problems; make policy. It's serious stuff. Gelb advocates security through organized procedures, using signature words of the spade (*problems, answers, think, goals, deal, guidelines*) and of the club (*order, security policy, maintenance, preventative action, establishment, institution*). His speech urges us to analyze and solve challenging problems (spade), and organize policies and institutions to maintain order (club). No wishful symbolism clouds this approach. Feeling and relating are not even onstage.

The analyzing and order-setting combination cautions us to think and act decisively. Evaluate issues, be thorough, have goals, base actions on prepared programs, manage or govern by policies, formulate and follow laws, establish organizations to promote safety, act responsibly, be tough, and persevere. Spade-club thinkers often name and number things, as in, "First, we must take stock." This is the domain of business managers, investment advisors, accountants, auditors, attorneys, administrators in government or military. They employ words that suggest the problem-solving process necessary for the success and preservation of the individual, group, institution, company, nation, or world order.

THE DIAMOND-HEART COMBINATION

Each side of the square, four-way system has its own distinctive voice and message. Let's now move to the directly opposite, diamond-heart side of the table. This combination links relating words with conceiving words: *dream, hope, together, flow, harmony, meaning, expand, open, like, rhyme, connect, relate, imagine.* It suggests poetry and art in general, everything from painting to music. Here is an attitude toward life that is an obverse mirror image of the serious, grounded—and conventional—spade-club reality. It is the world of artists and writers. It is also the realm of many helping professionals, for whom structure, systems, tests, conquest, and economic mastery goes against the grain. Diamond-hearted free spirits are most content to follow their dreams and promote a world of pacific coexistence with similar-minded people and with nature. An example of this disposition is seen in writer and psychologist Sam Keen, who advocates, in the following passage, that men venture out on a spiritual journey (italics added):

One of the disciplines of the spiritual life is the practice of *shifting perspectives,* turning the *diamond* to *see* each of its *facets,* holding to the complexities of the paradox. *Look* into the concave surface of the fun-house mirror and you see horror and suffering; look into the convex surface and you see *beauty* and *joy.* To get through the world alive *we have to care until our hearts break* and cram our lives full of enjoyment. . . . Only enjoyment and gratitude for our lives *create a spontaneous impulse* to *care for others.*

If I were asked to diagnose the spiritual disease of modern men I would not concentrate on symptoms such as our lust for power, our insatiable hunger for gadgets, or our habit of repressing women and the poor. I would, rather, *focus* on our lack of *joy.* . . . The most successful among us are far too busy to waste time on *simple* pleasures like *jasmine* and *friendship.*[6] ♦ ♥

Keen's visual and spatial words, such as *look, see,* and *perspective,* encourage open, conceiving (diamond) attitudes. The use of the word *jasmine* stimulates rich, imaginative associations. The relating process (heart) is evoked by words like *care* and *friendship*; this is about connecting with other people. And, of course, the words *diamond* and *heart* say it all. (The above quotation differs from a religious mandate, that we should uphold a higher law; here, spirituality is achieved by breaking out of our conventional needs for power, success, and timely efficiency, to seek a more spontaneous, caring, and joyful way to live.)

The conceiving/relating side of the square encourages us to expand connective associations, open ourselves to new experiences, and relate to others through song, art, humor, and myth. It seeks to create meaning, ponder possibilities, dream of a better world, give freely, abandon safe reality, avoid confrontations of power, and fearlessly bypass conformity. Diamond-hearted spirits are often artists, entertainers, designers, writers, or are involved in careers related to helping others. They create with images, symbols, metaphors, and expression. Life is about feeling and experiencing being alive.

THE HEART-CLUB COMBINATION

Next is a set of words from the relating and order-setting styles. The heart-club uses words like *love, care, should, maintain, law, responsible, together, save, harmony.* With a little elaboration on these, people build phrases and stories, and join other like-minded people to connect and preserve society. People of a heart-club orientation document communal attitudes. They weave fables and myths that guide others to diminish the spade's individualistic stance and experience their relating nature. This orientation, involving connective meaning, can produce powerful experiences that make one feel linked with the entire universe. The heart-club personality, valuing structure and loyal to authority, organizes churches and temples in which people gather and worship together. Rituals intrinsic to this way of thinking are woven into documents (scriptures) to record procedures of the order's faith. Because the fabric of organized religion is knit of these threads of relating and order-setting, it is rather oblivious to change, and sustains some of our oldest cultural traditions. *Religio* means "link back"—the connecting link.[7] Religion develops from concentration of the heart and club dispositions.

In the following informal talk, Catholic bishop John Myers speaks in terms of *we* rather than *I*. As a Christian theologian, his personal aims are put in the service of a higher, impersonal authority. His statement is steeped in ordered relating. Note how Myers's trust in religion and Keen's notion of the spiritual quest (the previous diamond-heart example) are quite different themes:

Theology is an activity of faith that is a particular way of our responding to God's initiative. We do so not because we are curious, but because we want to love—because we have already had the grace to turn our lives over to God. And this calls forth a basic trust in our God who has addressed this word to us. Theology has its birth in God's holy people—his church at prayer. It is there that people reflect and pray upon and come in contact with the Holy *Scriptures* and with the saving mysteries present for us in each of the *sacraments.* . . .

Theology aims at truth, not at power. The problem of some theologians, including some feminist theologians, is that they want to make their own program—their own experience—paramount. They desire to put lenses on, if you will, so that they exclude from God's revelation those things that do not square with their own experience or make them uncomfortable. Our ability to reason is our great *gift of having been created by God in such a way so as to share and reflect* the very image of our Creator. It is *ordered to a purpose.* And this purpose is to understand the truth of our existence as it has been perfectly expressed in Jesus Christ.[8] ♥ ♣

Expressed here is a duty to serve others. Myers is not curious; he tends to close off further exploration and takes issue with those who would initiate change. Rather, he prefers established procedures set down in *Scriptures* and the *saving mysteries* of the *sacraments*. This club message is furthered by his remark that life is *ordered to a purpose*. Fittingly, he joined an order devoted to preserving tradition and perpetuating ritual. Myers's heart theme is voiced in these phrases: *we want to love; gift of having been created by God in such a way so as to share; come in contact with;* and *pray*. A less apparent heart message is his acceptance of power residing in another being other than himself, as expressed in the words *faith, trust, turn our lives over to,* and *not at power*. This deference to authority is a basic fact of life for many heart-styled individuals, particularly introverted ones, because so often people of other styles are in charge.

The relating-ordering pair implores us to follow procedures, work for the common good, respect authority, adhere to community standards, promote security, and care for the welfare of others. It invites us to trust, join the club, and appreciate life as it is. It advocates traditions and values. People of this orientation might become teachers, nurses, social workers, businessmen or -women, salespersons, or even lawyers. Whatever they become, they bring to their career a commitment to the virtues of rules, ties, and actions intended to stabilize relationships with others.

THE SPADE-DIAMOND COMBINATION

Moving around to the opposite side of the square, strung together now are words of the analyzing spade and the conceiving diamond: *imagine, question, reason, evaluate, dig, expand, name, dream, identify, explore*. This combination suggests the analytic and visionary mathematician, architect, or psychoanalyst. It is also descriptive of groundbreaking, theoretical science. Science conceives and evaluates perceptions to identify causes and effects. Those involved in analyzing often don't understand people who prefer relating (and vice versa), because they specialize in wholly different thought processes and speak separate language styles. The language of science is fundamentally opposed to the language of formal religion. Thus, Sigmund Freud could diagnose religion as a collective neurosis.

Once developed, a profession favoring a pair of thought processes attracts new entrants who tend to think along the same lines. But from any combination of processes—in this case the spade and diamond—there are many different career interests represented. This only attests to the diversity of the human mind. For example, auto repairmen, scientists, and foreign-policy analysts all tap the diamond-spade integration of creative analysis, but they refine their methods and terminology for varied applications. (Henry Kissinger once said that Americans think of foreign policy as a "subdivision of psychiatry.") While individual practices and jargon may seem quite different, all of the above examples of diamond-spade specialists must possess a certain vision and an ability to narrow a spectrum to make choices. Consider Donald Trump; note in this next example how the spade-diamond combination manifests in his expression of entrepreneurial inventiveness:

> Deals are my *art form*. Other people paint beautifully on canvas or write wonderful poetry. I like making deals, preferably big deals. That's how I get my kicks. Most people are surprised by the way I work. *I play it very loose.* I don't carry a briefcase. I try not to schedule too many meetings. I leave my door open. You can't be imaginative or entrepreneurial if you've got too much structure. I prefer to come to work each day and just see what develops. . . .
>
> My style of deal making is quite simple and straightforward. I aim very high, and then I just keep pushing and pushing and pushing to get what I'm after.

> I like thinking big. I always have. . . . Most people
> think small, because most people are afraid of success, afraid
> of making decisions, afraid of winning. And that gives
> people like me an advantage. . . . I also protect myself by
> being flexible. I never get too attached to one deal or one
> approach.[9] ♠ ♦

Trump exploits possibilities with a cool passion to push them into reality. He avoids both schedules and structure (club methods) and, instead, advocates diamond spontaneity by *playing it very loose,* and *being flexible, open,* and *imaginative*—coming to work each day to just see what develops. He considers business deals to be his *art form.* The spade part of his message is expressed in these words: *decisions, success, winning, thinking big, aim, straightforward, advantage, pushing, pushing, pushing.* Moreover, Trump avoids attachment. Deals are not motivated by relationships with others. Rather, he separates himself from the pack and attempts to stay one-up. From the above frank statement concerning his drive, one senses a single-minded competitiveness toward triumph, at all costs, that is characteristic of the spade's edge.

The analyzing-conceiving side of the square independently strives to break free of old ways of doing things, to invent new systems, develop alternate approaches, achieve gain regardless of hurt feelings, charge fearlessly forward, take a chance, challenge authority, abandon tradition, change the rules, think of the future, and create a new world. Spade-diamond thinkers use language designed to alter the existing order—if necessary, at the expense of broken ties.

Note the self-centeredness that can emerge as an aspect of anyone in full mastery of his or her own decisions. Some might call it an overblown ego. But consider how spade thought processes actually allow the ego to develop in the first place. From childhood on, an individual defines himself or herself by a selective capacity to narrow and separate one's own self-identity from the world at large, an act of reductive analysis. The ego is one's own realization of "this is who I am." As one matures, ego development comes to include self-definition of one's skills and unique capabilities, distinct from those of other people: "This is who I am, and I am very good at doing this." Because individuals who possess strong spade, analytical talents tend to quickly make choices and draw logical conclusions, they often grow quite self-confident in their abilities to decide on a best course of action or an optimum solution, and to challenge others to accept their ideas. They may know they have an advantage that allows them to win or succeed over others. So these individuals, firmly grounded in this analytical mode, often display a self-assuredness that we commonly ascribe to big or self-important egos. Consider how this trait opposes the subservient style of the heart-club example, Bishop Myers, in which his own personal interests yield to the greater good of a religious and social order.

AWARENESS OF LANGUAGE STYLE
DIFFERENCES CAN PREVENT CONFLICTS

You have now been all around the table, crossing over to opposing sides to see how the language styles and values of various professions differ from one another. None of the four people in our examples encompasses the whole truth represented by the table's full range of thinking styles. Since the whole truth includes pairs of opposite values, there is no way for any one person or particular way of thinking to embody the whole truth. Each career field (and each combination of thinking styles) is one-sided in presenting its own version of the truth and opposing another's version of the truth. Yet all are right insofar as they articulate their own particular piece of the whole truth.

With the understanding of language styles and the way most people's words, career preferences, behavior, and thinking all tend to be consistent within their personal style, you now have the big picture of how thoroughly this four-way structure pervades human life. Many of these aspects of individual differences are hard to define. Describing someone else's behavior, for example, can involve a lot of our own subjective interpretation. But knowledge of the four styles of language provides a more objective means of evaluating an individual's personality. A person's words, in speech and writing, are their instruments for articulating their beliefs and views. By interpreting what a person says according to their language style, you are better prepared to understand what they are truly driving at, with fewer of your own subjective biases clouding your perception of their viewpoint. Discern another's language style and how it might differ from your own, and you will be more able to listen to them without being offended or angered by what they say. By seeing that both parties can have valid positions but still be on different sides of an issue, you can attain a higher ground in interpersonal relations, with less necessity to slight another for their different orientation. The whole truth does not reside in any particular camp, but in the inclusion of them all. Issues are less a matter of "I am right, and you are wrong," rather, people simply disagree and see things differently.

This awareness also may help clear up feelings of guilt or a sense of personal inadequacy for not being able to fully accept, let alone support, the views and values of another style. For example, if you have strong spade-diamond tendencies, you might not be religiously inclined. Now you know why. Or if you exhibit heart-diamond traits, you may feel incompetent in the game of corporate politics, while others seem perfectly suited to the one-upmanship needed for climbing the organizational ladder. There is nothing wrong with you, but you may not be in a career or an environment where your own strengths are fully appreciated and validated.

The next chapter steps away from the public arena to apply the principles of language styles to daily-life situations at home and at work. We'll see how the misunderstandings between people of different styles are played out and resolved. And you'll learn that when you are actually in the act of disagreement with another person on everyday issues, your listening skills will be tested to the utmost.

CHAPTER FIVE

UNDERSTANDING THE LANGUAGE STYLES OF PEOPLE IN YOUR LIFE

Listening for Indications of What People Are Really Thinking

In real-life situations you don't often find people talking at length about their beliefs. Yet you can usually detect people's differences by paying careful attention to their language styles. Picture a couple, Maxine and Randy, who live in a comfortable suburban neighborhood in Arkansas. She is an attorney, and he is the town's mayor. This is an imaginary couple, you understand. And their dispute is over who will walk the dog, Puff. Randy starts the exchange with a request: "Honey, can you walk Puff? I've got to prepare for a press conference."

"If I do, I'll be late for my own meeting," Maxine says. "It's your job to walk Puff."

"Yes, and we should talk about that!"

"Not now," Maxine answers. "If you'd have told me sooner, I could have planned to walk Puff, but I'm prepared to meet a client at the IRS in half an hour."

"What does that mean? You're *prepared*, and I'm not. Is that it?"

"Well, dear, you're not, are you? If you'd have prepared last night instead of playing cards so late with your friends, you'd have time for Puff now."

"Why is Puff always my job? You're the one who wants him walked by eight every morning."

"Randy, dear, you like walking Puff. You always have stories of people you meet along the way. I thought you enjoyed your morning walk!"

"I do, but not *every* morning. It's a hassle *every* morning! Why can't you do it sometimes? You know, just on a whim? Or wouldn't you be caught dead walking the dog?"

"I don't mind walking Puff . . . sometimes."

"Yes, you do. You think it's beneath you."

"I do not!"

"Maxine, when was the last time you took care of Puff? You wouldn't walk the dog if your life depended on it!"

"That's a mean thing to say, Randy, and you know it."

Now, what is this all about? Is this only a matter of who will walk Puff, or does it expose a deeper rift between Maxine and Randy? Actually, the underlying argument is about their individual ways of thinking. The issue of walking the dog serves as an entry topic for their ongoing debate over their style differences. In the above conversation, Maxine and Randy have staked out two opposing sides at the poker table of their relationship. You quickly sense that Maxine is the decisive and prepared member of the pair, the one who typically sets the family procedures. On the other hand, Randy enjoys partying and chatting with neighbors on the street, and he doesn't much like the daily routine she enforces. From these clues, you already suspect that Maxine upholds the spade-club side of the game, and Randy represents the heart-diamond side.

With a knowledge of the card suit language styles we can better understand what fuels arguments such as this one. Here, Maxine joined the debate by remarking that Randy was not prepared, a typical club criticism. Randy responded with the diamond view that to follow the same routine every morning is a hassle. Maxine then questioned why that was a problem, since the walk was his daily opportunity to chat with neighbors. Still in the diamond mode,

Randy asked why Maxine couldn't occasionally walk the dog on a whim; then he immediately switched to a challenge to her spade ego ("You wouldn't be caught dead . . . You think it's beneath you")—thus turning up the heat of the argument. Maxine was so taken aback that, rather than return fire, she only denied the charge. Randy then played a heart trump card by observing that Maxine doesn't take care of Puff. Randy's emphasis on her non-relating nature felt mean to Maxine.

Notice the weapons each partner seized upon to challenge and wound the other. Maxine implied that Randy should give higher priority to preparing and organizing, rather than staying out late playing cards with friends. Randy insinuated that Maxine was too concerned about her own image to walk the dog, and because of this does not spend any time taking care of Puff. It is this last point that cut Maxine to the quick, because it hurt her to be reminded that she is not the warm, relating partner. In this dispute, each revealed a special knowledge of the other by pushing their "hot buttons." Such buttons press on the sensitive spots in one's personal style, which are—in this case—the deficiencies that the other spouse fills. In tapping these hot buttons, it is as if each one says to the other, "I know your weakness. Remember, this is what I do for you."

Had the argument been raised to an even higher pitch, Randy and Maxine might have gone beyond jabbing at each other's weaknesses, and instead resorted to hot buttons that actually taunt the core strengths of the partner's style. For example, Randy might have said that if Maxine cannot stand to be even a few minutes late for a meeting then she has no real control over her life—in spite of the fact that she customarily has matters well under control. And for her part, Maxine might have accused Randy of being crass and insensitive, even though he is typically a very sensitive partner. Such messages would have escalated the battle, because such hot buttons directly challenge the partner's essential nature.

Looking at their argument on a deeper level, Randy's question— "When was the last time you took care of Puff?"—may refer to his own sense of not feeling adequately cared for or loved by Maxine. Indeed, he hinted at this when in response to Maxine's first argument ("It's your job to walk Puff"), Randy said, "Yes, and we should talk about that!" This comment indicates his desire for Maxine to be more caring. Oblivious to Randy's somewhat covert message, Maxine responded to his plea in a cool, spade, matter-of-fact way. After this, Randy contrived a contentious, argumentative route to achieve the interaction with Maxine that he needed. The tiff wasn't a particularly pleasant way to further his relationship with Maxine, but it did serve his longing for an emotional connection with her. In just such indirect ways, people often attempt to express their needs within a relationship. If a person's relationship requirements are not met, they often resort to subversive approaches to attain them.

An alternative and more positive turn of events might have been possible if each partner had started with an acknowledgment of the other's style, then listened for the other's spoken indications of their needs. For example, recognizing that Randy favors the heart style, Maxine might have realized that Randy's phrase, "We should talk," meant that he had a need for a closer relationship with her. If at that point she had addressed this need in a positive manner, she could have circumvented his move to secure what he wanted by taking an argumentative course. After years of familiarity with Randy, Maxine might know that he must obtain the intimacy he needs by one route or another. Her best strategy would have been to listen for his language style and to validate his nature at the earliest possible opportunity. This, of course, does not mean that she must bend to each of his wishes or give up her own needs. It just means that the ability to recognize and accept, and even give a little toward the other's needs, goes a long way in a personal relationship. Indeed, it is much more important to be recognized, each of us for what we are, than to get our own way all the time.

Randy, for his part, might have achieved a better connection with Maxine if he had validated her spade nature and her ability to identify his weaknesses. He might have said, "Yes, you're right, I'm not prepared. You know me. But I work best when I come down to the wire. That's when I get good ideas. Like I should give you a kiss right now." Note, however, that a kiss primarily answers Randy's needs at the moment, not Maxine's. This is a busy morning, and she has a business meeting coming up that is important to her. In recognition of her priorities, he might be wise to postpone discussion of this issue (his routine responsibility for walking the dog) until the evening when they both have some free time. This morning, Randy could say, "This is not the best time to talk about walking Puff. But can we agree to discuss it after dinner?" Such an agreement would assure both Maxine's need to maintain control over her schedule and Randy's need for closeness. This mutual validation of their different needs allows both to affirm their own nature and that of the other, rather than simply picking on each other's imperfections.

HEARING OPPOSING LANGUAGE STYLES AT WORK

The same ideas concerning the clues that language provides apply at work. Let's follow Maxine to the office, where she is telling her legal assistant, Ron, how she wants a document done.

"Judge Holmes is very demanding about the details, so follow the deposition format of the Avery case carefully, and check your work for errors—twice. I don't want Holmes berating me again for missing words. You remember that last deposition."

"I remember," Ron answers. "I'm not stupid. Why do you always bring up the Avery case? I made a mistake and I am sorry. Can't we forget it?"

"Ron, I bring these things up so you will stay sharp and focused. Legal work is exacting. You must get it right or I lose face. You can't la-dee-dah it the way my husband does his work. When you make errors, the other attorneys and judges skewer me on all sorts of technicalities."

"But how do you think I feel when you tell me how to do everything? I'm not a child, you know."

"No, Ron, you're not. I don't mean to hurt your feelings. Why does everyone get their feelings hurt? Listen. I like you. You're a nice guy. But you have to be very accurate."

"I try."

"Ron, in this profession, trying doesn't cut it. You have to be dead-on every time. You understand?"

"I understand. You don't care how I feel."

"I can't care about how you feel, or we'd be out of work. Both of us. Ron, if you're going to stay in this job, you have to be as tough and demanding on yourself as I am."

"I'm not sure I can stay in this job."

"That's your choice. You control your own future."

"Yes, I do control it," Ron remarks as he walks away from Maxine's desk. Just beyond her door, he mutters under his breath, "Bitch!"

Maxine thinks to herself, "Flake!"

Again, a contrast of personal styles, reflected in Maxine's and Ron's use of language, drives this confrontation. Maxine is in her element as an attorney, and at the office she has greater control than she does at home with her husband. Perhaps she has even selected Ron as her assistant because he is somewhat like her husband. Yet at the office she is fully responsible for deciding how things are to be done. For his part, Ron is not mature enough to see that as an extroverted diamond with a heart bias, he might truly be in the wrong job. He, in fact, yearns to be in an environment free of details where he can work in close harmony with associates who are sensitive to his feelings. But he is employed under a very exacting boss whose requirements are at odds with his own favored style. Although working for Maxine is good training for his weak spade-club side, Ron realizes that too often he is reminded of his shortcomings and not recognized for his talents. Thus, he may decide to seek a new job. And Maxine may learn that she needs an assistant whose style is more like her own.

In her office, Maxine is more inclined to speak in spade and club language styles than she is at home. In the exchange with Ron, she made her point with words and phrases such as: *demanding about the details, follow the format, check your work, stay sharp and focused, exacting, get it right, I'd lose face, skewer, all sorts of technicalities, accurate, doesn't cut it, dead-on, can't care, tough, choice, control your own future.* These spade and club messages, when strung together in a discussion, define the type of thinking Maxine is advocating. She maintains themes similar to when she argued with her husband, Randy. Walking the dog and drafting the legal document are only a few of the continually emerging matters over which her spade-club style will clash with those of the heart-diamond persuasion.

Ron is somewhat overwhelmed by Maxine's demands, as she is indeed his boss. And she speaks for a profession that demands accuracy, detail, and sound evaluation. Since he is her subordinate, and theirs is a professional relationship, Ron is unable to play some of the trump cards that Randy can use with Maxine. In this argument, Ron sticks to simple messages: forgive my errors, and care about my feelings. But note that under the deluge of Maxine's unrelenting spade speech, Ron is dislodged from his own preference for relationship and affirms, "Yes, I do control it [my destiny]." You can feel the parting of ways implied in that statement, for this disagreement caused him to energize an independent line of thinking. In his final statement (under his breath), Ron expresses his own evaluation of Maxine and calls her a "bitch." In similar fashion, Maxine declares Ron a "flake." Because of his attitude that she should assign as much importance to his feelings as to his accuracy, Maxine decides that Ron is not grounded. And relative to her, indeed he is not. From the viewpoint of his own style, however, he is quite adequately responsible.

The terms "bitch" and "flake" are slam words that people use to berate other people's thinking when it seems inappropriate from the home base of one's own style. These slam words often elicit an immediate angry reaction. Ron and Maxine wisely muttered such words only to themselves, for such terms communicate in a very brash way, "I totally reject your style." They imply that the other's way of thinking has no value whatsoever. Slam words are most often uttered when a person feels frustrated with another's seemingly inappropriate behavior. We have a wealth of slam words in our arsenal to fire at the various corners of the boxing ring. Here are some examples:

Slam words	Aimed at
You ditz! (. . . flake, daydreamer, airy-fairy, space cadet, featherbrain, airhead)	♦
You anal old fogy! (. . . fuddy-duddy, nitpicker, stick-in-the-mud, control freak)	♣
You heartless (. . . self-centered, cruel, brassy, cold-as-steel, callous) son of a bitch! (or bitch!)	♠
You wimp! (. . . gutless, mama's boy, patsy, mushy, sissy, bleeding-heart, pollyanna)	♥

Maxine's arguments at home and at the office parallel each other, because both her husband Randy and her assistant Ron oppose her spade-club nature. If, however, either Randy or Ron were nearer to her own style, then the structure of the exchange would be different.

Let's give Maxine a new legal assistant, Gerald, and replay her instructions to him.

"Judge Holmes is very demanding about the details, so follow the deposition format of the Avery case carefully, and check your work for errors—twice. I don't want Holmes berating me again for missing words. Gerald, you remember that last deposition."

"Yes, I'm so sorry. I don't know how I could have missed an entire sentence. But I had so many things going on that day. I regularly check everything over and over."

"Sometimes, Gerald, you can get so caught up in the details that you don't see the big picture. If you had read that deposition, instead of looking for commas, you would have noticed that you left out the name of the deposed."

"Yes, you're right. It was sloppy of me to make such a mistake."

"You're not sloppy, Gerald. My husband's sloppy. You're anything but. Your problem is that you can be too meticulous. Sometimes you need to step back for a fresh look at things."

"I do my best."

"Yes, I know you do. But you have to stay sharp, and don't forget the whole point of a document. The name of the deposed is crucial information in a deposition. You know that."

"Of course I know. But there are so many details to keep track of. I'm not sure I can handle this job."

"Yes, you can. You're much more thorough than my last assistant, Ron. Listen, with everything you type, take the time to sit back from your desk and read the paper copy, as if you were reading it anew for the first time. Can you do that?"

"Sure."

"Okay, Gerald, now do it right this time."

"I will," Gerald says as he walks away from Maxine's desk. Just beyond her door, he mutters under his breath, "Bitch!"

Maxine thinks to herself, "Hopeless!"

The same slam word for Maxine still applies, but Maxine now uses another term to characterize Gerald's club style. And what she drilled on in this example was his deficiency in the broader viewpoint. Maxine criticized him for being too narrowly focused and unable to see the forest for the trees. With Gerald, she promoted a spade-diamond message with these words and phrases: *you don't see the big picture, you don't step back, fresh look, stay sharp, don't forget the whole point, take the time to sit back from your desk, do it right this time.* She attempted to draw Gerald into a more detached frame of mind that would allow him to better evaluate his own work. Her persistence grated against Gerald's nature, as it did in her discussion with Ron. But in this case Gerald and Maxine are closer in style, and the argument didn't have the same highly charged emotions as the previous one.

94

In the last two examples with Maxine, notice that a person can shift into two or more styles depending on who they are with, and also on whether they choose to ally themselves with—or differ from—the other's style. Of course, Maxine must occasionally reach the zone of compromise between other individual's styles and her own—even with those of opposing styles like her husband's—for without the ability to sometimes find common ground, people cannot remain together. In order for people at home and at work to achieve a comfortable balance, they must meet each other partway. If she is to be successful at interpersonal relationships, Maxine must, at times, throttle down her own instinctual style and let others— Randy, Ron, and Gerald—have their way, especially when they have more effective skills for a particular situation. Becoming a mature person involves learning to let others express their own opinions and recognizing that we cannot always be right.

LISTENING FOR SIGNATURE WORDS

Now it's your turn to practice your budding skill at recognizing the four language styles and listening for signature words. As you try out this technique over the next few pages, and as you listen for signature words in the everyday speech of people around you, keep in mind that all of us make some use of all types of thinking, and therefore use words of all the styles at one time or another. In order to identify a person's style in a conversation, attempt to discern their use of signature words as signals of their true beliefs or values, and weigh an individual's statements to decide which styles predominate. Listen for clues in speech that precede personal style messages, such as: "I really believe we can . . . " "It's most important that . . . " "My goal will be . . . " "Our job is to . . . " or, "We should . . . " Such statements notify others that what follows is likely to announce their style. Here's an example: "We should make sure that everyone sticks with the official policy." The club style was conveyed by the words *should, sure, sticks with,* and *official policy.* Now here's a phrase combining two styles: "I believe we can both inspire people to create progressive ideas, and also encourage them to refine the tools for making smart business decisions." This speaker began with a diamond message (*inspire*, to *create progressive ideas*) and combined it with a spade phrase (*refine tools* for making *smart decisions*). In all probability the speaker is expressing his or her preference for a combination of diamond and spade styles.

For practice, here are ten sentences to evaluate for language styles. See if you can identify which single style is being expressed in each. The examples start with words or phrases that were listed in tables 4.1–4.4 in the preceding chapter. Then words that were not listed have been added, requiring you to apply the key-word method to identify the style. That is, for a word you are deciphering, figure out which key word (*open, close, cut,* or *connect*) is closest in meaning, and you can determine which style of thinking that word represents. The answers for the styles of each of the following sentences are in the notes at the end of book.[1]

a. "First, decide which goals are critical to the company's profitability."

b. "We must band together to care for the common needs of our people."

c. "You should play it safe and check to make sure the expenses are legitimate."

d. "Neat idea! Explore your hunch. Forget the costs. Color outside the lines."

e. "Tell me when you schedule these dinners so I can keep some order in my life."

f. "Be spontaneous and open to doing something on the spur of the moment."

g. "How about camping? We can commune with nature and talk and, well, bond."

h. "Gimme a break. I want some time alone. Camping won't make the cut."

i. "There's no way I'll take a flyer and bet the ranch on that foolish scheme."

j. "Ah, but wouldn't it be fun to follow where it goes and discover if it pays off?"

In the above examples, note how contrasting attitudes were expressed in opposing sets of signature words. Every two sentences opposed each other in style (*a)* and (*b)* were opposites, (*c)* and (*d)* opposites, and so on.

Usually a person's words reflect their natural style, but not always. While a person normally expresses a certain mode or combination of modes, on occasion they may actually take the opposite tack. For example, imagine a diamond woman who typically is free and unrestrained and is married to a diamond man. They are entertaining a friend for dinner, having a relaxed, fun-filled evening of discussion at the table. During dessert, the woman notices that her husband has picked up his piece of pie with his fingers and is eating it as one would a sandwich! This awakens some deep-seated sense of etiquette in her, and contrary to her own diamond nature, she launches into a verbal assault on him about his improper behavior. "Howard, what are you doing? Have you no table manners? That's not the way we eat! You're making a mess with those crumbs. Put the pie down and eat it the right way."

Where did that come from? the husband wonders. Usually he is free to be as loose and unstructured as he pleases. They are with a friend who won't be offended by his manners. "Oh, lighten up," Howard tells his wife. "You've eaten pie this way yourself when it's just the two of us. Why do you have to be the manners cop?"

"Someone has to do it," she answered. "Someone has to enforce some rules around here. If I didn't, you'd live like a slob!"

Both the words she uses and the tone of her voice say that she is taking charge and setting standards for the remainder of the dinner. In this somewhat formal social setting, the wife takes on the spade-club mantle of labeling her husband's actions inappropriate and attempts to impart some dignity to the occasion, even though doing so goes against her preferred, rule-free way of living. Occasional flip-flops of this kind—from one style to its opposite—are normal to all of us. And if you think about it, they are especially necessary when two like-minded people marry, because couples seek balanced thinking in their relationships. If both partners are of the same style, each is likely to step out of character at times to challenge the other from an opposing corner. When people are continually called upon to represent styles of thinking and behavior that contrast with their own natural style, however, they are likely to become rather unhappy campers. Such match-ups of partners will be discussed at length in later chapters.

BECOMING ATTUNED TO PEOPLE'S LANGUAGE STYLES
You now know how to recognize different language styles and to assess the personal style of a speaker. If you listen, most people eventually give you enough key-word clues to interpret their slant on life. In fact, it will probably not take very long at all. In the weeks ahead, make a point of identifying several persons' styles by paying attention to their written and spoken words. Once you get the hang of it, you will hear language styles everywhere you go. You will hear spade, club, heart, and diamond language when family members and friends speak to you. And you will notice signature words of the four suits as you listen to dignitaries on TV.

You will also become aware of the four language styles at the office as people express their views, beliefs, needs, and desires. Your boss might say, "Here's what I'd do. Forget what Human Resources says and fire that turkey! Seriously, Homer couldn't make a decision on his own if he tried. His goals are worthless. He won't take a bold stand on issues. Frankly, I don't even like the wimp." Hmmm, you say to yourself. There's a lot of spade attitude in that boss. But Homer is good with people in his personnel work. He and the boss may just be opposites in style.

Back at home your mother might say about your brother, "What's wrong with Billy? He never comes over. He knows how much I like to talk with him. I'm so happy when we all can be together. But Billy doesn't seem to care about family. What's wrong with him? He's so distant. It hurts that he treats me this way." Hmmm, you say to yourself. Good ol' Mom has such a big heart. Billy is so busy as a new floor manager, and so independent—so spade. Opposition of styles between Mom and Billy. Wonder if they could ever accept that they're just different, that's all.

In another example, you might be at home working feverishly in late February to file your taxes for an early refund when your wife or husband calls over to you at the desk, saying, "Let's get away this weekend. You've been working on that stuff for weeks. I've heard the new impressionists exhibit at the museum is wonderful. We could drive in, see the exhibit, stay over, and explore the city. Wouldn't it be fun to forget all those tax forms?" Hmmm, you say to yourself. I've been into these club procedures for weeks, and it might be good to experience a little diamond spontaneity. The taxes could wait a few days.

As you develop a savvy for styles, their languages, and attitudes, you might want to zero in on a few relationships. For instance, pick a person who makes you feel uncomfortable, and try to guess his or her style by listening carefully to what they say. Make a concerted effort to decipher the language styles in their conversations. If need be, jot down their words, especially those that offend you, or even ask them to write out what they want you to do. You will probably find that you can more easily spot signature words in print than you can in speech. This will be part of the challenge as you move from reading about language styles in this book to experiencing them in the reality of your own fast-paced life. But be assured that if you truly listen for the languages of the four styles, they will soon become very apparent.

SUMMARIZING THE STYLES AND THEIR LANGUAGES

Now you have a good overview of the four personal styles and how they operate. This is summed up in the Summary Guide to the Four Personal Styles (table 5.1, next page), which is designed to be photocopied from the book for your easy reference. Note that it is arranged in the same way as the other diagrams in the book, with opposing suits located diagonally across the page from one another. This guide gives you a brief description of all four styles, the type of thinking each favors, its strengths and weaknesses, its emphasis at work, a few signature words, and prominent people who display such a style. You can use the guide to help you recognize styles as you read on and as you apply this understanding in your own life.

In the remainder of this book, you will see how the four styles affect the way people relate to each other in couples, families, and work teams. And you will discover some techniques to deal with differences in styles, no matter where they are found.

Summary Guide to the Four Personal Styles

TABLE 5.1

♣ THE STABILIZER

Thought type: Order-setting—Operational mode of establishing procedures and routines, putting things in sequential steps, rule-making, setting standards.

Greater purpose: To establish stability—Provides the base of orderly foundations, codes, methods and traditions for the group.

Strengths: Responsible, precise—Methodical, thorough, attends to detail, disciplined.

Weaknesses: Cautious, near-focused—Rigid on how-to's, risk-adverse, pessimistic.

Ideal work: Steady, able to be right—Clearly defined, time to do tasks, evoking correctness.

Language key: Close—Signature words: account, conscience, judge, keep, law, limit, maintain, organize, rule, save, schedule, should, steps, stock, time

Prominent examples: Janet Reno, William Bennett, Queen Elizabeth

♠ THE IDENTIFIER

Thought type: Analyzing—Perceptual mode of selectively separating things into parts by logic, assigning, evaluating, deciding, and identifying goals/courses of action.

Greater purpose: To manage our reality—Provides the decision-making capability to narrow down, choose, and define the group's program.

Strengths: Decisive, problem-solver—Determines goal, persists, gets things done, self-reliant.

Weaknesses: Insensitive, impatient—Inflexible, unyielding, demanding of others

Ideal Work: Individual challenge—Independence, variety, control, direct answers

Language key: Cut—Signature words: answer, cool, critical, decide, determine, direct, ego, evaluate, inquire, pinpoint, problem, question, resolve, separate, think

Prominent examples: Martha Stewart, Mike Wallace, Prince Philip

---

Summary Guide to the Four Personal Styles (cont.)

♥ THE UNIFIER

Thought type: Relating—Operational mode of associating, linking and harmonizing thoughts, people, groups with each other, layering, building meaning, assembling.

Greater purpose: To build togetherness—Provides cohesiveness and team inclusiveness to interconnect group members with environs.

Strengths: People skills, expressive—Communicative, supportive, loyal, consistent.

Weaknesses: Indecisive, conforming—Procrastinating, possessive, avoids controversy.

Ideal work: Appreciated in group—Works with people, secure, minimal conflict.

Language key: Connect—Signature words: associate, care, commune, easy, engage, enrich, feel, flow, give, harmony, like, link, love, peace, soft, soul, together, union, warm

Prominent examples: Oprah Winfrey, Bill Clinton, Prince Charles

♦ THE EXPANDER

Thought type: Conceiving—Perceptual mode of envisioning possibilities, manipulating symbols holistically, imagining new ideas or courses of action, mind doodling.

Greater purpose: To develop a new future—Provides broader awareness and innovation which allows the group to adapt and grow.

Strengths: Perceptive, imaginative—Long-term thinking, creative, can-do, optimistic.

Weaknesses: Lacks follow-through—Overestimates, jumps ship, loose on procedures.

Ideal work: Uncontrolled—Open to spontaneity, free of detail, risk-enabling.

Language key: Open—Signature words: bare, could, create, develop, dream, free, generate, grow, guess, hope, imagine, inspire, leap, out, possibly, seek, space, spirit, wish

Prominent examples: Madonna, Robin Williams, Princess Diana

PART 2

DEALING WITH STYLE DIFFERENCES IN COUPLES

CHAPTER SIX

SEEKING COMPLETION IN ANOTHER PERSON

Love's Engagement of Styles

Perhaps you've had this experience or seen it in a movie: A woman and a man meet, and before long are entangled in an argument over some matter. Then suddenly the spirited confrontation changes into a passionate encounter, and the heated words are replaced by hot lovemaking. In real life, after the pair settles into living with each other, the early magic that their differences helped to create often wears off. But the differences remain. The couple is still at odds, but without the initial spark that ignited their romance. Is it possible not only to understand and work out those differences, but also to rekindle the spark?

In this chapter and the next, you'll learn how personal style differences between partners contribute to their attraction from the start, yet also cause conflicts in their relationship. And you'll probably recognize some problems shared by you and your mate. With the knowledge of the four personal styles, however, common relationship issues will become less puzzling, and workable solutions will become more obvious.

Sometimes a couple's problems also involve one partner's personal search for self-identity. Such issues are more understandable as well when seen in light of the thinking styles and the card suits. In this chapter, we'll explore how thinking patterns learned in childhood may come up for readjustment later on in life, and how you can recognize and deal with this change in your partner or yourself.

THE ROOTS OF MATE SELECTION

Since the friction between two people is often rooted in the pairing of their styles, let's begin by discussing how couples come together. Recall the story of Prince Charles and Diana. It illustrates that people desire what they lack. Indeed, what is desire in the first place if not the yearning for a sense of fulfillment and completion? Perhaps there is nothing more essential to one's choice of a lover or partner than the urge to complete some still-unfinished aspect of oneself.

There is an often-told myth that all souls were once complete, being both male and female. But at birth they had to choose either the form of a man or a woman, leaving the other part behind. The myth goes on to say that as a result of this loss each person searches throughout life for his or her "other half." In this quest many people find lovers and partners who fulfill that yearning. This division between the masculine and feminine is supposedly the foundation of romantic relationships, and of the partnerships that grow out of them. But gender is not the only way in which people differ. Most aspects of human nature—such as talents, temperaments, tastes, and tolerances—vary greatly from person to person, and many of these also call out for completion. In such qualities individuals seek their counterparts.

When we meet someone who exhibits attributes that we either lack in ourselves or have kept hidden and undeveloped, we are likely to have one of two reactions. One is revulsion, and the other is fascination. The pair described at the beginning of the chapter experienced both, but ultimately fascination won out. Had it not, their story would have ended in ill feeling—perhaps even hate at first sight! It would be a tale of what psychologists call the shadow, in which one senses and often resents in others exactly those qualities lacked or denied in oneself. If this negative dynamic had gained the upper hand, this man and woman would not have entered into a relationship at all. But for this couple, mutual fascination was the overriding force, and they became partners. In due course, they must accommodate their differences in order to nurture the joy and fulfillment they first found in each other. Before delving further into these matters, however, let us look at the developmental beginnings of one's personal style, and how one's formative years sway adult relationships.

Throughout childhood we are influenced by the values, attitudes, and behaviors we witness in our families—regardless of whether these are natural and comfortable to us. The first expressions of our own style may be shaped by these early experiences, which can stay with us well into adulthood. Such early development might be highly influenced by a particular parent, or quite possibly by a predominant family style—meaning a style that the whole family more or less takes for granted as the correct way to behave. This predominant style may well represent the influence of one parent who dominates the rest of the family, or, if both parents are somewhat like-minded, it might be a blend of their styles. In either case, the young person grows up with a leaning toward this style, which might suppress his or her own strong suit. For instance, Prince Charles was very conservative as a young man, adopting the Windsor's predominant family style of clubs. Yet Diana loosened him up after several years of marriage. Similarly, any young person can be conditioned to think along the lines of the influential adults in their family, and may spend much of their early life shaped by family biases. Growing up under a predominant family style that is different from one's true nature can make a person feel invalidated for the kind of thought and behavior they prefer. Thus, the person may feel that they are "not okay" and lack the confidence that they might have gained in another developmental environment that supported their natural style.

If a young person acquires a thinking orientation that is not true to his or her own nature, this person may find it difficult as they mature to express their true personality. Then, when seeking a mate, they may be drawn to a partner who offers the potential of bringing them around to their natural way of thinking, which they themselves have not yet mastered. Think of Diana, for instance, as a live-in instructor in the diamond style, which Charles needed in order to become whole. At the same time, Diana—whose childhood was destabilized by the separation and divorce of her parents—may have been attracted to the solid, responsible club elements of Charles's life, which were not highly developed in herself. Diana and Charles each sensed something in the other that they needed in themselves.

If, on the other hand, a child grows up in a balanced family—one in which the parents may exhibit opposing styles and involve the children in all types of thinking—then the children have a better chance of cultivating their own styles. Of course, even when the parents are of opposing styles, they may still fall into a predominant family orientation if one is more outspoken or more available than the other. For a family balance to come about, both parents must be at liberty to endorse their own styles, openly engage in debate for the children to witness, and also allow the children to take on styles which may be different from their own. Since such ideal conditions are rarely met, and with single-parent households so prevalent, many young people enter adulthood operating under the influence of a predominant style, often swayed by a particular parent—this can cause them to choose a style that is not ideal for them.

Whether an individual grows up with a family balance or a predominant style can greatly affect their later mating attractions, for, when entering into a relationship, a person reared under a predominant style typically has yet to discover who they really are. One who has matured into his or her own true style, on the other hand, can intentionally choose the kind of partner who best complements their own nature.

SEEKING COMPLETION IN OUR RELATIONSHIPS
There is an old saying that opposites attract. But while people seek completion in their choices of romantic partners, this does not mean that they necessarily choose mates with styles that are the opposite of their own. There are many aspects to human nature that are instrumental in forging an intimate relationship. These include factors such as education level, personal goals, cultural origins, religious beliefs, and so on. Personal styles of thinking are just one of these determining factors, though a very important one. Moreover, we do not actually seek opposition so much as completion in our relationships. Were this not the case, we might end up with spouses entirely different from ourselves. In fact, much of the research on couples indicates that people usually mate with those who share common features such as cultural origins, education, leisure interests, etc. We do not look for opposites in most of these areas. Indeed, the evidence from all quarters makes it clear that too many differences between partners creates problems that may be impossible to overcome.

Even if the study is narrowed to personality characteristics associated with the four thinking styles, the research still suggests that many of the happiest couples have some traits in common. Life is easier if your husband understands your impulsiveness and intolerance for fussy procedures, or if your wife is equally fastidious, does not trash up the house with dirty clothes, and rolls the toothpaste tube up from the bottom. Thus, there can be fundamental attitudes and skills that individuals must share or work out with their partner, or else they find themselves living with an alien—and perhaps a hostile one at that!

Nonetheless, there are many ways in which people do seek completion in their intimate relationships. For instance, one person's quiet and reflective orientation may be complemented by a partner who is chatty and outgoing, thus making them a good team. Although you might consciously choose a partner for interests you hold in common, what is likely to make a person so damnably fascinating is not their similarities with you, but those hard-to-put-your-finger-on qualities that make you feel complete in their company. We tend to be attracted to and excited by potential mates who effortlessly exhibit qualities that we see as valuable but which seem beyond our own reach. When partners offer each other a different and complementary style of thinking, a sense of completion is achieved.

Actually, the people to whom we are attracted often exhibit ways of thinking or behaving that we ourselves would benefit from learning. Just being with them, we discover attitudes and values that are unlike our own. Their intriguing approaches to situations have the potential to change our lives for the better, as they prompt us to develop thinking skills that we may have neglected. We're drawn to those with different personal styles because they serve as a beckoning signal for our own personal growth.

Indeed, it's not so much that opposites attract, but that growth attracts. We are drawn into a connection with another person to learn something. Subconscious mechanisms tune in like radar to another person who can help us grow toward completion. And in fact the attractive power is not usually fully activated within us until we hear what the other person has to say, thus revealing how they think. The giddy sensations that often accompany the early phases of romantic infatuation can be felt simultaneously by two people if they both have something to learn from the other, or by one alone when the learning is needed only by that one individual. This explains how someone can be attracted to you, or vice versa, yet both of you don't feel the same romantic vibrations. It is only when each party finds something enthralling about the other that the mutual magic kicks in.

HOW A PARTNER'S INTERNAL STYLE CONFLICTS CAN TROUBLE A RELATIONSHIP

Because people are often "under the spell" of love and thus drawn into romantic relationships with those who are of different styles, some degree of discord is inevitable. If one is confident in their own nature, a person can accept a reasonable amount of opposition from their partner. That is the topic for the next chapter, which deals with the common issues of living with people of other styles. Relationship problems can also arise when one partner is undergoing an internal struggle between conflicting personal styles. Such personal struggles for self-identity often lend uncertainty to a relationship, making it difficult to pin down what your mate's differences with you really are.

For example, if in their formative years a person emulates the thinking of a parent whose style is different from their own, later in life this individual may feel a need to overturn parental attitudes and express their own natural style. When a mate's internal pressure to unseat such an unnatural thinking style erupts within a marriage, the awkward transformation process is likely to confuse and upset both partners. The conflicted partner's self-doubt about their true nature can make them uncommunicative or antagonistic toward their mate—and thus the relationship becomes destabilized. Such was the case with Shirley and Bob.

Shirley and Bob: Female Club and Male Diamond
Bob's parents were "Old World" in their values and held very traditional religious beliefs. His father worked in a steel mill and "ruled the roost," while his mother dotingly attended to their six children. Both parents struggled to meet the needs of their burgeoning family. Since having a secure job was so important to them, they never encouraged Bob to develop his considerable artistic talents. In high school, where Bob met Shirley, he enjoyed acting in school plays and designing stage sets. Shirley was active in sports and, since she lived with her aunt, was relatively free of family demands. Bob was attracted to Shirley's independence, her less conservative religious practices, and her active interests. Meanwhile, Shirley enjoyed Bob's debonair charm and lighthearted spontaneity. The couple fell in love, and, after graduation when Bob got a payroll job at the steel company, they married. For several years he was involved in community theater, but once their

children were born, Shirley convinced him to put aside his impractical interests and concentrate on job advancement. Their children rarely saw indications of Bob's imaginative nature, though occasionally, while making impromptu weekend breakfasts, he would charm them with his French-waiter act.

During their child-raising years, both Bob and Shirley had administrative jobs. Their dinner-table discussions often related to happenings at the office. Being the stabilizing partner, Shirley managed the household duties, which allowed Bob to focus on work. He was promoted to corporate headquarters and eventually attained an executive position. By his parents' standards—and by Shirley's as well—Bob had become a success. He held a respected office job that afforded his family a comfortable life. However, he was not happy.

Each day Bob approached his job as would an actor getting into a role. He awakened early, put on his business suit, read the paper during the long train commute, and by the time he arrived at the office, he had transformed into a steely-minded taskmaster like his bosses. Bob had been well-prepared for this role, however, by understudying his father's cool, patriarchal dominance. In fact, Bob had been taught that being a man meant being tough.

At work, Bob played a spade role to operate effectively with the incisive, analytical managers that prevailed at headquarters. And at home, he often did the same to carry on the patriarchal methods that he had learned from his father and to communicate with Shirley. (You'll learn about the ways that partners shift styles to communicate in chapter 8.) In almost all facets of his life, Bob suppressed his creative diamond talents and gave the appearance of being a quiet, assertive spade. Only on vacations and special weekends—away from routine work and family duties—was Bob relaxed, open, and a delight to be with.

For Bob, life was a matter of doing what he should do rather than being who he truly was. Events and circumstances had seemingly conspired to limit his ability to do what he wanted and to be himself. The incongruities between the role he played and his true nature produced within him feelings of discomfort and resentment. Much of the time Bob was surly and silent. After arguments with Shirley, he brooded that his interests were groundless to her. Indeed, from Shirley's club frame of mind, she could accept his independence but not his irresponsible, freewheeling whims. Not knowing what was bothering him, Bob tackled his wife's weekend "to-do" lists with a fated sense of resignation. But he would not go to church or even attend family weddings, though Shirley thought they should. He used his long commute as an excuse to spend less time with the family, and regularly went to bed soon after dinner. He transferred to a job that required him to travel, so that he could be away from both home and office more often. Bob's way of dealing with the angst of living out-of-sync with his true nature was to be curt with and aloof from those people who kept him in his artificial spade role.

Troubling consequences result from people adhering to a false style and living out-of-sync with their true nature. The ramifications can take many forms, but most involve uncomfortably difficult behaviors and attitudes, as well as deep insecurities. For, while a person's false style may seem valid in the eyes of other people (including their mate), such a masquerade undermines the individual's own sense of self. When a person does not acknowledge their feelings of insecurity and misalignment, they become unhappy.

DEALING WITH A PARTNER'S SELF-IDENTITY PROBLEM
Shirley grew increasingly upset by Bob's remoteness. But the couple had no knowledge of personal styles and no means for identifying the source of Bob's distress. They could not see that the major problem in their marriage stemmed from Bob's spade act, which kept him from exploring and developing his diamond strengths. He had followed his father's footsteps into a career he was not well-suited for. Bob's issues were compounded by Shirley's determination to keep him well-grounded and responsible, like herself. Both his work and his home life required him to use a combination of

spade and club thinking processes, which he did not favor. Yet neither partner knew this—and Bob had no way of realizing what joy he was missing, because throughout his adult life he seldom used his creativity long enough to experience a sense of freedom. Bob only knew that he yearned to retire from the steel company.

A self-identity crisis rooted in childhood attitudes may be difficult to resolve, because people may not clearly recognize how out-of-sync they are with their natural style. The styles we learn in childhood are such a basic understructure for our attitudes and behavior that we may not even think of them as false or unnatural. Yet in a very real sense, it is these learned, assumed, "second-nature" thinking patterns that one's true, "first nature" works to overturn.

If your own partner has not differentiated his or her own style from the parental attitudes he or she grew up with, keep in mind that the transition toward their natural style will not be easy. Even with your help or professional counseling, changes in personal style can take years to accomplish. In the case of Bob and Shirley, it wasn't until he took an early retirement that he was actually able to cast off his lifelong role and freely explore his own interests.

Of course, you need not wait decades until retirement to deal with such self-identity issues within your own marriage. You might encourage your partner to take the self-test in chapter 1 so they have a better understanding of their own personal style. Share with them your understanding of their natural style and which of their behaviors seem inconsistent with the way they like to operate. Indeed, your partner's condition may be more evident to you than it is to him or her. You can use your unique, up-close perspective to help them become more aware of their internal conflict. Offer them a notion of what they could be struggling against.

Once the problem is defined, however, you will most likely need to make some changes in your lives that could challenge your own values. For example, Bob needed a career move that would offer him the enjoyment of using his imaginative skills. But to Shirley, this might have seemed both risky and irrelevant, because from the standpoint of her orderly style, one did not abandon a sound, secure job for some far-out flight of fancy. Therefore, she might not easily understand the need for such a change on his part, and would counsel against it. Indeed, she might question which was worse: frustration over his dark moods, or anxiety about his following his own drummer and operating contrary to her way of thinking. But realistically, unless partners are allowed to be themselves, the relationship is doomed to continual unhappiness and anguish over difficult behavior. Moreover, keeping a partner in a false role may cause them to seek validation of their true nature in the company of another person outside the marriage.

EXTRAMARITAL AFFAIRS AND THE SEARCH
FOR ONE'S NATURAL STYLE

Sometimes extramarital relationships are driven by a need for completion or acceptance that doesn't seem available within the partnership. As we've already said, a deep longing for completion is a powerful psychological force that can attract people and lead to marriage—and it can pull them into other relationships as well. The same yearnings that attracted you and your mate can later draw you or them to another person.

This is not meant to condone extramarital affairs. The point is to understand that they are often prompted by an unresolved need for personal growth that is not provided for in one's life or relationship. Not only may one be attracted, like a beacon, to a person exhibiting the style toward which one is evolving, but a new relationship also stirs mental processes that promote change. With no regard for proper conduct, one's own unconscious, diamond-heart mischief-maker may prompt a romance in order to open new mental pathways.

Having an affair is a dangerous way to accomplish personal change, however, because it provokes marriage partners into a self-protective mode that damages an open, relaxed relationship. Yet if the faithful mate can get beyond the judgmental reaction and forgive the cheating partner, both may ultimately be able to focus on what's been missing, either internally or in their marriage, and make improvements.

When you look at marital problems in terms of individual growth, there is usually no need to blame either party. Issues often stem from the fact that one or both partners are still discovering themselves while perhaps feeling trapped in a situation that seems to block their growth. The search for one's own natural style is, for some, a lifelong journey.

THE SPARK OF LOVE—AND HOW TO REIGNITE IT

There is one experience of the mating process that is quite universal. It's the way that the initial spark of love makes us feel helplessly drawn into something over which we have no control. Recall your own sensations. When romantic infatuation takes hold, you feel yourself being pulled along by an unknown force. You might say that the loved one echoes a call in your soul. Coming to you from beyond your normal powers of self-regulation, love beckons you to follow its lead. You seesaw bewilderingly between your own independence and a loving connection.

Love's pull is so awesome, in part, because of its inscrutability. Our feelings and actions are driven by subconscious processes that cause us to break out of our stable, isolated independence and enter into a relationship with another. Essentially we are being buffeted by a shift in our thinking patterns. When we become infatuated with another, we unknowingly ease up on our usual spade and club constraints. We relax our analytic, critical side and our conservative, moral tendencies. At the same time we openly express our hopeful, spontaneous diamond impulses and also our warm, caring, and sometimes needy heart feelings. When we sense the spirit calling us to expand our limits and explore a connection with another person, our diamond and heart processes are temporarily overwhelming our controlling, spade-club tendencies.

While relaxing the ego's spade-club defenses in order to build an intimate relationship, our pull toward connection has us spellbound, and our mental experience during this period can be pure bliss. It is as if we have been drugged or intoxicated by the newfound joy of this love we are in. But once we have lived with the other person for a while and settled into a routine with them, the hope-filled, explorative stage draws to a close. Our initial state of bliss gives way to everyday life, which includes working out relationship problems and living arrangements. Nevertheless, as Scott Peck so aptly describes in his book *The Road Less Traveled*,[1] this is the point at which real loving begins. For although self-control now reasserts itself, both parties willingly set about reshaping their lives to meet the different needs of both partners. Both lives must be adapted to support a maturing love.

Fairy-tale myths portray the princess and her handsome prince living in bliss, happily ever after. Such beloved tales, like wonderful, old romantic movies, focus on the delightful expectations of a budding relationship. They don't prepare us, however, for the hard reality that the bliss will come to an end. After the dream of connection is realized, the couple returns to normal, everyday existence with only occasional moments when one or both of them feels the bliss. Anyone who expects the magic of that early period of love to continue undiminished, is living in, well, a fairy tale.

This is not to say that the love does not continue, but joyful bliss becomes a sporadic rather than a continuous experience. What does it take to revive this state of happiness? A combination of diamond and heart processes. The key to renewing your relationship is putting some of the original diamond adventure and heartfelt connection back into it. The trick is to discover unexpected, unpredictable ways to enjoy each other and show each other that you still feel the bond of togetherness. This might involve making love in surprising new ways, traveling together to new places rather than returning to the same vacation spot year after year, or spontaneous togetherness in whatever form it might take—

indeed, anything that provides both partners with exhilaration and opportunities for new growth.

One partner may have a better knack for energizing the relationship in such ways. This stands to reason, because one is likely to be more skilled in the imaginative, diamond processes or the connecting, heart processes than the other. If this mate realizes that it is his or her role to create ongoing opportunities for renewal, and if the other follows along in open anticipation, then both can enjoy moments of original magic rejuvenated in their lives. Not twenty-four hours a day. Not every day. But whenever they feel inspired to playfully and lovingly rekindle their sparks.

A couple's need to refresh their relationship becomes particularly acute if they are raising children. As every parent knows, there is a strong tendency to become so involved with the kids that the partners can increasingly lose sight of their own needs. It is so easy to give children all of our time and affection, while taking our spouse for granted. The sad result of this common situation is a couple who has forgotten the joy they originally shared. If a couple remains solely focused on the children, they will eventually experience the emptied nest as two strangers when the children leave, staring at each other and wondering what became of their enthusiasm for life. Not only is this a sad consequence for a husband and wife, it can also have unhealthy repercussions for children. Parents whose marriage lacks passion or closeness because they devote all their energies to the children are not providing a good example for those children. How are sons and daughters supposed to learn what a happy marriage looks like if their parents don't have one? No matter how well children are treated by their parents, if they don't witness a loving relationship between their mother and father, they'll probably find it harder to create a good marriage when they grow up.

In virtually all relationships, it is essential for you and your partner to find time for togetherness. After all, it is this heart component of your relationship that is most basic to your union. Think about the activities you enjoyed when you first fell in love. Did you go to plays and dances, go skiing or to sporting events? Why not set aside more time to enjoy each other in the unencumbered ways that brought you together to begin with? This may mean that you'll have to "schedule" an evening or weekend alone every now and then. But once you have carved out this time together, you'll remember how important it is to be a loving couple. Maybe you just need time alone every once in a while to talk. The key is to find ways for the relaxed enjoyment of each other, away from your regular work and family obligations. You'll discover that bliss is found in those free moments of open connection.

EACH PARTNER IS RESPONSIBLE FOR THEIR OWN BLISS
While one partner may be more capable of rejuvenating the relationship than the other, neither is responsible for the other's bliss. No one can make another person happy if he or she doesn't wish to be. Joy is a state of mind that calls for us to relax our prevailing controls. To attain it, we must switch off our spade-club seriousness and ease into a diamond-heart flow, letting go of the criticism and demands on others, forgiving past injustices, accepting people as they are, and experiencing a sense of freedom. This is a change in attitude that a person can make only on their own. A partner may help, but no one else can throw the switch for us.

Keep in mind that the four personal styles represent different kinds of thinking that are available to all of us. Each of us has the resources within ourselves to find the joy that can be tapped in the heart and diamond regions of our own minds. There are many ways to do this, but they all involve relaxing our spade-club inclinations. To attain joy, occasionally we have to put aside busy schedules and stressful environments and engage in activities that make us feel enthusiastically alive.

This is not solely a matter for couples, for each of us as individuals has the internal means available to develop our own bliss.

You might seek your own inner resources during quiet walks in the forest, or even in the city when you can enjoy the private pleasure of your own company. In many couples, each partner takes one night out of each week to spend alone or with friends. But do not overlook other, more personal resources, such as keeping a diary with your own reflections, wishes, thoughts, and even poems. Some people record their nighttime dreams as well, which they use to help them tap inspiring images and their innermost feelings. Doing some or all of these activities, even on a casual basis, can help you get in touch with the subtle heart-diamond processes that round out your whole self.

TWO DIFFERENT STYLES CAN PERPETUATE PERSONAL GROWTH

Relationships are not always easy, and the issues that develop between partners are often intricate. Differences in partners' thinking styles may be just one of many kinds of problems facing a couple. Indeed, it is difficult to draw a line where the conflicts over personal style differences leave off and other heavy issues begin. However, there is a common thread to the wide-ranging set of problems that frequently beset relationships. All of them—including the personal style differences—involve the perpetual need for personal growth. The attractions that draw us to a mate for our own sense of fulfillment and completion, and the tempting vibes that later may attract us to another person, operate on the same principles. Love and attraction break us out of the status quo and, among other things, incite an expansion of our thinking.

When we enter into a loving relationship or marriage, we share a commitment with another person who might have quite a different approach to life. We need to remember that our original attraction to this person may have been born out of our search for completion, in the hope that our partner's style might broaden our mind and supply us with what we need emotionally. Yet it is often the very qualities that drew us together that later come to frustrate us the most. Our partner's thinking, so different from our own, provides special benefits to the partnership; but their contrasting traits can get on our nerves and entangle us in bitter quarrels. As we will discover throughout the rest of this book, however, adapting to someone with a style different from our own can both inspire our personal growth and become the foundation of a good relationship.

CHAPTER SEVEN

IT'S A BATTLE OF STYLES, NOT SEXES

How Different Styles Affect Relationships

All it takes for disagreement is two people. Actually you can disagree with yourself. But that's another story. The subject of this chapter is how to better understand and live with a mate of another style. In this chapter you'll also see how stereotypical attitudes regarding gender can undermine relationships, whereas understanding a partner's card suit style can reduce the negative effects of gender expectations.

A popular method for understanding the opposition that couples experience is to represent the sexes as being from different planets—men from Mars, women from Venus.[1] Women are depicted as caring partners who take more interest in family matters and promote communication. Men are seen as dominating partners who are less interested in relationships, unemotional or remote, and mainly interested in their work. Even though a person's style may vary from the stereotype for their gender, we still attribute differences of behavior to their sex—to hormones, perhaps—and say, "Ah, that explains it." Then we assume that if men and women learned to squelch their differences, the disagreements would end, and couples could settle into peaceful harmony. Of course, things don't work that way, because people need to express their opinions. Partners who suppress what they really think become unhappy, and they lose the benefits that different views offer to any team—a dynamic, open approach is best for everyone.

Attributing communication difficulties between men and women to their gender differences seems valid because mates usually do vary in style. Also, there is a tendency for the sexes to play out culturally accepted roles. People expect men and women to act according to time-honored styles typically ascribed to each gender. The stereotype for men generally fits the profile of the analytical spade, but also includes the diamond's perceptiveness and the club's rule-forming qualities. And of course the "typical" man has difficulty reaching across to the heart's connectedness. Indeed, a man with these traits is often called a "man's man." Similarly, the stereotype for women is consistent with the relating heart, with aspects of the diamond's openness and the club's duty to family responsibilities, and deference to her mate. Everyone loves a heart, for rather than challenging others, they usually seek connections. So here is the commonly accepted divvying-up of roles that balance the family. It is assumed that men will take on the masculine/spade side of the equation and women will uphold the feminine/heart side.

In our society, we expect the sexes to fulfill these customary roles in their thinking and behavior. We also teach children to take on these gender roles. So it should not be surprising that the male and female concepts often fit, in part because we've been taught to live according to these stereotypes. We conform to them so that we'll be regarded as normal. Whatever the cause—be it the expectations of our culture or actual physiological differences—men and women are, in fact, biased toward different styles. When asked to choose between analytical thought (spade) and feeling processes (heart), about 60 percent of men identify with the former and 60 percent of women favor the latter. There are differences between men and women. Club and diamond processes, however, are chosen about equally by both sexes.[2]

But such comparisons between sexes miss the larger point: With the population so well distributed among all four styles, most men are not spades, and most women are not hearts. Clearly, then, the images of "masculine" men and "feminine" women cannot address everyone's issues.

Since there are four basic personal styles, there are actually sixteen types of couples—together representing all the possible combinations of the suits.[3] Each combination presents distinct issues for a couple, as indicated in table 7.1. In the 1-in-16 chance that a relationship presents a case in which the man is a spade and the woman is a heart, the prevailing concepts of the masculine/feminine stereotypes may work quite well. However, in the greater likelihood that your style or that of your partner falls outside those stereotypes, then you cannot trust conventional wisdom to fit your problems. If you carefully observe how your mate operates, you may discover that your man is just masquerading as a "typical" male, or your woman gives only the appearances of an "ideal" female heart. This makes a world of difference in your relationship. People can spend many hours in psychotherapy working toward the removal of such masks in hopes of discovering their real nature. To the extent that the male/female stereotypes perpetuate expectations that men and women should think and behave in certain ways, the old, "two-planet" symbolism does us a disservice—the reality is likely to be far more complex.

Each style has its own unique slant on life, with its own characteristic attitudes and behaviors. In the many possible ways that they combine, each of the sixteen kinds of relationships has distinguishing traits, as listed in table 7.1. After you review the summary table, we'll go into more detail regarding the kinds of issues that are likely to affect relationships containing different combinations of styles.

Combinations of Styles in Relationships

TABLE 7.1

Style of the male partner	Style of the female partner	Characteristics of the Relationship
♠	♥	This couple most represents traditional, Western, masculine and feminine stereotypes. The caring female yearns for togetherness with the analytical male, who may dominate and be critical. If they come to terms with their sharp differences, they can make a very strong partnership.
♠	♦	In this couple, creativity struggles against logic. The logic-oriented male often challenges the creative female, who finds it difficult to express herself in the face of his deductive approach to every problem. If they work together, her creativity can give originality to his reason.
♠	♣	This couple can seem to fit the gender stereotypes, as the female may follow tradition and undertake the heart role. The independent, competitive, risk-taking male pursues adventure, while the conservative female stands for safe practices and avoiding risks within the family.
♠	♠	An ongoing power struggle may persist between these two headstrong partners who both want to call the shots. They will often challenge each other but may make an unusually powerful team.

Style of the male partner	Style of the female partner	Characteristics of the Relationship
♣	♦	The creative female is balanced and sometimes hampered by the solid, steady, conservative male. She puts up with his more methodical behavior, taunting him to lighten up. He finds her creativity stimulating, yet her lack of organization prompts him to urge her to attend to details.
♣	♥	The well-organized male plans and directs the accommodating female, who is thoughtful of others and easygoing. While appearing similar to the gender stereotypes, this can be an unusually steadfast and compatible couple.
♣	♠	This couple may struggle against the stereotypes. A competitive, decisive, risk-taking female can be a threat to a methodical male who wants to handle things in a prepared, conservative way.
♣	♣	Both partners often play traditional gender roles and tend to be conservative. Each partner is generally steady and trustworthy. However, each may wish the other were more lively and spontaneous.
♦	♣	The impulsive, optimistic male may depend on the disciplined, reliable female to help him keep his feet on the ground. During impasses, he may shift to the male's traditional spade independence and lose his openness.

Style of the male partner	Style of the female partner	Characteristics of the Relationship
♦	♠	The creative man and the rational results-oriented woman have different visions. Each might want their partner to have more of their characteristics. He may wish that she'd mellow out and be less challenging, while she may urge him to be more realistic and to follow through.
♦	♥	The inspiring, creative male may overshadow a nurturing, supportive female. She cares for the family responsibilities, enabling his free-thinking independence.
♦	♦	Both quixotic partners may take turns at hard and soft roles; neither wants to be responsible for routine details. They exhibit unusual openness and creativity but may lack stick-to-itiveness.
♥	♠	In a reverse of the usual gender roles, here the man is warm-hearted, and the woman is competitive and logical. The self-assured female gives them resolve; the engaging, participative male comforts her.
♥	♣	In this near reversal of gender stereotypes, the social, compliant male lets the dependable female manage their routine. She may wish he had more initiative; he may seek the authority traditionally granted the male.

Style of the male partner	Style of the female partner	Characteristics of the Relationship
♥	♦	The gentle, cooperative male is challenged by the open, enthusiastic female who wishes he were more spirited. If he seeks authority in the relationship, he may appear to be conservative and stodgy. She may seem quite independent.
♥	♥	Both sympathetic, caring partners work toward peaceful tranquillity in the relationship and stymie independence. Demands of the workaday world can be a real challenge. As the male attempts to uphold his gender's spade role, he will seem like a teddy bear in disguise.

Before we delve into style differences in couples to see how specific issues unfold according to particular style combinations, it is important to remember that no one can be defined by one suit alone. A partner who is essentially a heart will also have secondary traits that are closely identified with at least one of the other three styles. And the same goes for a spade, club, or diamond partner. We are each a blending of styles. For our purposes here, however, couples are identified in the following scenarios by each partner's strongest suit.

RELATIONSHIPS BETWEEN OPPOSITE STYLES

The first couples to be profiled here are opposites, since their issues are easiest to define. "Opposites" refers to partners whose individual styles are diagonally across the illustrative poker table—a heart with a spade partner, or a club with a diamond.

Libby and Sean: Female Spade and Male Heart
Picture a couple in which the woman is the "fix-it" expert and has an exact approach to her handiwork, from installing window treatments to wiring lighting. Libby likes to do things on her own and gains a sense of achievement from her efforts. She is a departmental manager in a computer technology company and is conservative and decisive in financial matters. Her mate, Sean, also holds a responsible job but is more people-oriented. His strength is his expressive salesmanship. At home, Sean is eager to be involved in Libby's projects because he likes to do things with her. However, he is not as skilled as she is. He makes blunders that can be costly, and money is not as much of a concern to him as it is to her. You can imagine their arguments.

Libby and Sean do not occupy the customary female and male seats at the card table—yet they think they should! This in itself can cause many problems as they negotiate their roles. While a male partner may be of the heart style deep down inside, he has been taught to think he must uphold the spade tradition, and so he believes that he should do all the "manly-man" fix-it projects. But Libby would rather do them herself. At the same time, she is confused about why Sean can't do them well. She judges this as a weakness in him, just as Sean sees Libby's preference for fixing things over cooking as a flaw—a lack of "womanly" domesticity. Sean and Libby have a spade-heart opposition, but their styles are also opposite from the culturally prescribed roles for their gender. Thus, each is tormented by the fact that the other does not operate according to expectations. Each may see such "failures" clearly in their mate, but not in themselves.

For example, Libby has made regular advances into senior management jobs but knows that much of the staff does not like her direct, aggressive manner. Sean, on the other hand, feels bypassed and alienated from the managers where he works, but is well-liked by his clients and coworkers. At home he consoles Libby about the remoteness she senses from people at work. For her part, Libby challenges Sean to stand up for his own self-interests at work, to set goals, and go after a promotion. Libby wonders what's wrong with him that he doesn't want to take control of his life. Her dad says Sean has no ambition. Is her dad right? And Sean wonders what's wrong with Libby that she can't be friendlier so that people will like her. His dad says he's never felt real warmth from Libby and questions whether her parents were loving people. Is Sean's dad right?

Over the course of Libby and Sean's discussions and arguments, these doubts about what's wrong with the other partner may have been voiced as demeaning remarks. In the positions they take on various issues, each remains true to style. Libby upholds her independence, makes the hard choices, and promotes new challenges. She plans for the future, has clear goals for what she wants the couple to achieve, and exercises her right to decide whether or not she wants to have children. Sean, on the other hand, wants them to spend more time with each other, brings about their special moments together, sells Libby on the joys of family, and comforts her when she has self-doubts. He stays in his job because he likes the people he works with.

Think of these partners as sitting at opposite sides of the round poker table, Libby at the spade quadrant with arms outstretched to both club and diamond, and Sean at the heart, reaching to diamond and club. Faced off against each other, they each grab halfway around the table, their hands virtually touching. It seems that on every issue they confront each other and sparks fly. Indeed, the attraction of these opposites was very likely forged in the exhilarating clash of emotions during such skirmishes. As issues come and go, they each readjust their stance a bit, shifting slightly from their favored base, but not very much.

Libby and Sean experience many of the same kinds of problems in their relationship as do Maxine and Randy (see chapter 5). Although they may reside in different parts of the country, have different jobs or incomes, and live among different friends and families, they actually share similar challenges. Both Maxine and Libby are strong-minded managers at work and at home, whose decision-making capabilities exceed those of many people around them—including their mates. Both are smart and cool thinkers, which is perceived as "unladylike" by those with traditional values. They are amid a challenging contingent that advances women's opportunities—often in law, policy formulation, or corporate enterprise. Randy and Sean, for their part, are dedicated to the concerns of people, which drew them to government and sales. They are warm, likable, and masters of the interpersonal exchange. Some might call them soft, for they are not at ease making tough decisions. Both Randy and Sean rely to some extent on others, and especially their mates, for goal-setting and critical thinking.

When partners are at odds with common gender stereotypes, they encounter almost predictable difficulties. Not only do they face opposition with each other in matters of opinion, but they also must cope with the fact that they don't fit the customary expectations for their gender. Unfortunately, people often try to adapt to the expected roles before they figure out how to simply be themselves. For example, Libby, our female spade, may attempt to be warm, caring, and relational to fit the image of what is expected of a woman. She may even think of herself in this way, because from her point of view she is sufficiently warm, caring, and relational. But from a heart's point of view, there is a cool distance in Libby's manner of relating. Her style of caring may be seen by others as stiff and businesslike. Rarely do people say that she is genuinely warm. If Libby does have children, it is possible that she might be insensitive to their emotional needs and may try to manage them as she would her office staff.

Naturally Libby's independent style stirs Sean's relating mind to wonder, how can Libby be so indifferent to others? so insensitive? so calculating? and at the same time, so on-target in evaluating his weaknesses? so capable of making the tough choices leading to their success? He might expect these traits in a male, but not in a female. Sean struggles with the dichotomy between stereotype and reality, both in his mate and in himself. And Libby is doing the same from her side of the table. At times she even wishes she were a man, because that would make it easier for her to be her natural self.

If such couples act in ways that are expected for their gender (that is, moving around to the opposite sides of the poker table— Libby to heart and Sean to spade), they only temporarily satisfy their expectations. If Libby, in the Donna Reed tradition, plays the dutiful "womanly-woman" role, staying home to fix Sean a fantastic meal and dote on his every whim, he may feel more "manly" for the moment. But he will still rely on her for all the spade functions she fulfills for them. Sean may initially have been attracted to Libby because she represented the spade-based half of his mental operations; so one might say that what irritates Sean most about Libby—her deficit in heart, which is the typical expected role of the woman—is the very trait that he is trying to develop within himself. Yet coming to this realization in the face of all the macho male portrayals in the media is not easy.

For couples like Libby and Sean, the key to solving their problems is for both partners to change their expectations of each other. Each partner must accept their mate for who they are. To aid that change in awareness, at the end of this chapter is a section on "Understanding Yourselves as a Couple." There you'll find ways that partners can work together to acknowledge their personal styles and develop mutual respect for one another. In the next chapter are techniques for improving communication between partners of different styles. To make effective use of these methods, however, partners must first acknowledge their style differences and then accept that they are beneficial, since they serve to round out the skills available to the couple.

Lisa and Mark: Female Heart and Male Spade

After Libby and Sean's perplexing set of problems, the issues in a relationship between a man and a woman who match the gender stereotypes might seem easier to handle—that is, unless you're in such a couple. In this next example, the new players are set halfway again around the table. Mark is a quiet spade, a respected analyst for a think-tank firm. Lisa is an extroverted heart, a people person who loves to get together with other people socially. She works for a travel agency, but that is mostly her hobby. She is not as committed to a career as Mark is. At home Mark is the family decision-maker and likes his household to run smoothly and be shipshape. Lisa takes care of the children and enjoys dealing with their joys and trials. She often encourages them to put up with their father's commands. Mark limits the time he spends with his children, preferring to read in the evenings rather than involve himself in their bedtime activities. On Sunday morning, Mark goes off to a coffee shop to read the newspaper. Lisa is upset by his aloofness, his insensitivity to her and the kids, and his lack of social interests. It is an effort just to get him to go out with friends for an evening. On the occasions when Lisa can provoke him to argue—perhaps for the closeness she needs—he tends to scoff at her flimsy notions. He frequently responds by questioning her goals, which sets her off like a rocket. "It's not about goals," she objects.

"Of course not," he observes, "you have none. You can't even make a decision."

Now the battle is fully joined.

"All I want," she says, "is a little communication. I want us to be open and spend time together like ordinary people! Sometimes I just want to go out and have a good time. All you do is sit here in the den and read your book or watch CNN or . . . God, you're hopeless!"

You get the idea. In fact, you probably know couples like Lisa and Mark, or perhaps your own relationship is similar to theirs.

In Mark and Lisa's case, the struggle between them is consistent with traditional gender stereotypes. He is less relational and more ana-lytical about managing the issues that affect their lives. She is not decisive. She doesn't identify solutions to their problems. Rather, she cares mostly about promoting family unity. They argue over objectives and communication. Her objective is open communication.

His communication is focused on achieving sound objectives. Mark upholds spade-club thinking patterns and values, while Lisa counters with heart-diamond feelings and hopes. She believes he is overly logical. He thinks her interests have no strength of logic, but he loves her regardless of her sappy sensitivity. And she loves him despite his calculating remoteness. Indeed, subconsciously, they probably love each other for these very traits.

WHY SOLUTIONS BASED ON GENDER DON'T WORK
In both of the above examples—Libby and Sean, and Lisa and Mark—the couples cope with an opposition of styles. But what might be appropriate guidance to the man or woman in one couple would not be equally useful for the same partner in the other. For example, let's take a page from popular psychology and suggest to both Mark and Sean that they develop their own "feminine sides" in order to improve their relationships with their mates. By now it may be obvious that this essentially refers to becoming aware of the mysterious heart and diamond processes of one's own mind, in which females are typically better-trained than males. To Mark, who is of the spade style, "getting in touch with his feminine side" probably sounds like psychobabble. He is so solidly grounded in conventional, logic-based reality that he is likely to assign this other, feeling side of himself to the same category as he would alien creatures from Venus—not in my universe, not in my lifetime. He may become more open to this sensitivity as he grows older, especially if he encounters traumatic hardships. If, however, by his ongoing success Mark is able to maintain his confident self-control, he probably will discount this suggestion and consider the feminine side as Lisa's province; so this advice has little meaning to him, even though this is exactly what is missing from his awareness in order to understand her better.

Sean, on the other hand, would take the suggestion of getting in touch with his feminine side in an entirely different manner, because he already is in touch with his heart-diamond modes. Therefore, he might willingly enter into family counseling or therapy, or join a men's bonding group to explore his feelings and spiritual side— any of which could bring out missing parts of Sean's own self-development. Yet such remedies could compound the couple's problems, rather than solve them. The heart-based therapy could encourage Sean to urge Libby to be more sensitive and caring— which might alienate her and work against the togetherness he seeks. Unless they acknowledge that their personal styles are distinctly different, their arguments will continue to be driven by expectations that "you should be like me."

Since not all men think alike or have the same personalities— nor do all women—simplistic, gender-based solutions can't represent the unique issues and interplay of styles that challenge most couples. Indeed, if the customary advice really worked, there wouldn't be so many couples still seeking help to resolve their problems. In order to make real headway in dealing with their issues, couples must first recognize that they are two individuals who prefer to think and behave differently from each other. And their preferences may vary from the gender stereotypes. Rather than judge such differences as wrong, partners must learn to value the unique set of skills that each one brings to the table. You'll find suggestions on how to go about this process in your own relationship toward the end of this chapter.

CLUB-DIAMOND RELATIONSHIPS

There are two additional types of relationships between opposite styles—the club and the diamond—with the man or the woman holding either of these positions across the card table. In these combinations, each partner has a part of themselves that fits the gender stereotypes and another which doesn't. On some occasions they will experience clashes like Libby and Sean, and on others, like those of Mark and Lisa. That is, either the diamond or the

FINDING YOUR STRONG SUIT

club partner—man or woman—might exhibit the spade's cool, grounded logic or the heart's warm, relating behavior. Indeed, they may take turns doing so, although many couples tend to follow cultural tradition, with the male covering the spade and the female sustaining the heart. So the application of conventional Mars-Venus wisdom to these club-diamond relationships is often a "yes, but" proposition. Parts of it make sense, but something of significance is missing. What they may not recognize is that their opposition is fundamentally between the club's tried-and-true, safety-oriented procedures for doing things, and the diamond's tendencies toward openness and spontaneity. In relationships between these styles, there might be arguments over risk-taking as opposed to financial security, doing what's responsible versus having fun, sticking with known activities rather than trying new experiences, etc.

Hope and George: Female Diamond and Male Club
Remember the argument between George and Hope in chapter 1? The discord in their club-diamond relationship was about the gulf between George's prepared, saving, conservative style and Hope's more capricious nature. It was her desire to drive a car that reflected the openness with which she engages life. But like many entry topics for kindling debate, the convertible was a symbol for a self-awareness she was trying to manifest. Hope wanted them both to see that she doesn't have the same interests and motivations as George does. The two very different ways each preferred to deal with money—Hope's inclination to enjoy life now and George's need to save—represented their unique styles.

In a club-diamond disagreement, the tone of the words and issues has less of a "hard versus soft" quality, and are different from the previous spade-heart examples. This is not to say that a spade-heart couple would not argue about a car. Rather, the way they do so would sound different and involve different motivations. If Mark and Lisa debated a new car, Mark would probably seem more boldly authoritative in his challenges than George did. And Lisa might not take the dominant stance of threatening to trade in either George's car or George himself, as Hope did. Mark and Lisa, however, would be less likely to argue about her need for a convertible in the first place—in fact, they both might want a sportier car. Nor would Mark have such singular footing in their financial security, for both partners would share this concern.

Gender expectations are less significant in the club-diamond combination. While one can easily picture George standing for budgetary responsibility, it is not difficult to imagine another couple in which Georgina, a woman, takes a similar stance in opposition to a free-spirited husband. In the case of Georgina and her husband, their dissension would not be so heavily laden with cultural expectations for their genders as in those couples where a club-styled male shifts into the spade role as a matter of tradition. We are not actually biased to expect that it is the natural function of one sex to be either responsible or free-spirited; however, partners often tag such traits as gender-related, because that is the way in which they perceive their own differences.

Of the two partners in a club-diamond relationship, the club is the one most likely to hold to values which they believe to be appropriate for their gender, whereas the diamond is prone to shift in and out of hard/spade and soft/heart messages. These shifts are popularly called "mood swings." In the example of George and Hope, she expressed most of her views in an attitude of relating and sharing her feelings. But in the end, when she could see that George didn't understand her point, Hope's mood shifted to a calculated, independent spade stance, by which she totally dominated George's methodical approach.

The key to coping with club-diamond differences is to understand the characteristics of each partner's natural style. With that awareness, both George and Hope might appreciate why each has unique requirements for a car, and see that their debate is part of an ongoing process of defining who they are.

RELATIONSHIPS BETWEEN NEIGHBORING STYLES
Harriet and Jay: Female Heart and Male Diamond
Now let us turn to relationships in which the partners are neither total opposites nor of the same style, but are occupying adjacent corners of the boxing ring. See figure 7.1 for the next example, Harriet and Jay. In such cases, one partner's predominant style is a secondary style for their mate, and vice versa. The set of processes that they share between them (on one side of the ring) is their favored way of being together. For Harriet and Jay, this is the diamond-heart side.

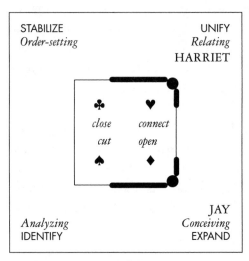

FIGURE 7.1

Yet to remain in this zone would leave the opposite processes (the spade and club on the far side of the ring) unattended by either of them. If each partner is mature and proficient in three of the four types of processes, then each may combine their dominant style with one particular secondary mode to achieve necessary balance in the relationship. In Jay and Harriet's case, Harriet fulfills the heart-club, and Jay the diamond-spade. Therefore, as they interact on everyday issues, their stances often preclude them from sharing their favored side (in this case, the diamond-heart) which is their common bond. This point will be more understandable after you get to know this couple.

Jay heads a computer-software design department. He is a creative, diamond-styled innovator who is as clever as Tom Sawyer. Confident and witty, he constantly challenges traditional attitudes. His optimism is useful at work for sparking his department's new ideas; but at home this quality can annoy Harriet, who is a quiet family caretaker. She is a volunteer nurse at the local hospital, and, true to her heart nature, sincerely likes to help people. Her mother was a civic-minded librarian, and, like her, Harriet tends to respect tradition. Yet Harriet was not always so staid. After college she ventured into community theater where she met Jay. Even now she loves to freely express herself at times. But their relationship at home seems to call upon her stabilizing duties, and she still hears her mother's prudent voice in her mind. Jay, meanwhile, takes flying lessons, befitting the independent side of his nature, but at home he frequently dons the customary male/spade role in behavior and tone. Were you to see him only with Harriet, you might suspect that the spade is his primary style, since he carries it out so well. At work, however, his free-spirited diamond nature prevails.

Jay and Harriet often argue about money (for neither likes financial management) and also about the use of leisure time. She likes church functions, but he prefers the outdoors and parties. His outgoing good humor makes him popular in groups, while Harriet avoids the limelight. Jay doesn't understand how Harriet can be so stuck in old habits, especially when he recalls the whimsical woman he so much enjoyed when they met. And why is she always instructing him about what to do? Harriet feels that Jay is insensitive to her inner needs. Why is he always badgering her? She can't compete with his ever-confident personality. Sometimes she wants to step out of his shadow and escape his incessantly upbeat antics.

On the positive side, Jay urges Harriet to independently expand her interests and touts the same suits (diamond-spade) that he does at work. Because he is so outgoing, however, she tends to be intimidated by him. For her part, Harriet provides Jay with the same caring support (heart-club) that she gives her hospital patients. Occasionally his imagination and her warmth spark with each other, and they share special moments of intimacy and being simpatico. Neither, in fact, likes to drag the other down and be the grounding, structuring force. There is tension in their relationship, however, because Harriet takes on the club role and Jay the spade role, even though neither is solidly based there. They fall into their secondary roles with each other by default.

Early in their relationship, Jay's combination of strong, confident, perceptive capabilities with an easygoing spirit may have been just what Harriet needed to break free of the upright training she had received from her family. At the same time, the solid values which had become a part of Harriet's style may have been very appealing to Jay, who was allured by her giving heart. As years went by, however, they came to rely on the other person more and more for the traits that are secondary in their own personalities. Now, when they are together, Harriet is stuck in her heart-club mode, and only with other people does she find her heart-diamond openness. Similarly, Jay wears the diamond-spade mantle at home, yet he, too, seeks his diamond-heart connection with others. Thus, they both feel that their needs are not met within their relationship, because each partner's hold on their own primary style blocks the other partner from embracing what would be the secondary side of their nature.

Since Jay and Harriet have neighboring diamond and heart styles, it is difficult for them to achieve a comfortable counter-balance. Because they are not opposites, each person's natural way of thinking do not fully complement the other's. Therefore, they tend to adopt roles that are different from their preferred styles in order to achieve balance. In this couple you sense that a secondary style of thinking in one partner is forestalled by their mate's domination of that very style. Thus, because of Jay's stronghold on his diamond style and his avoidance of club qualities, Harriet compensates by constantly setting the order. In so doing, she is stuck in a club role and can't express her more easygoing, diamond side, normally available to a heart. She accesses that freer side of herself with her friends but rarely with Jay.

In encountering each other, Jay and Harriet seem, like boxers, to each have one arm clinched by their mate, so that each punches only with the arm that swings loose. Harriet hammers away with her club hand, laying down procedures and financial concerns that hit Jay squarely between his diamond eyes. And Jay pounds with his spade hand, showing her a cold independence that breaks her sensitive heart. Only when they free themselves from this clinch can they lovingly stroke each other with the heart-diamond hands that actually connect them.

Jay and Harriet's manner of relating was locked in by gender-role conditioning, parental influences, and mutual dependence on each other. In their relationship, the clinching effect leaves each of them with only "one arm" to use—each contributing just a pair of processes that oppose their partner's pair. Thus, at home they tend to be one-dimensional and unable to access the full range of their being. They rarely share the sides of themselves they had originally cherished in each other.

Yet both of them need to feel loved and accepted in exercising the full range of their own styles. This means that Harriet needs to let go of the club and explore her diamond openness and spontaneity. Jay, meanwhile, needs to back away from his spade role and tap the sensitivities of the heart. One way that both partners might rediscover their own diamond-heart dimensions is to get away from family responsibilities for an extended period of time, to renew their relationship and discuss how each of them needs to reawaken traits that they had ceded to the other.

Female Diamond and Male Heart
If Jay and Harriet's table were turned around, and the woman was the diamond extrovert and the man the heart introvert, then things would be different. He would be the one struggling in her shadow. In this case, she might urge him to loosen up. She would be the one with the lively, light personality. And she would be the one people would seek at social events. By comparison, he would be quiet and uptight. Yet there would be a hidden depth to his concerns for helping others and in his love for his family. He might retreat to his garden to wrestle internally with her one-upmanship.

This would be more arduous for him than for Harriet, because he is expected to be the dominant partner—so his struggle would involve gender doubts as well. The woman might taunt him, saying, "What are you, man or mouse?" He might then counter-attack in order to look more tough. Following his conservative bent, he might try to appear to be more "manly," in the club manner. As a result, she might see him as closed-minded. In this way, he might be displaced from his natural relating style, and not be himself with her—because his true heart style has been reserved for women's roles. If his partner succeeds in dislodging him from the heart role, then she might even occupy it herself, as feminine turf. On the other hand, if he stood firmly based in the heart, then she might be diverted into a decisive, independent, spade role (traditionally reserved for men), and therein encounter gender-stereotype issues herself.[4]

WHY NEIGHBORING STYLE PARTNERS ARE "FORCED INTO CORNERS"

When mates are neighbors in style, rather than opposites, it can be difficult for each partner to use "both arms" of their style. This is because one of these "arms" is being held in check by the dominant style of the mate. This strains relationships in a way that is different from the direct challenges of natural opposites in the prior examples. Unless people are aware of and securely rooted in their own styles, partners are apt to be driven to behavior that is outside their true nature.

In the preceding examples, you saw an unhappy dynamic that runs through a surprising number of neighboring-style relationships. The tendency is for one or both partners to get pushed into a particular corner and be kept there, like it or not, by their partner's seeming unwillingness to occupy it. For example, if one partner is always late paying bills, neglects dirty dishes, and tosses clothing about the house as if it were a rag bin, then inevitably the other person—even if by nature an easygoing diamond—may take on these club responsibilities, not because he (or she) likes doing them, but because he or she can't stand it otherwise! This sort of thing is quite prevalent in neighboring-style relationships. Someone gets "assigned" the role of guardian, disciplinarian, financial manager, social coordinator, or whatever role the other partner has defaulted from. If they enjoy the role, then fine. If they do not—if they have been forced into it by the refusal of the other partner to help out—then they may come to deeply resent their situation. To make things even worse, it is unlikely that such a person will receive any thanks for their efforts, and may well come to actually bear a grudge for having to carry out this role.

For example, how often is a woman who is a diamond or club, forced to make virtually all the decisions in her relationship with her heart husband?—ranging from what movie to rent on Friday night, all the way to whether or not to put the house up for sale. Does her husband appreciate that she steps in where he refuses to tread? Not a bit! More likely, he feels resentful that he has no authority or say over family matters. What started out as a simple division of responsibilities, either by choice or by default, has become a standoff in which both partners are unhappy. In fact, this is the darker dimension to the neighboring-style relationship, in which couples start out complementing each other and end up resenting their roles. In such a situation, nothing can be done until both partners talk to each other openly and plainly about their feelings. This may not be easy, as both must be willing to acknowledge their own deficiencies and make compromises on the allocation of family tasks. But the results in terms of their happiness and peace of mind will be well worth the effort.

In discussing Jay and Harriet's problems, we have concentrated on just one type of neighboring-style relationship: heart-diamond. But similar principles apply to the other types as well: heart-club, club-spade, and spade-diamond. In any of the four kinds of neighboring-style relationships, partners may be precluded from exercising the full range of their styles due to the couple's need for balance. Sadly, each partner may sense that they are not fully themselves when they are with their mate. If this is the case in your own relationship, notice what it is about your own thinking and behavior that you enjoy in the company of others, but seems repressed when you are with your mate. This self-knowledge will enable you and your partner to discuss which of the four styles you need to "re-own."

While neighboring-styled partners can shift about to cover all four processes, they rarely take on the thinking styles of their opposite sides. Each side of the square gives us a significant portion of complete, balanced thinking. If one side is neglected, however, a weakness will result. Table 7.2 shows various types of issues that can haunt relationships between neighboring styles. This table lists combinations of styles in partners, along with potential strengths and weaknesses that can grow from each match. This is not to say that if you are in a relationship involving neighboring styles, you automatically will have the problems listed here. They may not manifest if both parties are skilled in their secondary processes. On the other hand, if a couple has deficiencies in one style or more, this can result in resentment and conflicts that are emblematic of the kind of thinking lacking in the relationship.

Neighboring-Style Couples

TABLE 7.2

Match	Potential Strengths and Weaknesses in
♦♥	*Strengths*—Inclined toward creative relationships; can often experience lighthearted joy when having fun together; especially sensitive to each other's feelings and those of other family members; caring and devoted as parents; prone to unconditional acts of kindness; generally optimistic and egalitarian; receptive to new ideas; casual and free-spirited about going wigh life's flow. *Weaknesses*—Neglect for logical, grounded thinking—the kind exemplified by evaluating problems and implementing responsible solutions, identifying economic goals and preparing for financial security, judging how an idea or behavior might be deemed inappropriate by society, or cautiously assessing the probable outcome of a particular act.
♥♣	*Strengths*—Inclined toward steady relationships; caring and loyal to each other; honor family traditions; teach their children to be responsible and thoughrful of others; impart a reverence for moral and/or religious values; hardworking; often volunteer their services, care for the sick or handicapped; respectful of social obligations; ten to be solid citizens. *Weaknesses*—Neglect for imaginative and analytic thinking that is found in dreaming of new futures and taking risks, creating innovative ways of doing things, considering alternate lifestyles and accepting those who live differently, participating in entrepreneurial ventures, or working toward individual realization of a compelling idea.

Neighboring-Style Couples (cont.)

Match	Potential Strengths and Weaknesses in
♣ ♠	**Strengths**—Inclined toward individual responsibility; respectful of well-established ways for doing things, yet can be open to new ideas; proficient in fiscal matters and planning; steady of purpose; firmly set limits for children and provide a civilizing structure in a well-ordered home; oriented to achievement that drives family toward successful completion of goals.
	Weaknesses—Neglect for intuitive, spirited thinking—represented by relating to others with spontaneous emotion, taking a break from work to have fun or celebrate; experiencing fantasy and that which lies outside one's established reality; appreciating the imaginative efforts of others; valuing the non-measurable; or being sensitive to people's whims and feelings.
♠ ♦	**Strengths**—Inclined toward individual spontaneity; spur each other to try adventurous activities; willingly take risks and (by example) encourage children to do the same; independently minded; exceptionally open to new ideas; usually successful and good providers for the family; exercise ingenuity; look for the better way; develop a lively and often competitive living environment.
	Weaknesses—Neglect for the order-setting, relation-forming activities that are associated with esteem for established social and cultural values, reverence for religious belief and ceremony, regard for institutions (organizations, clubs, education), respecting moral codes, honoring social contracts such as marriage, or building long-standing interpersonal ties among the family.

Before moving on to the next broad category of relationships, let's review several important points. First, couples need balanced thinking for long-term success. Second, individuals can adapt their thinking and adjust their style to take on characteristics that are different from their true nature. Third, people are most comfortable when they can operate from the solid base of their natural style, which includes their two secondary suits (as a mature, "two-armed boxer"). And last, a person can be inhibited from carrying out the full range of his or her style when a mate is usurping some important aspect of it. This can cause such a person to feel troubled, since they are not fully being themselves.

With these understandings, you can see that while true opposites like Libby and Sean, George and Hope, Maxine and Randy, or Mark and Lisa may get on each other's nerves and frustrate each other to no end with their differences, their issues are distinct from those of people in neighboring-style couples who can't spread their wings, so to speak, because a mate has blocked them from some aspect of themselves. In most cases, partners do not intentionally checkmate each other's expressions of their natural styles in ways such as those we have seen with Jay and Harriet; rather, it just happens. And usually people can't articulate what's going on inside of them, or why they feel uncomfortable, because they can't exactly define what part of them is missing. Unfortunately, partners may not know which aspect of themselves they've been cut off from until they find it restored after leaving the relationship. Indeed, many divorced people report that they are more at ease with themselves than they were in marriage. Affairs, separations, and divorces are often brought on by a partner's need for self-development. Later in this chapter, the section on "Understanding Yourselves as a Couple" offers techniques for dealing with such problems before they result in the destruction of a relationship.

WHEN PARTNERS HAVE THE SAME STYLE
With an understanding of how partners of neighboring styles can checkmate each other, it should be apparent that a similar situation

can occur with couples in which both partners are of the same personality style. Here the strengths and weaknesses of the couple will tend to parallel the strengths and weakness of the style that they favor. For example, if two clubs are married to each other, their partnership will probably include more conservative attitudes, fewer risks, and less openness to other styles than a relationship between a club and a non-club. As another example, we frequently read of movie-star couples, often both diamonds, each of whom has been in and out of marriages one after another. Caught up in the exciting fun of a new relationship and operating with a notion that the grass is greener in the next pasture, there is not enough non-diamond stability in these partnerships to hold them together. No matter which style a like-minded couple expresses, they will be challenged to reach the worthy aspects of the suit that opposes their style.

In a partnership between two people of the same style, one of them (or both partners at various times) usually has to play certain roles that do not suit them. For example, in a marriage between two hearts, one may be forced into the spade role, just to give the household some direction.

Holly and Greg: Two Diamonds Together

Consider the case of Greg and Holly. Greg grew up in a family with a predominantly club style, and he had not cultivated his own natural diamond side at the time he found himself attracted to Holly, also a diamond. When they married, Greg performed the club duties because, by family training, he was better-skilled at doing them. Yet he felt angry when he had to nag Holly about being on time, recording the checks she wrote, planning trips to the grocery, and the like. Their arguments often sounded like those of a club-diamond couple such as George and Hope, but the issues were much more complicated. For though Greg and Holly were both diamonds, the family balance they established required Greg to handle the club role, which, unbeknownst to either of them, was entirely unnatural for him. He could carry out its functions, but did so with deep discomfort and resentment. This is because while he was learning his own natural diamond style from Holly, her stronger claim on this style precluded Greg from fully developing into it, especially when they were together. At work Greg could be free and creative, but with Holly he seemed a mere shadow of himself. It wasn't until after they had separated that Greg felt at ease and realigned with his own true nature.

If both Greg and Holly had been completely mature and comfortable in their own styles as they entered into their relationship, they might have recognized that neither truly liked taking on the club role. With this knowledge, they could have negotiated a more equitable allocation of those duties. Greg might not have felt the need to nag Holly if he, too, could live in a more relaxed manner, with the responsibilities of organizing and carrying out the household details shared between them. They might have turned to advisors for handling the financial matters and taxes that neither enjoyed. Such solutions would have required that each partner acknowledge the other's wish to be a free-spirited human being. Yet the fact that they could not come together in this more effective way was no one's fault. Indeed, when they married, neither Greg nor Holly was fully aware of their own true nature. It was only within their marriage that they began to develop this type of self-awareness. Neither party needs to be blamed for their lack of wisdom about themselves, or for causing their relationship to slowly unravel over the years. Their love for each other and their ultimate separation were stages in their lifelong development.

Helen and Jacob: Two Clubs Together

Many couples get along reasonably well covering just three of the four suits. A common pattern for same-style relationships is for one partner to uphold one of their secondary modes, and for the other partner to champion the opposing secondary mode. In this case the partners seem to be opposites, because in disagreements they typically shift to their respective secondary corners and argue from those positions. For example, both Helen and Jacob are clubs. They have agreed on an orderly and predictable family life for their two sons, and both children seem to do well with the limits their parents have set. But every now and then, Jacob allows the older son to deviate from the rules without the usual consequences. And it upsets Helen when Jacob treats their two children differently. Recently the older son came in after curfew, apologetic and upset that the movie had ended later than he'd thought and that his girlfriend's house was clear across town. Jacob appreciated his son's honesty and did not want him speeding to get home. For the most part the older son had conducted himself reasonably, and no point would be served in grounding him, preventing him from attending a long-awaited young-people's concert at church the next night. But Helen contended that it set a bad example for the younger son, who had been grounded repeatedly that summer for coming in late. She reasoned that the same rules should apply to both sons. Actually, both parents are reasonable and loving people. Jacob is not irrational; rather, he tends to go with what his heart tells him about his children. Helen is not unfeeling, but she stays alert to the dangers of treating the two boys differently. Helen takes the stance of the club-spade, and Jacob the club-heart.

Since Helen and Jacob repeatedly debate from opposing secondary positions, both of them feel inauthentic in the roles they serve. Helen dislikes having to be the "mean witch" of the family who enforces the rules while Jacob wins his sons' friendship. She always seems to be ousted from the role of the caring mother whenever her husband is home. For his part, Jacob feels that he never has any authority at home. Helen is forever challenging his decisions about the boys, undermining his control. Worse than that, Jacob can't understand why she must be so tough on them so he also sees her as the "mean witch." If they could step back and look at the dynamics of their relationship, they might recognize that each partner cedes aspects of themselves—Helen her heart, and Jacob his spade—to the other partner when they are together. In order for each of them to feel more fully alive, they will need to discuss ways that they can back out of their routine roles and begin to exercise the parts of themselves that they have long relinquished to each other.

UNDERSTANDING YOURSELVES AS A COUPLE: FOUR INITIAL STEPS

Even when both partners have a mature knowledge of themselves and are comfortable with their own personal styles, couples can still have problems. With this in mind, here are a few guidelines that may help resolve some long-standing difficulties with your mate, no matter what combination of styles the two of you have.

Step One

Both you and your spouse might take the self-test at the beginning of this book and share your profile results with each other. Then set aside several hours so that together you can read aloud the characteristics of each other's personal style found near the end of chapter 2. Discuss each set of traits, strengths, weaknesses, and motivations, so that both of you are fully aware of the attributes of each of your individual thinking styles. Talk about the differences and the similarities represented in your profiles and discuss what they mean to your relationship. Acknowledge the ways each of you may favor different approaches to situations. Or, if your profiles are actually similar, note where voids are represented by your lowest scores, and talk about these ways of thinking that one or both of you dislike. The discussion might bring to the surface feelings of hostility, but in this session it is best to agree ahead of time not to make judgments about each other or to let arguments erupt. Instead, look at each of your styles in a rational, objective way so that both of you begin to understand the uniqueness of each other's behavior. By the end of this session, make it your goal to begin to endorse each other's styles, accepting the fact that each of you is unique. Begin to validate each other's personal styles as being right for each of you. Acknowledge that each of you has a right to your own way of thinking.

Then take yourselves out for a day or an evening of enter-tainment, doing something that suits both of your styles and is a pleasure for you both. You deserve it! Do this frequently as you work with the material in this book. As time goes by, explore the range of pleasurable activities you share as a couple. Learn to enjoy each other by engaging in these experiences.

Step Two

With your partner, decide on a period of time—perhaps a couple of weeks—when you will try to avoid starting arguments about the ways you each behave. If you disagree about particular matters during this period, include the attitudes and perspectives of your dif-fering styles in your debate. That is, in the process of disagreeing, clarify why it is natural for each of you to take different stances that follow from your individual styles. During this period, watch and listen to your mate for indications of their style. Compare your obser-vations with what you learned about your mate from their profile in Step One. Look for a pattern of actions and words to emerge which clusters around one of the styles, and also note which of the four types of thinking they tend to avoid. At the same time, try to make similar observations about yourself. Note which style (or styles) you favor in various situations. Are you consistent at home, at work, with friends, and with family? Or do you shift styles depending on the people you are with? Which situations make you feel uncomfortable? Where do you feel most at ease? And with whom?

Step Three

At the end of this period of mutual observation, get together with your partner again and discuss what you've noticed about each other, and about your relationship. As before, try to avoid arguments, and remain objective. Take turns talking, first about your understanding of each other, and second, about your awareness of yourselves. Simply share what you've both learned about each other in the past few weeks. By the end of this session, make it your goal for each of you to list out loud at least five things that your partner does, about which you can say, "I now know why you. . . . want me to save; . . . are cool to my family; . . . need your space; . . . always want us to talk, etc. As you each come up with your lists, write them down. When you've listed several of your mate's behaviors which tend to bother you, compare them to the characteristics of your mate's style that are summarized at the end of chapter 2. Keep your lists as ongoing reminders of how you are different, and add new items to them as you continue seeing your partner in a new light.

Step Four
You are now ready to put your new knowledge into practice. When you clash over daily matters, attempt to discuss them with an understanding of why you each take different stances. Be aware of style differences as the source of hostile feelings. Instead of feeling that your partner's position is an assault on you personally, recognize that he or she is providing a counterbalance to your own views and values. Think of disagreements as a process in which both of you add enough weight to your own sides of the scale for it to reach equilibrium. The objective is to strike an overall balance that is comfortable for both of you.

If after a month you have not yet reached a frame of mind where you can avoid arguing about your partner's traits, then you might mutually agree to repeat Steps Two and Three through several cycles of observing, understanding, and discussing your differences, after which you will try Step Four again, repeatedly if necessary. If after several months either you or your mate is not satisfied with your progress, it may be appropriate to turn to a counselor for outside help in improving your relationship.

THE PROCESS OF CHANGING EXPECTATIONS
Let's apply the four-step process to the issues in the relationship of Marnie and David. Marnie manages the grocery store in the shopping

plaza where she met David, whose shop sells surfing equipment. They soon discovered their common interest in sports, began dating, and within a few months decided to live together at Marnie's apartment. That's when their relationship started to deteriorate, because the free-spirited fun they once had had surfing or climbing mountains gave way to wrangling about their joint responsibilities. Marnie managed the household, scheduled their activities, and paid most of the bills. She began to test David by giving him an important bill, form, or vacation offer. Invariably, David misplaced the document and did not find it again until weeks later. Sometimes he would lay it atop the pile of surf-shop paperwork on the seat of his pickup truck. Sometimes it went into the glovebox. David would say to himself that he'd take care of it the next day. He really didn't want to let Marnie down. But as much as David would have liked to do things in a timely manner, he had the tendency to put things off until the next day. Marnie would eventually receive the late-payment notice or the vacation-offer deadline would pass, and she would feel let down again.

As David flunked test after test, Marnie became increasingly angry about his carelessness. "You're so disorganized!" she told him. "How can you run a surf shop if you can't even pay our phone bill on time?"

"That's just it," David answered. "There's only so much of that stuff I can handle. You've always paid your bills here. Why give them to me?"

"Grow up, David. You live here, too."

As their battles became more heated, David felt that Marnie lacked sensitivity to his needs, as well as to those of other family members. When David's dad was sick, Marnie made only a brief visit to see him. And David was the one to attend Marnie's brother's soccer games, not her. When it came to family ties, it seemed that David could find the time to be the responsible partner while Marnie remained disinterested and aloof. Within several months of living together, each of them thought there was something wrong with the other one.

Identifying Styles—Step One

One of Marnie's friends who was familiar with her complaints recommended that the couple look into their differences in personal styles. They began by taking the self-test in chapter 1 and discovered that Marnie's strong suit was the spade, while David's was the diamond. Then the partners devoted an evening to discussing what this meant to their relationship. They began by studying the characteristics of each partner's style (from chapter 2), taking turns reading aloud each other's strengths, weaknesses, interests, and other traits. Although some traits didn't fully apply to them individually, most of the descriptions were right on the mark.

"'Diamonds may be loose on procedures,'" Marnie read, "'make light of obstacles, and fail to follow through to the finish.' Boy, David, that's you to a T."

David nodded, chuckled, then read about Marnie's style: "'Spades may be insensitive to the feelings and interests of others, impatient, and inflexible, with a cleverness that may border on scheming.' Yes! That's what's been bugging me about you," he said. "You're more interested in testing me than caring about my needs."

Marnie felt David's remark was a criticism, so she counted to three. "Okay," she said, "that may be true. We're not going to argue. That's the way you feel, and it reflects our differences."

They read on through both lists, paying special attention to the positive aspects of their styles. They also compared the profiles of their test results and found that Marnie's strongest secondary suit was the club, while David's was the heart. Each of their secondary strengths was their partner's weakest suit. Marnie recognized the implications. "Now I see what's caused our problems," she said. "I've been expecting you to be as organized as me, and you've been expecting me to be as attentive to others as you are."

"That's almost it," David replied. "I would have said that I was expecting you to be 'understanding of others' or 'caring.' It's not the same as being 'attentive.'"

"How so?" Marnie asked, and they began discussing the shades of difference in their thinking processes, and what was important to each of them.

After talking for over an hour, David said, "This is the first time that I feel I've begun to really know you. We're not finding fault. We're simply talking about the two of us as individuals, openly and objectively. This is a good space for us to be in."

"Yes, it's our space," Marnie answered. "Why don't you invent a good way for us to celebrate?"

Observing Patterns—Step Two

During a weekend getaway to the mountains, the couple decided to set aside the next two weeks to avoid arguments and to carefully observe each other's actions and their own feelings. By the end of the first week, Marnie realized that she had stopped giving David tests. Rather, she took on all of the household paperwork herself, so there were few occasions for them to clash. However, she also noticed that she was not happy about having to handle all of these duties. She asked herself, "Why should David not have to do this work?" Instead of confronting him, however, she wrote down her thoughts and feelings to discuss them with him after the agreed-upon hiatus. And David did the same, noting that after Marnie had done their weekly bill-paying, she seemed particularly cool to him. The next day he surprised Marnie by picking her up after work and taking her to dinner and a jazz club. They both enjoyed the departure from their nightly routine of eating at home and watching TV. She asked what gave him the idea to do something they hadn't planned. David smiled and said, "It must be my diamondness. I'm the spontaneous one, so I decided to give it a try. And I felt that you could use a break."

Both of them observed that the evening out had restored them somehow. Marnie was unusually sensitive to David's needs, while he went out of his way to help with some household chores. But as their two weeks drew to a close, David had a crisis at his shop. He received an eviction notice for being consistently late paying rent. He turned to Marnie for advice about how to deal with the problem. "First of all," she reasoned, "they want you to stay. The plaza's not doing so well that they want more empty storefronts. This is a tactic to get you to be more organized. Second, you'll need to prove to the leasing manager that you've set up a program to solve this problem. And third, you need to respond to the notice now. Don't put it off."

"That's what I love about you," David said. "You know exactly what to do. But what kind of program would satisfy them?"

"You could set up a direct-payment plan with your bank."

The next day David went to see his contact at the bank, then delivered a letter about the payment plan to the leasing agent, who canceled the eviction proceedings.

Sharing Understandings—Step Three
On the next Sunday afternoon, the couple set aside time to share what they had learned about each other. David started by saying that he had a very different understanding of Marnie. She had been exactly on target in helping him escape eviction. His worries were over in one day. In the past he might have fretted for weeks while he figured out what to do. He had a new appreciation for Marnie's analytical skills. Although he disliked her coolness at times, as he had experienced after she paid bills, he could accept that trait as part of her nature.

Marnie said that indeed she had been upset about having to do all of the paperwork, and she was feeling unhappy about David not having to do the same. Yet she felt closer to him. She loved their jazz night and realized that he had been more aware of her needs. She was surprised they'd been able to get through two weeks without arguing, and attributed this to their having considered their differences before reacting in the emotion of an angry moment. She also encouraged David to become more organized and not rely on her so much. She didn't like paying all the bills.

"Why not set up a direct-payment plan at the bank?" David suggested.

They laughed. "Good idea," Marnie said. "That's what I love about you."

The partners then began writing their own, "I now know why you . . ." lists. Marnie's was as follows: "I now know why you . . . are more disorganized than me, . . . inspire me, . . . seem happier all the time, . . . want me to be more caring, . . . light my fire with your spontaneity."

David's list was: "I now know why you . . . want me to be more responsible, . . . seem cool to me, . . . irritate me at times, . . . are needed in my life to help me grow, . . . are so exciting when you challenge me."

Living with New Expectations—Step Four

This session of mutual understanding put Marnie and David's relationship on new footing and changed their expectations of each other. They acknowledged their different personal styles. Each also recognized that their partner offered guidance for developing their own weaker sides. Still, they didn't always agree. For instance, they soon debated whether to make a lasting commitment to each other. While Marnie valued her years of independence, she felt she was ready to marry David and plan their lives together. But David was reluctant to make permanent ties. He prized his freedom and saw no need to alter their relationship so soon after making it work. Although he loved Marnie, David did not have the same internal need to make a choice and tie the knot as she did. "Look, David, I understand that we have different views about things," Marnie told him, "but eventually we're going to have to come to some agreement about this, one way or the other. I don't want to go through life with you just hanging around here from one day to the next. You need to get serious."

"I know that," David said. "But see, it's not easy for me to settle down. It's not that I don't love you. I just need time to adjust to our being together."

Later, after Marnie and David reflected on each other's positions on the marriage matter, they saw how their differing views were consistent with each partner's personal style. Since they understood their differences, they were able to deal with them in the spirit of acceptance and appreciation of their partner's strengths. Did they eventually marry? Of course.

DEVELOPING THE RIGHT-RIGHT ATTITUDE

It doesn't take much difference in styles to ignite arguments in couples. And when it comes down to important matters, it can be hard to remember the many ways that another person's style may differ from your own. Even so, it's often useful to look for style characteristics before assuming the worst.

When a relationship contains marked differences in personal styles, both partners need to make real efforts to honor and savor the differences between them as individuals. They must learn to value even their disagreements, for these serve a vital purpose. When arguments occur, each partner should make their cases as honestly as possible, then give consideration to the other's views. Above all, however, try to avoid forcing your partner to follow your own line of thinking. The goal should not be to prove that you are right and your partner is wrong, but rather to understand that there are truths in both sets of opinions which, together, must be reflected in the outcome.

If a relationship has been built around "right versus wrong" attitudes, the transformation to a new "right-right" approach will not be easy. And despite full acceptance of the many ways in which you think differently, your differences will be frustrating at times. You both will continue to reach your breaking points and blow up over small things. When you do so, however, it will no longer be marked by the reaction, "What's wrong with you?" Instead it can be framed in the realization, "I see where you're coming from." And this change in perception makes all the difference for people openly accepting, respecting, and validating each other.

In the following chapter we'll explore methods for communicating with a partner of a different style. But to apply those techniques you must first be willing to accept your partner's differences. You will not be able to bridge communication gaps unless you recognize and affirm the points of contradiction that together you are attempting to connect. With this in mind, take the time to gain a deeper understanding of the differences in styles between you and your partner, and then validate each other's uniqueness before you undertake the methods described in the next chapter.

Differences in character are part of the wonderful richness of human nature. As you deepen your awareness of your own personal style and that of your partner—and you learn to validate and appreciate your differences—you will increasingly find that your lives together can be much more rewarding.

CHAPTER EIGHT

SHIFTING GEARS TO RESOLVE COUPLE CONFLICTS

How to Use Other Styles to Improve Attitudes and Communication

People are most comfortable when they live according to their natural styles and champion their own true beliefs. However, if everyone held rigidly to the attitudes of their individual styles, we would become locked in conflict and find it almost impossible to live with others. To have a successful relationship, you must learn to "shift gears" by communicating in a style that works with your partner's style. This chapter shows you how to resolve disagreements by employing your secondary styles while at the same time remaining true to your primary one.

But perhaps most fundamental to enjoying a good relationship is a couple's ability to interact with an open and accepting attitude. So we'll start by discussing how you and your partner can shift your thinking to end conflict and develop positive attitudes toward each other.

THE CLOSED-MINDEDNESS OF CONFLICT

Thus far, the words "disagreement" and "conflict" have been used interchangeably to describe people at odds with each other. Yet "conflict" is the harsher term. It implies the hardening of dis-agreement into the intractability of a running feud, the solidifying of viewpoints so that one party identifies the other as the one at fault. Each time the parties meet, they return to an ongoing battle and accumulate arguments to escalate the war.

Let's try to understand conflict by applying what we know about language styles. Consider the words used to describe conflict. They're affiliated with the spade-club side of the mind. A person is unable to relate openly when judging another as being flawed or at fault and their mind is locked into evaluating them that way. In feuding, the mind remains stuck in a judgment/attack posture, continually dredging up old issues and attempting to get even for past injustices.

The key to resolving a long-standing conflict between you and your partner is to defuse the judgmental, spade-club mind-set inherent in most feuds. Instead of closing yourself off from your mate with alienating accusations, you can open the lines of commu-nication by tapping into your diamond mode of thinking. But in order to do so, first you must decide to stop paying attention to your own internal club case against your partner. Make a conscious choice not to revisit old arguments as a matter of routine. Then you can open yourself to the possibility that you and your partner can create a new way of relating that involves meeting each other halfway. Note that in this process, you incrementally go around the card table from one suit to the next. At each step along the way, you shift out of a mode of thinking that is provoking conflict and shift into the mode that moves you closer to openheartedness.

Think of your relationship as a car with a manual transmission and four mental process gears through which you can shift. If the car isn't moving the way you want it to in one gear, you have the ability to shift to a better gear. Often you have to shift through several gears to reach the right cruising speed. Once you become familiar with the distinctions between the four kinds of thinking represented by the card suits, you'll be able to shift styles in a way that will help you and your partner interact more comfortably.

TRUSTING YOUR DIAMOND AND HEART ABILITIES
TO TRANSFORM RELATIONSHIPS

The most challenging part of shifting mental gears to end conflicts is that we often have little awareness of two of the four gears—the diamond and the heart. Brain research shows that Western languages are processed primarily in the brain's left hemisphere, its spade-club specialist. Language, for the most part, is an identifying and ordering of signs (words, letters) to represent objects and situations. So we're usually quite adept at making a case against our partner. We can readily identify anything that doesn't meet our standards. We label and list criticisms, assign blame, and save it all in a mental file containing the complaints against our partner. Then, during an argument, we can retrieve the file and recite any part of it at a moment's notice. Putting an end to this spade-club habit of defensively rehashing old arguments and coldly stating our position requires shifting into the club's opposite—the open, expansive, diamond attitude.

But recall the times when you have come up with new ideas. You may have discovered that creativity doesn't always come about by conscious effort. Creative ideas are more likely to pop into your mind as if by magic from some outside source, and they seem to form according to their own timetable. Yet imaginative insights can be applied to every area of your life—including your relationship. Since most of us lack the experience of dealing with relationships in an open, creative way, however, we tend to rely on the readily available, dirty-laundry list of complaints about our partner which the spade-club side of our brain produces. We don't have the faith to toss that laundry into the unconscious wash to see if it comes clean.

In order to switch on the inventive processes that will help you to find new ways to relate, you must deliberately turn off the filing mechanism that maintains that same old list of resentments—the ones that you can recite backward and forward. How do you sidetrack a boxcar full of well-documented arguments? You trust in the hunch that a better train of thought will appear.

When it comes to accessing the less conscious diamond and heart processes of our minds, all of us are at a disadvantage—no matter what our personal style. That's because our culture places prime emphasis on training our spade-club capabilities. The "3 Rs," basic work skills, and competitive games hold priority over the arts, creative design, and music. And if we have interests in the spiritual side of our mental powers, these days we tend to develop them on our own. So even diamond- or heart-styled people typically have ready access to their well-trained spade and club skills, but may not be aware of the other processes they use. Some people—perhaps your mate—may not even perceive that the non-rational, diamond and heart modes are a part of their own mental capacities![1]

Therefore, one aspect of a couple's problems may result from a lack of awareness of these mysterious processes. After all, how can you shift to two gears you don't even know are there? How do you begin to trust the creating and relating processes as equal partners with the thoroughly analyzed and well-ordered programs that are very conscious within your mind? Frankly, it's not easy.

The great choreographer Agnes de Mille once observed, "Living is a form of not being sure, not knowing what's next or how. . . . We guess. We may be wrong, but we take leap after leap in the dark." That's essentially what's required to end conflicts. Step out of the well-rehearsed frame of mind. Let go of the list of complaints. Then leap from judgment into a new attitude of openheartedness.

Use your own past experiences to guide you. Recall the focused intensity of heated confrontation. Then feel the sense of release that is found when an argument stops. Your attitude swings into peaceful acceptance and you feel at ease. If you are attempting to end a conflict with your partner, keep in mind that you have conscious control over bringing about this shift in attitude from maintaining discord to seeking accord. It simply requires that you decide not to rely on those old complaint files. When both partners choose to create an easier relationship, it will come.

HOW PERSONAL STYLES AFFECT ATTITUDES
ABOUT CONFRONTATION

Your attitude sets the course for what you expect to achieve in the relationship. Since virtually all of us possess the four modes of thinking, we all can shift our attitudes at will to bring about the results that we seek. However, shifting into an openhearted attitude to end conflict may not be what some people actually seek. To some degree, attitudes relate to a person's style.

For example, spade-styled individuals often challenge others to debate in order to hone their own expertise in logical analysis. If they take on someone of another style, the spade often wins by the force of their keen arguments and dominant manner. In victory the spade gets an ego boost from their skillful mastery. It makes them more self-confident, and better at their game. A special problem arises, though, if their need to win prevails over other motives for debate. Then the contest is a power struggle, and they may not be concerned about negotiating agreement or even actual outcomes. They won't want to end the dispute until they've clearly triumphed and satisfied their own sense of being top dog. Occasionally, circumstances can bring out this spade trait in someone of another suit. Listening carefully to what's being said by your partner may offer clues that you're involved in a power struggle, rather than a style dispute.

Club-styled people often have an altogether different motive for continuing a conflict. Since clubs tend to support proper behavior, laws, and established social standards, they often have well-grounded reasons for holding steadfastly to their causes. If your actions fly in the face of a club's strongly-held values, they won't quickly forgive and forget. They may concentrate on the details of the matter, letting you know how you have let them down. Clubs often focus on blame, right versus wrong, and acting responsibly. Once you're in their doghouse, they won't readily let you out. Indeed, they may revisit you in the doghouse to remind you why you're there! In doing so, clubs take comfort from having been proper and correct themselves.

Because conflict serves hidden motives of clubs and spades to promote their strengths, they may be more reluctant to end contention than diamonds or hearts. (In fact, some people even make careers out of confrontation—consider attorneys.) But this is not to say that spades and clubs are the only ones to carry on conflicts.

Heart-styled people can easily get their feelings hurt and may hold resentment toward anyone who makes light of their unifying interests. They are most likely to become contentious when they are ignored or not accorded sensitive consideration. In addition, they may even start an argument (although they might not call it that) in order to engage in communication. Given the heart's longing to relate, even an antagonistic relationship is better than no relationship at all. But they much prefer peaceful, easygoing relations and will avoid confrontation if at all possible.

Diamond-styled people can get their feathers ruffled if someone tries to curtail their freedom, stifles their creative expression, curbs their ability to explore new experiences, or pushes them to be more deliberate and systematic. Whenever they feel pressured in this way, they may confront anyone who seems intent on controlling their expansive interests. However, once such limits are relaxed—and if their feelings have not been wounded by bitter accusations—diamonds are usually willing to forgive and forget. In fact, out of all four styles, diamonds are least likely to hold a grudge.

One way to short-circuit conflicts with people of all styles is to go directly to their ego needs: acknowledge a spade's logical superiority, a club's correctness, a heart's harmonizing talents, or a diamond's originality. Once you validate anyone's strengths, they are more likely to discontinue their critical, judgmental attitude and warm up to you in a new way.

SHIFTING STYLES TO IMPROVE COMMUNICATION
Let's now turn to some practical ways to shift through the four mental gears in order to improve communication with your partner.

These methods won't end disagreement. What they will do is enable you to shift the wording of your message into the language of your partner's primary or secondary style, so that you can get your ideas across. That way, your partner will be more inclined to listen, rather than dismiss your words out of hand.

The communication techniques that we will be discussing here follow from the principles of language styles presented in chapters 4 and 5. You'll recall that the four key words—open, close, cut, and connect—characterize the core messages of the four styles. Language styles branch out from these basic roots, and the words that people use often trace back to the key word of their style. But as shown in figure 8.1, opposing styles (located diagonally across the diagram from each other) have key words that oppose each other in meaning. The heart's key word *connect* has the

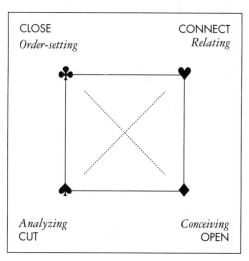

FIGURE 8.1

opposite meaning of the spade's key word *cut*. Similarly, the diamond key word *open* opposes the club key word *close*.

So if you and your partner happen to be of opposite styles, the clusters of words that each of you uses to represent how you think— your individual language styles—may clash in meaning. If you're a heart, you may be promoting connecting, relating, and linking-together, while your spade mate focuses on cutting, separating, and analyzing situations. If you're a club, you may want to set limits and assure safety and routine in your life, but your diamond mate touts freedom, taking risks, and exploring new possibilities. When opposing-styled partners carry on conversations, their messages are often in stark contradiction. This causes each partner to disagree with the other's thinking and become frustrated that they're not speaking the same language—which is precisely the case.

Even when partners are not opposites in style, they may hold down opposite roles to achieve balance in the relationship, as discussed in chapter 7. Therefore, their arguments may be waged across such poles of opposite thinking. This may cause them to appear as true opposites in style.

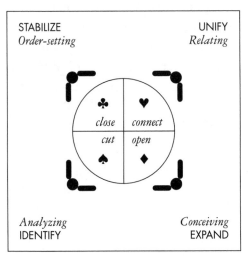

FIGURE 8.2

Luckily, people don't speak in one language style alone. Usually, two or three styles are evident. As represented in figure 8.2, the "arms" of people's styles—and the words they use—reach out from their primary suit to their neighboring, secondary suits as well. But they don't easily reach across the table to the opposing suit.

If you and your partner are arguing across the table from opposing positions and your language styles are clashing, try shifting into a secondary style that you and your partner share. That's where you might meet on common ground. We'll give you some examples of this technique in the following pages.

HOW OPPOSITES CAN SHIFT INTO SECONDARY STYLES TO COMMUNICATE

In order to shift your words into another style, you'll first have to shift your thinking. For instance, if you and your partner are in an argument that pits spade ideas against the heart, one of you will need to introduce diamond or club messages, or both, to reframe the debate. To shift your thinking into one of these alternative positions, simply recall a few signature words of the suit that you want to shift into. To shift to diamond, think of "open, conceive, expand." Or to shift to club, think of "close, set order, stabilize." This will direct your thoughts and words into whichever secondary style you've chosen. The whole point of this strategy is to reword your ideas into messages that don't conflict with your partner's preferred way of thinking. This opens new channels of communication for possible resolution with your partner. So let's practice shifting.

Jane and Tom: Female Heart and Male Spade

We'll start with the case of Jane and Tom, who have been married several years. Jane wants them to spend more time together and says she doesn't feel appreciated for all she adds to Tom's life. Tom can't understand why Jane feels this way. He loves her and has been faithful, even though he tends to want some time to himself. He likes tinkering in the garage with his old Corvette, which sometimes bugs Jane to no end. Yet he is there for her whenever she needs his help in solving her problems, Tom contends. What more could she want? Why, he wonders, does she feel unloved and unappreciated?

To work through their differences, both Jane and Tom must recognize each other's styles, which are heart and spade. Jane is the unifier, who likes to build relationships, whereas Tom is the identifier whose strongest skill is independent problem-solving. Once they see that it is each other's nature to be as they are, then they can better articulate both their interests and how they are at odds. So the first step involves identifying and accepting each other's styles.

The next step is to gain a better understanding of the opposing language styles that each of them uses. Couples often experience communication problems, because both parties enter a conversation expecting to hear their own favored language style being spoken by the other partner. Jane, for example, assumes that in a discussion about their need to be together, Tom should use words like *share, trust, tender, sympathetic, ties,* etc. She filters his speech through the expectations of her own heart style, and thus is disappointed that he rarely uses the words that she responds to. Likewise, Tom does the same, expecting Jane to speak his spade language of *challenge, decide, goals, hard, focus,* etc. Because she doesn't, Tom may even think that Jane is simpleminded.

In order for these two opposites to communicate, they must learn to shift out of their prevailing styles. Now, it is unlikely that either of the partners is going to abandon their natural interests and convert directly to the language style of their mate—although doing so occasionally may work wonders to get a partner's attention. Indeed, Tom would be shocked if Jane said to him, "Tom, I've studied our problems, and I think it's time to initiate some changes. Let's skip the crap and focus on answers. Are you with me? Okay, what's your solution to my getting a piece of your time?" Tom might realize, "Whoa, she's serious," and say, "Okay, I read you loud and clear." In adopting Tom's spade style in the negotiation for togetherness represented here, Jane shifted into a calculating, problem-solving mode to face her husband head-on. At times she might succeed in doing so. But over the long haul, using this technique would feel artificial to Jane, because she would be operating in a manner that contradicts her own interests and strengths.

A more natural approach is for each partner to preserve their own integrity and engage the other in their secondary styles—in this case diamond, club, or both. For instance, Jane might ask her husband, "Tom, what would you think about putting some adventure in our lives? Say we took your 'Vette out on the road and got away this weekend. Where would you like to go?" Here, Jane appeals to her husband's exploring spirit and encourages him to whisk them away in his beloved car to someplace of interest to him. She has not clashed with his style, because she does not plead for togetherness. Rather, she has opened him up to pursuing a dream of his own to see new territory. She also gets what she wants: time together with Tom.

But she refrains from asking for it outright, since such a direct request could fall on deaf ears. If Tom and Jane go on their trip and enjoy themselves, their return trip home might be a good time for Jane to say, "Tom, we really had fun this weekend. You know, I think it could be good for both of us to do this on a regular basis. What would you think about scheduling a getaway once a month so we could visit places we each want to see? If something comes up at work, we could postpone it until you have the time, but it is just so relaxing to do something different every once in a while. What do you say?" This club strategy to regularize a schedule of weekends together followed her diamond appeal to draw out Tom's imagination; Jane's favored heart style was not employed.

This may sound sneaky. But if both partners can satisfy their needs without a frontal assault on each other's styles, there is nothing wrong with employing such a strategy. You've probably always known that there is strategy involved in dealing with your mate, and here is the key to it: Learn to communicate in language styles that do not clash with your partner's favored style. To improve your chances for meeting on common ground, avoid using words and phrases that are associated with your mate's weakest suit. Refer as needed to chapters 4 and 5 on language styles, and particularly to tables 4.1–4.3 for the favored vocabularies of each of the four styles.

Naturally, the same strategy could work for Tom as well. He might say to Jane, "Now that we've got some extra money, I think it could be good for us to budget some funds for our individual interests. You've talked about taking that floral-design course. You've mentioned piano lessons. How about it?" This prompts Jane to imagine how she might develop her hobbies, while Tom, of course, thinks of the next car restoration project he'll do during Jane's class time. Tom's suggestion encompasses both diamond and club messages in one appeal. It inspires Jane to explore her personal interests, and it also suggests a program of classes that would become their routine. They both would get what they want. Jane would enjoy the lessons, expanding her abilities and being with other people. Tom would get more independent time to fix up his 'Vette.

Much like the previous example, Tom avoids arguing for his self-interests using his own spade language style, for that direct approach would likely anger Jane. But by structuring the message to include the diamond and club secondary styles that they both share, he directs her thinking into those modes where they might agree.

Hope and George: Female Diamond and Male Club

Let's now apply this same communication strategy to the other pair of opposites: the diamond and club. We'll return to Hope and George's argument about buying the convertible (from chapter 1), and restart it as they began. Then we'll see what happens when they shift into secondary styles to redirect their debate into a more conciliatory outcome:

"I'm tired of driving that old clunker every day," Hope says. "It's no fun. I want a sportier car, so I feel more alive."

George falls into his regular response, "You know we planned to save for retirement. Buying a new car now wouldn't be responsible. We should stick to our plans."

Hope already recognizes that the use of her diamond style to sell George on her needs for a car would only lead to their mutual frustration. Therefore, she shifts into spade-heart persuasion. "I agree, George. We must plan for the future. And you are doing a great job of investing our money. I'm only suggesting that we adjust our spending habits so that we could have a car that we could truly enjoy together."

"Isn't that why we bought the Buick?" George asks.

"Yes and no," she answers. "The Buick is good for long trips and going out with friends. But I'm thinking we could trade in the old Chevy for a convertible that we could hop into on warm weekends and go golfing together. Or when you golf with the guys you could take the convertible and show them how sporty you are."

George warmed to the idea. "I like the sound of that. But how would we change our spending to afford it?"

Hope reevaluates her priorities, "Well, I could stop buying new clothes for six months. We could postpone redecorating the living room. . . ."

In making her new appeal, Hope first acknowledged George's financial skills. Then she introduced a spade message that they would have to reanalyze their spending habits. After that she shifted to the heart style to promote a car that could aid both their togetherness and George's relationship with his friends. The clincher was Hope's insight that the car could be a symbol for George's sportiness as well, to boost his self-image in an area in which she knows he struggles for well-roundedness. She avoids attacking George's conservative ways, and instead makes use of them in advancing her cause.

HOW NEIGHBORING STYLES DEAL WITH DIFFERENT COMMUNICATION PROBLEMS

If two partners have neighboring styles, their communication problems are different from those of true opposites like Jane and Tom, or Hope and George. For while neighboring-styled partners do have different interests and motivations, their major clashes occur when they step into opposing roles that serve to balance the relationship. In order to do this, they rarely battle from opposing corners of the boxing ring, rather they almost always take opposing sides. However, since the common ground upon which they can reach agreement is the side that stretches between them, they each have only one secondary style that will work with their mate. They don't have the flexibility to shift into two secondaries as opposites do.

Harriet and Jay: Female Heart and Male Diamond

Let's see how this applies to Harriet and Jay (from chapter 7, and also represented here in figure 8.3). In the diagram each partner is shown with one long arm, which represents the particular combination of styles that each one tends to use in their relationship: Harriet upholds the heart-club side—unifying and stabilizing the family—often reminding Jay to carry out his responsibilities; Jay reaches out to the diamond-spade side—expanding and identifying the family's course—often urging Harriet to make a decision of some sort. They have become so stuck in these one-sided roles that they've forgotten how to enjoy being together. Jay

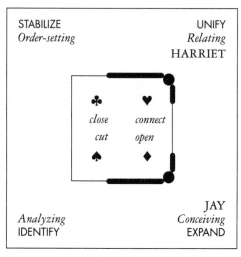

STABILIZE   UNIFY
Order-setting   *Relating*
            HARRIET

♣   ♥
close   *connect*
cut   *open*
♠   ♦

             JAY
Analyzing   *Conceiving*
IDENTIFY   EXPAND

FIGURE 8.3

knows Harriet will bring up something he should do. Harriet knows Jay will tell her how she must think for herself. With such constant "punches" against their mate's primary style, each signals their displeasure with their obligatory roles.

In order to achieve a more pleasant line of communication between them, Harriet must forego her nagging, club requirements, and Jay must avoid being the cool, spade driving force. The only two language styles that truly work for them are the heart and the diamond. This calls for a great deal of forbearance on both of their parts, as we'll find in the following sample of their everyday issues.

For instance, Jay arrives home after work and asks Harriet, "What's for dinner?"

She says, "I don't know yet. I just got home myself. Did you stop at the bank and make that deposit?"

Jay shakes his head no in disgust, and Harriet does the same.

In less than twenty seconds, the couple has already set the stage for their nightly clash. She can't make a simple decision. He can't carry out a simple task. These seemingly minor breaches of their duties have been going on for years. So long, in fact, that the looks of disgust now serve as a quick substitute for the once-raging battles about "Why do you always disappoint me this way?"

Normally they stew about the matter. Jay retreats to his computer, and Harriet takes to the kitchen. But this evening is different. While still shaking his head, Jay's expression changes to a wry smile as he says to her, "You know, I don't know how you've put up with me all these years. I forgot to make the deposit, but the bank's still open. How about going with me? We could stop at the grocery, figure out something for dinner, then cook together."

"And just leave the kids here?" Harriet frets about her duties to their teenagers.

"Sure. We'll tell them we're going. We won't be gone long. We could chat."

This spur-of-the-moment change in their routine is what Harriet needs to open her heart-diamond mode and let go of the club procedures that she typically imposes. On their way to the shopping center, she notes that they haven't grocery-shopped together in years. She likes having Jay involved in their mealtime plans and sharing the daily burden. As they fix dinner together and talk about their workaday lives, there is no cause for argument. They both engage the two modes of thinking in which they best communicate.

Because their personal styles—heart and diamond—are adjacent along one side of the four-way diagram, Harriet and Jay have only the heart-diamond combination of thinking processes available to them for optimum communication. Whenever their discussion turns to decisions or responsibilities, one partner or the other is likely to become peeved. This makes it difficult for the couple to talk about economic goals, financial planning, legal matters, and the like. Discussion of any of these topics inevitably requires that one or both partners shift to their weak suits, which perturbs them. Rather than handle such matters themselves, they might turn to experts for financial management and legal help.

Although Harriet and Jay have a more limited range of thinking and language styles for reaching common ground than opposites do, the neighboring-style couple is generally more in tune with each other's needs, interests, and ideas than opposites tend to be. When Harriet and Jay bring themselves around to sharing their heart-diamond zone, they can be exceptionally compatible and understanding of each other.

ACCEPTING THE COMMUNICATION GAP
IN YOUR RELATIONSHIP

If partners always thought alike, relationships would be very boring. Fortunately, most of us experience enough differences between ourselves and our mates to prevent such boredom from setting in. But can't communication gaps—another name for differences in language styles—cause serious problems in relationships? Not necessarily.

Throughout this chapter we've explored how "shifting" into secondary thinking styles can help us to prevent misunderstandings and improve communication with the one we love. Employing this strategy doesn't mean that we'll miraculously begin to think and feel as one—nothing of the sort. It does mean, however, that we can learn to give our partner at least some of what they want and at the same time get at least some of what we want from the relationship. It means we can enjoy each other's company and come to appreciate how our partner's differences define who they are—the person we initially fell in love with!

Part of the solution for improving your relationship is to get beyond the need to eliminate the communication gap, and instead work around it. Eliminating the gap would mean limiting each partner's ability to think for and be themselves. There is nothing wrong with a communication gap except that we find it frustrating. Why not focus on validating our individual uniqueness and that of our partner, and accept the fact that communication gaps are inherent in our individual differences?

While your partner may not be able to converse in the style you most enjoy or fully share your interests, there are many other people who can provide you with the conversation and camaraderie that you seek. These people are your friends. It is perfectly natural to find emotional nourishment from friends and relatives with whom you share interests or sensibilities. And it takes the pressure off your partner. Besides, once you're aware of the four suit styles and realize that no one person could ever exhibit every trait in all four styles, you'll no longer look to your partner to satisfy your every need. And you'll no longer expect to have perfect communication between the two of you. With this new understanding, you'll both feel more relaxed about the relationship and about being yourselves.

THE INTERESTS GAP—AND HOW TO BRIDGE IT

Words aren't the only barriers to good communication between different styles. Different interests can also create rifts that are difficult to bridge. To see how such divisions affect relationships, let's return to George and Hope, who debated buying the car. He is a club stabilizer and she is a diamond expander. In order to understand this couple's "interests gap," we'll recap their styles—this time with an emphasis on how the partners spend their time.

Clubs tend to be involved in organizational and administrative details, setting up routine procedures, planning ahead, and generally keeping things in order. At home, a club-styled partner might spend their time cleaning and straightening up, making lists of things to do, managing financial matters, scheduling social activities, coordinating civic responsibilities, and guiding the family on how to uphold laws and moral principles. Indeed, they take on the administration of so many family responsibilities that they enjoy being able to check things off their list. They feel satisfied when they've completed a necessary job.

In contrast, diamonds are interested in exploring new ideas and experiences, understanding the world at large, and expanding awareness. At home, this can mean pursuing their interests when and where the spirit moves them, having fun, adventuring off to some new place or into a facet of themselves that they haven't yet experienced, suggesting activities for the family to do on the spur of the moment, taking on creative projects (even messy ones) without a corresponding need to finish them, and chatting with friends to share ideas. A diamond may keep many projects going all at once to stimulate their creative imagination.

Note that these are not exclusive traits of people who exhibit the club and diamond styles. A person of any style never exhibits only that style's traits. Diamonds can be clean and neat, and clubs can be fun-loving and take time out to pursue a craft. Rather, the point here is that there is often a tendency for people of these styles to be pulled in the direction of the concerns and interests described above.

George exhibits many of the club traits, from handling the couple's financial matters and maintaining a neat, well-run, orderly home, to serving on the boards of several civic organizations. By contrast, Hope leaves these concerns to George and pursues her diamond interests. She prefers to spend her free time on her graphic-design business, taking meditation classes, or producing creative meals. Hope accepts the traditional woman's role of managing the household and most of the cooking, but there are often disputes between her and George over his more rigorous standards of neatness. A typical night might find George working on their stock portfolio, while Hope is reading about Zen. If the choice for an evening's activities comes down to listening to George talk about stocks or calling a friend to go to a movie, you know Hope will opt for the movies. On weekends George is inclined to work through his "to-do" list of home projects, but Hope itches to head for the beach or go shopping—anything to be out of the house.

So when George and Hope converse at the dinner table, there are sharp distinctions not only in their language styles, but also in their basic interests and motivations. Hope wants to discuss the new ideas or ways to be that she has experienced during the day, perhaps the concepts for one of her graphics projects. George, however, continually talks about methods or things to do, such as coordinating their calendar for the next few days or describing in detail an investment recommended by someone at work. Hope could care less about George's friend's investments, or even their own, for that matter. She longs for a meaningful discussion with George about her evolving spiritual awareness, but he doesn't seem to relate to such interests of hers. Rarely can George draw Hope into a conversation about the details of their life together that he considers necessary and important, and he reads this disinterest as irresponsibility on Hope's part. On the other hand, Hope is rarely able to get George to talk about creating more adventure in their lives. Neither partner seems motivated by or interested in the other's area of true expertise.

While George and Hope occasionally talk about each other's interests, these conversations tend to be somewhat halfhearted as compared to the conversations that they have separately with their friends, who share in their individual ways of thinking. Hope finds that chats with her diamond friends are rich and inspiring, while George thrives on informal conferences with his club friends about investments. But at home, together, neither partner can fully share their own deepest interests with their mate. Nor are Hope and George ever likely to change in this regard.

While Hope and George may not be able to effectively communicate using their own preferred diamond and club styles, they can become involved in each other's interests when they shift into the secondary styles that they have in common—heart and spade. To see how this works, let's summarize the interests of hearts and spades.

Hearts tend to enjoy building relationships and finding meaningful connections between diverse aspects of life experiences. In daily life, these interests may be applied toward taking care of family members and others outside the family, making social contacts and maintaining lasting ties with friends and associates, playing a musical instrument, writing poetry, sharing stories, taking up environmental causes, volunteering, joining team activities, participating in religious groups or peaceful causes, and any other activities that foster unity and connection. Thus, the heart serves as an advocate for many kinds of togetherness.

Spades are often masters at evaluating, analyzing, formulating goals, identifying needs and solutions, and problem-solving. At home, these skills may be employed in setting a course for the family and making decisions, maintaining discipline, independent problem-solving (as in home fix-it projects or car repair), participating in or watching competitive sports, playing games and doing puzzles, coaching, heading civic groups, picking investments, starting entrepreneurial ventures, urging scholastic excellence, reading information related to work, and doing work at home. All the while, the spade tends to be the leader and capable of cool independence.

Let's see how George and Hope can use the secondary strengths that they mutually share—the spade's evaluation and analysis, and the heart's connection and relating—to reach each other and share some of each other's interests. Neither can fully relate to each other's worlds: his procedures on what they should do, and her vision of how they could be. But they can meet each other in making choices and decisions that affect their daily lives and in voicing their own opinions. For instance, Hope might willingly help George evaluate the growth potential of two alternative stock purchases, but leave the routine investment details to him. George might enjoy discussions with Hope about her business clients, but avoid involvement in the creative aspects of her graphic-design work. The two of them can also share their feelings, discuss mutual friends, and otherwise engage in togetherness.

Jane and Tom, the heart-spade couple you met earlier in this chapter, have differences that often boil down to the issue of "togetherness versus independence." Tom is quite comfortable being on his own much of the time—tinkering with the car, watching football, tracking his stocks on the computer, reading management guidebooks, etc. Other than Jane, his only real friends are his tennis buddies. Tom talks with the neighbors, and on social occasions he debates people in interesting discussions, often challenging their views. But Tom is not truly social, for he doesn't seek relationships. He has a tendency to one-up others, rather than treat people as equals. That alienates many people, except for the ones who are similarly involved in Tom's game of one-upmanship. And Jane is not one of those. She is frustrated by the way that Tom takes on and shuts out other people—even her friends—and can't see how he could live with himself having so many people mad at him.

Indeed, Jane is almost never combative with people (except Tom). Actually, she avoids disputes and prefers a happy, peaceful coexistence with everyone. She is well-liked by her friends and coworkers. She enjoys going out with them to shop or catch a movie. But this causes Jane to feel guilty that she is leaving Tom home alone—guilty that she is having fun and he isn't. From her perspective, Jane can't understand how anyone could have a good time without involving other people. But Tom is refreshed by his independent tinkering time. When he can work on his car without having to contend with people, he's in his element.

These differences in their interests and motivations underscore their daily actions. Tom uses conversation with Jane and others to convey his solution to how one must think, while Jane is sensitive to how people would feel. Neither partner really comprehends the other's interests. Neither would be comfortable living the life of their partner. And in their communication, neither can fully engage in the type of discussion that stimulates the other. Tom finds talking about the incessant happenings of people's daily lives as just so much drivel. Jane considers Tom's world of technology, games, winning, and keeping score to be soulless—sometimes frighteningly so. While they both enjoy spending an afternoon together watching a football game, this is not the togetherness that Jane seeks. On the other hand, it perfectly suits Tom's idea of quality time with one's partner: two independent people participating in an entertaining activity that does not entail sappy connection.

Tom's energy is sapped by relationships, but Jane's is restored by them. Thus, they can't draw each other into the types of heart or spade activities and conversations that they themselves enjoy. Yet they both can engage each other in the diamond realm of their imaginative adventures, or in the club matters of handling the details of their lives. In these secondary modes, they are able to relate effectively. They may have their disagreements, but at least they can get through to each other's interests using these alternate routes.

There are many activities that involve both the diamond's imaginative exploration and the club's arranging details, such as boating, camping, travel, investigating wines, and gardening, to name just a few. Therefore, Tom and Jane can plan such activities together and enjoy the pleasure of each other's company while doing them. But if you were to ask each one what truly interests them about a particular activity, such as camping, they'd probably give very different responses. Tom might say that he likes being self-sufficient and independent with no one else around, having to solve problems that they hadn't anticipated, and staying alert to unknown dangers. Jane, however, might say that she likes them being together without TV games or household projects competing for Tom's attention, talking with him in the coziness of their small tent, and snuggling to the peaceful sound of crickets chirping. They involve each other in such activities by applying their secondary styles, which they share in common. But they each filter the experience through the individual interests of their own strong suit.

The way to bridge Jane and Tom's interests gap is not to insist that they both have the same interests. Rather, the solution is for them to take part in activities together that allow both partners to satisfy their own unique interests.

Since each of the four styles serves a particular purpose in life's four-way scheme of things, it stands to reason that people's different interests and the words they use generally reflect the fundamental outlook of their personal style. In figure 8.4, Tom, Jane, George, and Hope are located around the table as representatives of their individual styles, along with a shorthand description of their style's basic perspective on life. George upholds the organizing concern for

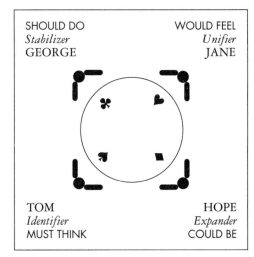

FIGURE 8.4

what he and Hope should do. Hope sparks the possibilities of what she and George could be. Tom focuses on what he and Jane must think. And Jane urges Tom to consider how people would feel. Although each of them has capabilities that apply all four modes of thinking, they each tend to speak up for the particular interests which stem from the essential functions of their own style.

Within your own relationship, it is useful to keep in mind how the basic perspective of your own style can conflict with that of your partner. When your partner engages in interests that clash with your own, they merely are upholding their side of the table, involving the partnership in things that you may dislike doing yourself. The frustration you feel when your partner promotes different interests or motivations is the price you pay for their carrying out their part of the bargain.

As you and your partner learn to shift your thinking into your own secondary styles, you'll find that your relationship no longer needs to be at loggerheads. The shorthand phrases for the basic perspectives represented in figure 8.4—*should do, must think, could be,* and *would feel*—can be useful for guiding your thinking into your secondary styles to bridge the interests gap and the communication gap as well. Once you identify which of the styles you and your partner share in common, make a written note of the shorthand phrase(s) associated with your common ground. Post it on the refrigerator, if you like. Do whatever it takes to remind both you and your partner how easy it is to shift styles in order to bridge the differences between you.

FINDING COMMON GROUND VIA YOUR SECONDARY STYLES

Knowing that you and your partner are of different styles will help both of you to grasp why you don't communicate or enjoy activities together in the ways you'd like. Acknowledging your individual and secondary styles will give you insight into the language styles and interests that are difficult for you to share, and also those that are your common ground for reaching each other.

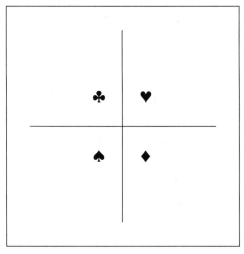

FIGURE 8.5

As an aid to this process, indicate your own style and secondaries in the appropriate quadrants of figure 8.5. Put your initial in each of the squares of the thinking styles that you use the most, and underline the one that is your strongest suit. Then do the same for your partner. Next, look for those suits in which both of you have indicated either a favored or secondary style, and in those cases circle the symbols of these suits. These circled suits are the thinking styles in which you should find common ground.

If your underlined suits are in squares that are diagonally across from each other, thus indicating a pattern of opposition, it is likely that, however you struggle to change your mate, communication will be thwarted whenever you use either of these styles. Your best opportunity for sharing easy conversation and engaging each other's interests will be in the suits you have circled as being your common ground.

If your underlined suits are in adjacent squares, you are likely to experience discord in a different way. Here, each of you may inevitably feel it necessary at times to balance your partner's strengths by drawing on your own secondary suit that opposes your mate's strongest suit. During these acts of counterbalancing your partner, you may feel that you are not being yourself. And you may get angry when you are operating beyond the two neighboring styles in which you and your mate communicate most easily. To change this pattern, tell your partner how you are feeling. Encourage them to find the internal balance to address their own weaknesses themselves, without your always having to play the role of their counterweight.

If the underlined suits of both you and your partner are in the same square, you may have remarkably similar interests and "speak the same language," yet still experience conflict. Your communication problems are likely to occur when one or both of you shifts into another style to achieve balanced thinking in the relationship. Both of you must recognize that it's not easy for either of you to uphold these other styles, but occasionally it is necessary to do so. As you return to the kind of interaction that allows both of you to enjoy your natural style, you may remember what it was that you loved about each other in the first place, and place less dependence on either partner to serve as the balance wheel. Indeed, each of you will need to reach for these balancing traits within yourselves, rather than carp at your partner to satisfy such needs.

No matter which pattern you and your partner exhibit, keep in mind that your friends can satisfy your needs for communication without the awkward gaps you may be experiencing with your mate. With a friend, you will probably talk about your mate and laugh at his or her strange ways, which seem alien to you and the friend. But remember, your friend may urge you to change your mate to be more like you. And this just sets you up for another showdown with your partner. So appreciate friends for the camaraderie they provide, but in your relationship with your mate, you must be the one to decide when and how to "shift gears." That way you'll be less likely to lose sight of your objective: common ground and a more rewarding relationship with your partner.

LOVING YOUR DRIVING INSTRUCTOR

A source of conflict for many couples is that each partner assumes the other partner's thinking is like their own. Therefore, each spouse's seemingly inappropriate speech and interests indicate there must be something wrong with them. For example, in the case of Jane and Tom earlier in this chapter, Jane thought Tom didn't love her, and Tom thought Jane was overly emotional. What they had not realized was that each one's thinking compensated for the other's weakness—neither could see their partner as a live-in "driving instructor" who could teach them how to shift into less commonly used gears.

Too often, however, couples unconsciously go overboard in playing the role of the "driving instructor." Perhaps you've seen those driver training cars with two sets of controls, so the instructor can jam on the brakes when the learner is driving dangerously. That's what Tom and Jane unconsciously did for each other. When Tom drove off into independent aloofness, Jane applied her set of heart brakes. When Jane became too cloying, Tom applied his spade brakes. And, of course, each responded by saying, "Why did you do that? I wasn't operating dangerously. Why did you brake me?" It is extraordinarily difficult to see one-sidedness in our own thinking.

To some extent, the presence of the instructor (your partner) next to you with his or her own controls may serve as a crutch, so that you don't have to shift into less-favored gears yourself. You come to depend on your partner to handle the opposite kind of thinking in your partnership, yet you get mad at them for doing what you have been unable or unwilling to do yourself. A common problem in relationships is that each partner is stuck in their own favored mental gear—this is what often breeds arguments that can escalate into conflict.

The key to a enjoying a better relationship is for you and your partner to validate each other's personal styles and to acknowledge each other's right to be yourself. Then as you both learn to shift to your secondary modes of thinking, you can resolve differences in a way that you'll both find acceptable. If you regularly practice the techniques for shifting styles, you'll find that the conflicts you and your partner have experienced will eventually yield the right-of-way to mutual respect and love.

DEALING WITH STYLE DIFFERENCES IN FAMILIES

CHAPTER NINE

IS YOUR FAMILY FEUD A QUESTION OF STYLE?

Style Differences in Families

For a treasure trove of insight about division within families, turn on the TV any evening. Study any current family sitcoms such as *Dharma & Greg* and *Frasier* or reruns of old shows such as *Cosby*, *Roseanne*, or *All in the Family*. What makes them funny? Style differences, and the recognition that we all have to deal with them in our own families. If you consider the arguments you've had with members of your own family, they might also seem funny, but only in retrospect. Yet how can you laugh now when you were so furious at the time? Because in hindsight you see that the actions of each family member perfectly match who they are, reflecting their own unique differences. You might now realize, "Yep, that fits with how Mom and Dad are." But it sure wasn't easy to acknowledge family style differences at the time.

A FAMILY'S PREDOMINANT STYLE

Most families have their own characteristic way of looking at the world. That perspective typically is formed by one dominant parent or by the parents in combination. This becomes the family's predominant style, against which other family members may find it necessary to struggle. In the 1970s classic sitcom *All in the Family*, father Archie Bunker set the tone for the family. He lorded it over his wife, Edith, and their daughter, Gloria. When Gloria's boyfriend, Michael, entered the scene, however, the warfare began. Archie's pronounced differences with Michael—the "Meathead," as Archie called him—were classic. And on many issues, Gloria, and even Edith, challenged Archie when Michael rallied them. Without Michael, Gloria and Edith tended not to have the strength to go against Archie, the family's patriarch, whose views held sway by force and habit.

Archie Bunker often advocated traditional, club principles that were passé, but he voiced his opinions with spade authority. In doing so, he eclipsed the heart-styled members of his family, Edith and Gloria. The family's predominant style was club, in which mode Archie and Edith often met on common ground. But Michael's diamond views contested the family order. He opened Gloria and Edith to their diamond-heart sides, which clashed with Archie's narrow-mindedness.

No matter what combination of thinking styles may be involved, many families display a similar pattern: one vocal parent establishes the predominant style, and his or her attitudes are often the ones instilled in the children. While the other parent may sometimes take issue, the prevailing messages are conveyed by the most outspoken, strong-minded, or most available parent. A grand-parent or other member of the household may also fill this role. Although today's parents tend to share the dominant role, most of us are likely to recall that one parent's opinions set the tone for the family and were most instrumental in our formative years.

Perhaps your family's predominant style happened to match your own natural style. In this case you may feel that your dominant parent effortlessly shaped the way you view life. But with four possible styles, the odds are against that happy coincidence. In a majority of cases, children grow up with values and attitudes that they at first take for granted but later must overturn—or at least adjust to accommodate their own natural style. The parent's attitudes are often taken for granted initially, since the prevailing instruction is all the child knows. Only later, through education and experience in the world beyond the family, does the child encounter different approaches that spark a glimmer and then a flame of opposition to the parent's style.

THE DIFFERENT WAYS FAMILIES
HANDLE DISAGREEMENT

In a family where parents have opposite styles, the inevitable disagreements between them can actually help a growing child to understand that opinions differ, and can give the child confidence to take stands in life. They learn firsthand about the challenges they'll face throughout life. If the arguments and debates are constructively drawn so that each parent respects the other's differing views and does not characterize the other as wrongheaded or stupid, they can be positive lessons for the child.

If, however, the disagreement is fueled by the attitude that "I am right and you are wrong, and foolish for even thinking that way," then one partner feels unloved, and the self-confidence of both that partner and the child is eroded. This is what was so objectionable about Archie Bunker's approach. Even those who might have agreed with some of his opinions usually were disgusted by the mean-spirited way he treated his family. Whenever he was challenged, Archie's typical response was, "Aw, wouldya just stifle!" In other words, "Shut up. Only a meathead would think that way. If you can't agree with me, keep quiet." Because he treated anyone who disagreed with him as if they were emptyheaded, he was the one who actually seemed the emptyheaded Neanderthal. This single-minded Bunker mentality is like a monkey wrench thrown into a family's growth dynamic, bringing it to an abrupt halt.

The "I am right, you must lose" attitude toward family differences stifles those who are out-of-sync with the predominant style. Children are often the ones most inhibited by a dominant parent's style, because they are handicapped by their fragile sense of self and lack of confidence. When parents create an environment in which a child is inhibited from developing and revealing his or her own style, that child is more likely to develop psychological problems. Once confidence and self-esteem are squelched in the crucial early years of development, these are difficult to restore. Indeed, it is the responsibility of caring parents to nurture the self-esteem of their children, rather than force their own styles or biases onto them.[1]

While it can be damaging to be criticized for differences of opinion, it is worse to feel stifled from disagreeing at all. In the latter case, a predominant style is promoted like propaganda, and democratic debate is forbidden. There can be many reasons for such single-minded dominance. For instance, the family may have a controlling "leader" who takes it upon himself to be the sole voice of the group. This may be a carryover from the old, patriarchal family system in which the father ruled the roost, in keeping with traditional gender stereotypes. However, the suppression of disagreement also occurs when parents impose a policy of not arguing in front of the children, or of not arguing at all. This may come about by dictum from a dominant parent, and it has the effect of suppressing any ideas or messages other than those of the dominant parent.

The reason for such a policy might involve a parent who had been similarly stifled in childhood, perhaps exposed to physical or emotional abuse surrounding their parents' arguments, or damaged by their parents' alcoholism or substance abuse. Or the parents actually might both be hearts and dislike confrontation. Whatever the reasons, the barring of disagreement within the family results in children failing to learn how to get along with those who are of different styles. Under a single predominant style, with little divergence, the child sees only one approach to life and may not question the one-sidedness of that training.

STYLE DIFFERENCES WITH PARENTS

Let's now turn to the ways that personal styles affect relationships between family members. There are myriad variations of style differences in families. Remember the sixteen possible types of couples we referred to earlier? With more family members, the potential number of style combinations grows even larger. In this chapter, we're going to focus on some common style-related issues that arise between parents and children, couples and in-laws, and siblings.

Among these, difficulties between parents and children are most prevalent, but such clashes typically do not turn hostile as quickly as do those involving in-laws or siblings. Since parents are the authority figures who gave us our childhood training, we tend to give their views the benefit of the doubt. Out of respect, we often defer to a parent and may not speak our mind as directly as we might with other relatives. Even though we disagree with the parent, we may keep the differences of opinion to ourselves, at least for a while. However, when they irritate us, we still save such incidents in our mental file for future recall.

The severity of our discord with parents is often rooted in the degree of our style differences with them—that is, whether the parent is of an opposite style, an adjacent style, or the same style. For example, Carolyn gets along with her father, Ken, but not with her mother, Joan. When Carolyn was a child, Joan continually challenged her daughter to be more outgoing and fun-loving like Joan herself. Although Carolyn had many school friends, she was never as lively and exuberant as her mother, who was active in community theater and aided causes for the arts. Being a real-estate agent, Joan was away from home at various times of the day and night, so Carolyn felt that she could not depend on her mother. She typically turned to her father instead. Ken was a quiet, gentle, home-loving dad who, to Carolyn, seemed much more responsible than her mother. His secure, nine-to-five job as a case manager for a health-benefits company enabled him to be home most evenings. He helped Carolyn with her homework, participated in school volunteer efforts, encouraged her to play in the band, and even organized her birthday parties. With Joan's unpredictable schedule, more often than not it was Ken who cooked dinner for Carolyn and himself.

When Carolyn became a teenager, she increasingly felt that her mother took advantage of both her father and herself. Carolyn had to do household chores, including the cleaning and laundry. Actually, she doesn't recall ever being assigned these duties. Rather, they seemed to fall into her lap by her mother's inattention and lack of time for family obligations. As Carolyn accepted the chores as a matter of routine, Joan treated her daughter as if these tasks were Carolyn's responsibility. On Joan's way out the door to attend a meeting or tour houses with a client, she left chore lists that gnawed on Carolyn's sensibilities. Yet whenever Carolyn confronted her mother about her feelings of servitude and Joan's lack of interest in everyday family matters, such arguments accomplished nothing, and the patterns of their behavior never changed. Carolyn felt like a domestic Cinderella in the castle of a fly-by-night queen.

As Carolyn matured into adulthood, married, and had a family of her own, the pattern of relationships with her parents continued along the same lines. She remained close with her father, but the issues with her mother became more strained. When Carolyn had her first child, Joan stayed a week with Carolyn to lend a hand. After several days, Carolyn grew frustrated that her mother paid little attention to the diapers to be washed, cleaning to be done, beds to be made, etc. Eventually, Carolyn voiced her anger: "Mother, are you blind? Can't you see what should be done around here? Are you here to help or not?"

"Yes, dear," Joan said, "I'm here to lighten your load. Just tell me what you want done."

"Why do I have to tell you what to do?" Carolyn vented. "You're the mother, for God's sake. Can't you figure out what to do?"

"Carolyn, I'll gladly help, but this is not my house. You know what should be done—"

"Right, I've always known what should be done. Even in your house! You never took your family responsibilities seriously. You always dumped them on Dad or me. You were never home. I don't think you really loved us."

This flare-up left a lasting scar on their relationship. Carolyn had expressed the bitterness that had simmered within her for years. In doing so, she made Joan feel that she had not been a loving mother, which most certainly was not the case. When Joan returned home, the two women stopped talking to each other for weeks. Ken, however, served as intermediary, turned their attentions to the new grandson, and patched up the wounded feelings.

Years later a related incident occurred after Carolyn had resumed her job in the county auditor's office. The staff undertook a computer-training program that was to run past normal office hours. Carolyn anticipated a problem in retrieving her son from nursery school on time. She made arrangements with Joan, who looked forward to some playtime with her grandson and offered to return him to Carolyn's home early that evening. True to her habit of running late, Joan and her grandson arrived at Carolyn's at nearly seven o'clock, an hour beyond the time they had set. "Oh, we had so much fun together," Joan explained. "We went to the zoo but got caught in traffic."

"I was really worried," Carolyn said. "Why didn't you call?"

"My car phone's on the fritz. Sorry, dear."

"What did he have for dinner?" Carolyn asked about her son.

"Well, we didn't have time for dinner yet. We had some popcorn at—"

"I can't believe it!" Carolyn fumed. "You didn't feed him? We always eat by six, at the latest. You know that. I give you one responsibility to pick up your grandson, and you blow it! I can't trust you to do anything right. God, if Dad hadn't cooked, I might never have eaten."

Understandably, from the point of view of Carolyn's procedure-oriented club style, Joan seemed to be a bad mother who could not carry out basic family responsibilities. Joan, on the other hand, did not assign the same high priority to schedules and routines. It was her diamond style to seek fun and enjoyment with her grandson—especially since Carolyn had once accused her of being an unloving mother. Joan, therefore, had opted for a creative activity to do with her grandson and disregarded the child's normal routine.

In this family of Joan, the diamond-styled mother, and Ken, the heart-styled father, the predominant family style was diamond because Joan was so extroverted. Carolyn's life was a struggle to recognize her own different strengths, which opposed those of her mother—her female role model. Carolyn had more in common with her father's more conservative and caring style, but as much as she loved him, she also considered him too weak for his own good. After all, he rarely stood up to Joan's irresponsibility and inclination to take advantage of his good nature.

What about all those chores that Carolyn had to do as a teenager? To a great extent, they were the product of Carolyn's own doing. When she began to exercise her own skills within the household, she was recognized for her ability to do them well. She became a valued member of the family team, helping it become better-organized. The more Carolyn donated her orderly strengths, the more her family depended on her doing so. In time, her contributions came to feel like obligations. Indeed, her organizing efforts worked against her own sense of freedom and happiness.

What is perhaps most troubling about this particular example is that the mother and daughter showed telltale signs of carrying on a feud. They did not recognize their opposing styles, and they attacked each other for behaving so differently. Carolyn was very vocal about her displeasure with her mother. Joan, however, appeared to do battle using her actions rather than words. This sort of silent feud can be very tormenting, for one of the participants is not saying what they think, but is challenging the other nonetheless.

In situations such as this, both parties will not only need to acknowledge their differences, but they also must defuse their blasting remarks and soothe the hurt feelings that arise. Both Carolyn and Joan need to engage in some long, heartfelt talks. If they don't, their feud is likely to escalate to ever-greater levels of retaliation.

STYLE DIFFERENCES WITH IN-LAWS

What is it about in-laws that causes some of the most emotional disagreements we ever experience? Why would the parents who produced the person we love cause us such strife? To a great degree, the problems are attributable to clashes in style that test all of the assumptions that we formed while growing up in our own family. As much as we may differ with our own parents, at least we typically have two decades of ongoing adjustment to the ways they think and the values they hold. The individual styles of our parents, and the predominant style of their union, form the groundwork for our own understanding of how life works. If we've grown up in a normal, nurturing family, we grow to accept our parents' teachings and beliefs as the right way for people to live. In fact, many of us hold the notion that since all people are created equal and think alike, then, logically, other people would share our own family's values if only these other people would see the light and change their ways. We are seldom prepared for the challenge of all our familial standards that comes with marriage.

When we marry, we face totally new sets of values and attitudes that have been shaped by our partner's parents. The in-laws' styles and beliefs significantly vary from those we've known. And our partner is promoting these different standards, just as we are trying to influence the partner to accept our own. Moreover, this usually is happening at a very awkward and confusing time for us, when we are learning to live with another person. Sometimes all of this change is more than we can handle, as we'll see in the following example.

Megan grew up in a very progressive family. Her father was a charismatic charmer who developed and owned a large, successful advertising firm. Her mother was a staunch feminist and had served as president of their state's women's organization. Of the two parents, Megan's mother was the stronger personality and her decisions tended to prevail. Together, Megan's parents made a very successful, free-thinking partnership. Likewise, both of their children were liberal-minded. The family did not practice their religion. They spent much of their time independently involved in their own personal interests and causes, as Megan's mother had always done. And her mother set very high goals for Megan: to go to Yale Law School and become a leader in the women's movement. Megan herself was more interested in psychology than law, but she yielded to her mother's ambitions.

In law school Megan met Scott, who was warm and genuine. He was deeply attracted to Megan's open-mindedness and uninhibited spirit, and she liked his constant attention to her. To Megan, Scott seemed like a confident, sensitive guy who was very well grounded and had high integrity. But the very best part was his smile, which seemed to welcome Megan into his very soul.

Megan liked Scott's parents, too. His father, Leo, was a good-natured, well-respected financial consultant who had many clients. Scott's mother, Betty, was a wonderful person who quickly made Megan feel at home in the family. Megan worried, however, about how she would relate to Betty, because Scott told Megan that his mother had always been a housewife. But Betty was such a warm-hearted person that Megan immediately liked her, regardless of what Betty might think of feminism or Megan's mother's causes. Actually, the topic rarely came up in the months she dated Scott, because Betty tended to avoid controversy of any kind. Megan respected Betty's peace-loving nature, and found that it struck a chord within herself. Megan came to enjoy her conversations with Betty as well as with Scott.

The first major signs of trouble with Scott's parents surfaced when Megan and Scott announced their engagement. The issues then seemed to be about religion, because Scott's family was Catholic and

Megan's was Protestant. His family was upset about the couple's plans to marry in a Presbyterian church and Scott's abandonment of his Catholic traditions. In this instance, Megan's mother supplied all of the needed fortitude for Megan to stand up for her own convictions, regardless of pressures from Scott's family. As for Scott himself, he hated to see the families divided over the matter. Yet his love for Megan was greater than the obligations he felt to marry someone within his own faith.

As they began their lives together, Megan and Scott often talked about the wedge that had apparently been driven between them by the families' religious differences. Megan felt resentment from Scott's father, Leo, over this matter of faith, or so it seemed to her. Of course, the families also differed in their political views as well. Scott's family voted Republican, while Megan's family typically favored Democrats or Independents. So the young couple quickly became embroiled in both religious and political debates no matter which family they visited. In response to the rifts they felt when they were with either set of parents, Scott avoided both families. Naturally, Megan's mother told Megan that Scott couldn't simply bury his head in the sand and wish the problems away. He needed to be more bold and assertive. But anything that Megan said to Scott about his meekness only drove him further into his cave of seclusion.

About a year into their marriage, the couple experienced a tragedy that brought all of these conflicting views to a head. Early in Megan's first pregnancy, medical tests revealed that their baby suffered from a rare brain disease that would cripple its mental functions, if it survived at all. Megan and Scott had to make the painful decision of whether or not to abort the fetus and attempt another pregnancy.

Predictably, Scott's family fought against the abortion, while Megan's parents supported her right to choose. Caught in the middle of these opposing positions, the couple felt the horrible weight of this decision looming upon them with no consistent support either way they turned. Scott tended to side with his own parents, who stood for the sanctity of life no matter how incapacitated a child might be or what consequences the couple would suffer. Long-standing moral principles supported their case. Megan, on the other hand, leaned toward her parents' views that the impaired child would not enjoy a normal, healthy life, and the complications of supporting a very severely handicapped child would strain the couple emotionally and financially. Yet neither partner wanted to go against the wishes of the other, nor against their partner's family. Unfortunately, either decision would be wrong in someone's eyes.

The sharpest disagreement Megan experienced over their anguishing choice was with Leo. He even told her that this kind of situation was exactly why he thought that Scott should have married a Catholic, because a Catholic never would have questioned the right to life. His comment torpedoed Megan's tender emotions and made her doubt her choice of Scott as a life partner. Through her tears, she told Leo that he was living in another age, for many of her Catholic friends she had known in college would certainly examine their own conscience on a matter of abortion and would not automatically follow any religious dogma.

While this painful controversy seemed to be waged over religious principles, Megan's discord with Leo was truly a matter of style differences set into religious arguments. If they were both of the same religion, Leo might have described their differences in political terms—with Leo expressing a Republican, "Moral Majority" stand against Megan's liberal, Democratic views. If they were both of the same religion and same political party, then Leo might have identified Megan's feminist upbringing as a reason for their disagreement.

No matter how they framed the issue, in essence, Leo's traditionally oriented club values clashed with Megan's developing diamond style. Moreover, this difficult dispute with her in-laws was shaped by the pattern of Megan and Scott's family styles, which opposed each other. Megan's spade mother and diamond father had taught their daughter an independent, progressive set of ideas. Scott's heart mother and club father had promoted traditional, social values and beliefs in their son, who was also a heart. The couple's marriage brought into play these differing ways of thinking, forcing each family member to deal with and resolve their own internal contradictions. This was not easy for young Megan and Scott. The process of accepting and integrating such opposing styles takes many years— all the while, each partner typically endures critical remarks from the other and their in-laws, makes derogatory comments about them that they wish they'd never said, and suffers confusion from one round of arguments after another.

At the end of this chapter is a section on "Dealing with the Differences in Your Own Family." The process that is presented there will be helpful in coping with your own in-law problems. Indeed, with so many family members involved, resolving prolonged difficulties with in-laws may require your utmost skills in diplomacy.

STYLE DIFFERENCES WITH SIBLINGS

Since brothers or sisters often have differing personal styles, it is quite normal for them to experience clashes. In fact, if you and your siblings have a perfectly cozy relationship, consider yourselves lucky—or well-trained in the art of getting along with others.

Typically we enjoy our friendliest relationships with people whose styles are similar to our own. But in a family we must interact with sisters and brothers who are different from us. These are our first lessons in dealing with the variations in thinking that we later undergo with people outside the family. Even if our parents were good coaches in resolving sibling rivalries, we still are likely to be annoyed at times by what a brother or sister says or does. The discord may last all our lives. Be it at age eight or eighty, family irritants tend to remain true to form.

Consider the issues between Christine and Ed, the children of Lois and Edgar. Ed was four years older than his sister, and he was a watchful help to Lois when Christine was a toddler. Indeed, Lois noticed that throughout their childhood, Ed was much more responsible than his sister and attributed this trait to Ed being the firstborn child. He was the more studious one, got better grades, was active in sports, and rarely got into trouble. Christine, on the other hand, was more unruly, something of a tomboy and explorer, and got only mediocre grades. Yet she excelled in art and won several scholastic awards for her watercolors. These honors inspired her to be an art major in college where, unbeknownst to her family, she had a rather adventuresome sex life and even experimented with drugs. Eventually she settled down and applied her talents to magazine illustration. Ed majored in political science, interned in their congressman's office in Washington, D.C., successfully ran for a local office, then was voted into the state legislature.

Lois and Edgar were proud of both children's accomplishments. Lois loved them equally, and her care and support aided their self-confidence to take very different career paths. Edgar, however, had a tendency to be exasperated by his son's steady, plodding style. He often wished that Ed had Christine's daring. They had never had an easy father-son relationship, even though Ed had been a model child. Edgar shared in his son's interests in school sports. Later in life, Edgar was pleased that his son's political office provided tickets for big sporting events. At a game, Ed could count on his father to interpret what the opposing political party thought about local issues.

The sibling relationship between Ed and Christine was regularly strained by their noticeable differences in temperaments. During childhood, their problems often revolved about rules. Ed told his parents when Christine violated the rules; Christine teased and ridiculed Ed for being such a stickler for his "precious rules." Often the problems between them would arise not from what they said, but from what they did. It was their different styles of behavior that galled each of them most. Ed seemed so prim and proper about everything—from the clothes he wore to the friends he had. Among her own friends, Christine was embarrassed that her brother was an Eagle Scout. Ed, in turn, was troubled by Christine's loose behavior, particularly as she became a teenager. Occasionally he was sent out to look for her when she was out late, but she got away with doing things that he never would have attempted.

In their adult years, Ed and Christine saw each other a few times a year and kept in touch only minimally, even though they lived in the same city. When they met at family gatherings, they rarely had deep, personal conversations. They mostly talked about their jobs, their career goals, and such. Typically, the closest they came to airing their differences was in arguing politics. Their discord intensified, however, when Ed learned that Christine had taken a job with a gay-rights magazine. He was furious when he saw a copy of the magazine featuring one of her illustrations, with their last name boldly signed across the bottom. Ed immediately called his sister. "What possessed you to join such a group?" he asked her. "Haven't you thought about how this will look?"

"To whom?" Christine answered. "My friends know I'm not gay. The magazine likes my illustrations. What can be wrong with working for them?"

"What's wrong? . . . My constituents don't know that you're not gay, and this is a very conservative district," Ed admitted. "What will they think?"

"Who cares what they think? This is my life!" Christine said defiantly.

"But can't you see that this could cause me to lose the next election?"

"Look, I don't tell you what you should do. You can't tell me what I should do. I like the job at the magazine," Christine added. "I believe that their cause is just. They have every right to—"

"Their cause is abominable," Ed steamed. "It goes against all of our principles. . . ."

This skirmish between Ed and Christine was waged over their difference in styles. Ed's club manner opposed Christine's diamond openness. While they may have thought that their opposition was caused by their different politics, different genders, or even different positions in birth order, their disagreements all boil down to variations in the ways that they think. Birth order may have helped make Ed even more responsible, and his role in government may have strengthened his attention to moral values, but he would still have been irritated by his sister's behavior even if he were the second-born or wasn't involved in politics at all. It was the variance between these siblings' own natural styles of thinking that provoked their discord.

Keep in mind that the traits of the four styles as portrayed in these examples are not absolutes. Not all diamonds are Democrats, support gay-rights causes, or sanction abortion. Not all clubs are Republicans, side with the Moral Majority, or denounce a woman's right to an abortion. Rather, the tendency is for people with these styles to take such sides. Indeed, in a family that has been affiliated with a particular political party, all of its family members may find ways to support that party, even when that party's basic tenets run counter to the values of their own individual thinking styles. The same goes for a multitude of causes and beliefs.

For Ed and Christine to resolve their feud, they first must be able to articulate the basic differences in their thinking, and not get stuck in arguing over issues. When they reach the understanding that both sides have value, then they can redirect their efforts from jabbing at each other like boxers, to taking their places at the card table and finding the right balance between their positions. In making this advance, they will need to engage their secondary styles, in which modes they will be able to meet each other on common ground. Ed ventured toward a heart resolution of their differences when he asked Christine to consider how her actions might cause him to lose the next election. Unfortunately, she countered with an independent, spade rebuff in advocating her own self-interests, which furthered their division.

To effectively bring about an end to their standoff, both siblings must shift their attitudes into open acceptance of each other, as was discussed at the beginning of chapter 8. The same techniques for shifting attitudes and language styles that applied to couples, work with family members as well. In addition, at the end of this chapter you'll find more suggestions on ways that you can understand and resolve your own differences with family members, be they siblings, parents, in-laws, or other relatives.

Adam's Family: A Spade Son with a Club and a Heart for Parents
In the following story of Adam's family, we'll link all of the various kinds of relationships to see how a person's style influences their "life story." For at every stage of life, the complex maturation of one's own style significantly affects interactions with all members of one's family. When an adult child has ongoing struggles with a parent, he is often wrestling with that parent's conflicting style as well as with inauthentic aspects of himself that were shaped much earlier by that parent. Such is the case with Adam.

Adam's father, Lyle, has always been the most vocal member of the family, but his mother, Fran, sets the rules. Lyle is a good-natured sales agent for his own insurance agency, and Fran handles customers' claims and the bookkeeping. When their children were young, Lyle coached soccer teams, and for decades he sang with the church choir. Fran served as a board member of the Women's Guild at church and volunteered her time doing taxes for the elderly. Lyle and Fran experienced little of the marital turmoil they saw in other couples. Their easygoing daughter, Amy, was a school cheerleader and member of the Future Nurses Club. They were a conservative, religious family and well-liked in the community—truly the model of a loving, responsible, civic-oriented family.

Their son Adam, however, seemed like an intruder from hell! Three years younger than Amy, he was the diametric opposite of his "perfect," caring sis. He was brooding and rebellious. He hated school. As a teenager, he smoked, had his hair dyed into a punk-rock style, and couldn't wait to turn sixteen to buy an old car and get out with his friends. Indeed, Adam was a challenge to his parents from the word go. Fran and Lyle couldn't understand what was wrong with their son. He wouldn't go to church, although this may have been a blessing since Adam was often an embarrassment to them in public. Lyle attempted to establish a meaningful father-son relationship with Adam, but the more he tried the more Adam pulled away from him. Lyle coerced Adam to meet with their minister for counseling, but it didn't help. When Adam was required to attend a church youth-group event, he went silent for a week. While Fran could get Adam to at least pick up the trash from the floor of his room, he often barricaded himself behind his door while playing computer video games. He was a terror to his sister, who couldn't wait to go to college to escape his constant disruptions to the family's otherwise calm style.

For his own part, Adam seethed with frustration and couldn't wait to escape his family. Just before his eighteenth birthday, he traded his car for a motorcycle. When Lyle wouldn't insure Adam's new wheels, Adam split. He took off across the country and did not stop until he got to the Coast, where he settled in and began an independent life. Adam took a job packing computer software, and was soon making enough money to rent a studio apartment. A month after he left home, he called his mother at the office to tell her where he was. But Adam refused to speak to his father. Lyle was hurt by his son's refusal to talk with him. He wrote Adam several letters, but none were answered. Their minister suggested that Lyle let go, and leave the resolution of such troubling family matters to higher powers. Lyle had done all he could to have a relationship with his son, but nothing he did seemed to make a difference. They were always at odds.

As years went by, Adam changed jobs and began working for a computer manufacturer. He became interested in computer technology, took electronics courses, and was promoted to the position of supervisor of his assembly team. Adam had a quick mind and worked hard. He signed up for a management-training program, and more jobs came his way. Eventually he was made supervisor of the entire plant. About that time, Adam met Sarah, who was an interior designer hired to renovate the company's offices. Adam and Sarah quickly fell in love, and within weeks she wanted to meet Adam's family.

It had been eight years since Adam left home. He had returned for holidays during the last few years, but it was never comfortable for him. On such occasions he could talk with his mother about work and his accomplishments, but he had not resolved the long-standing discomfort with his dad. Whenever they were alone in a room, Adam felt as if he were returning to his childhood, and old feelings of alienation and insecurity would flood back. These usually erupted when Adam was telling Lyle about his job. Lyle would say how proud he was of his son, then go off on a well-worn path: "You get along so well with the people at work, Adam, why can't you get along with your family? We so rarely hear from you. Your mother is heartbroken that you don't call her more often. What would it cost to call every now and then? We just want to hear that you're Okay, and say that we love you. Is that too much to ask?"

Adam would grimace and agree to call more often. Then Lyle would continue: "Son, it would make your mother so happy if you went to church with us on Sunday. It would be good for you, too. I can tell that you still have a hardness in your heart that keeps you from knowing true peace. Are you happy?" Adam would roll his eyes a bit and say that he thought so. Lyle, however, would then escalate the pressure: "One of your mother's and my greatest joys is all the friendships we share with so many people at church. All those won-derful connections give meaning to our lives and restore our souls. And you could feel that blessing too, son, if you gave it chance." Then Lyle would remind Adam that Amy actively attended church and proceed into a series of lessons that included the story of the prodigal son. Usually about that time, Adam would tell his dad that he had something to do, and steal away.

This pattern of Adam's independence and remoteness from the family, and Lyle's efforts to draw him back into the fold, continued unchanged for over a decade. Lyle could not get through to his son, and Adam never told his dad how much his sentiments annoyed him. Once when he was home, Adam even dreamed that he was a dog that had fallen into an underground beehive. In the dark burrow, he was surrounded by sticky, sweet honey. All the while, bees were crawling all over him, ready to sting at any second.

If Adam had an understanding of personal styles, he might have recognized that the honey hive symbolized his father's heart style, which felt inauthentic to Adam's spade nature. Adam's way of dealing with the internal discord between Lyle's teachings and Adam's own developing style was to put distance between them. That is exactly what Adam needed to do within his own mind to resolve his true nature—he had to isolate his father's ways from his own.

As a heart and a spade, Lyle and Adam are opposites. Adam's strength is in analyzing, decision-making, and goal-setting, which his employer saw in him when making him plant manager. Lyle's talents, on the other hand, lie in his ability to relate to people, to share their concerns, and offer them friendly support, which made him a well-liked and successful insurance salesman. In conversations, they each expected—or at least hoped—that the other would share their interests and motivations. While Adam enjoyed having a problem of logic to solve, the only one his dad ever presented to him was Adam's problem of not being more like the rest of the family. Indeed, Lyle rarely raised any issues that called upon his son's interests or strengths. Instead, he droned on about the need for Adam to be a better son and to go to church.

Adam struggled against his parents as a unit comprised of his father's heart style with his mother's club style, all melded into a singular parental attitude that spoke of religious interests. Lyle felt that his son was so cold and arrogant that he missed out on the simple pleasures of being with people. Adam's insensitivity, toughness, and the way he operated around his parents were, to Lyle's mind, the very traits that religion could alleviate in people. It was as if Lyle had been personally presented with a mission to bring about Adam's transformation, to soften his cold heart and make him a caring human being. For Lyle, helping Adam find the peace and joy that he himself had long known became a kind of calling.

Because father and son each remained locked in their individual modes of thinking, they did not venture into their secondary styles, which might have enabled them to find common ground. If Lyle had drawn Adam into a diamond discussion about his vision for the company or his own personal dreams, they most likely could have communicated. If Lyle had shifted to club and asked Adam how he carried out supervision of the plant, Adam might have told his father about his management procedures. But it never occurred to Lyle that there were alternate routes to achieving the closeness that he sought. Likewise it never entered Adam's mind that Lyle might have certain business problems for which Adam's own strengths could be helpful. If Adam had shifted to diamond and asked his dad to imagine the future of his insurance business, Lyle might have told him of his worries about keeping his agency current with advancing computer technology, which was Adam's own specialty. Or if Adam had shifted to club and asked Lyle about insurance needs for his own company's assembly plant, Adam might have learned something useful for his work. But neither of them had found a way out of the rut of judging one another and angering each other with their single-mindedness.

This pattern with his father had existed for decades before Adam met Sarah. However, when she entered the picture, Adam's relationship with his parents took a new turn. Sarah was not willing to maintain the isolated stance that Adam had held with his folks and his sister. When she went with Adam to meet his family, she found Lyle, Fran, Amy, and Amy's husband to be nice people. Sarah usually got along with people, and she had an optimism and light-heartedness that most found charming. So Adam's family took to Sarah immediately. Moreover, when Sarah, Adam, and Lyle talked, all three of them got along wonderfully. They chatted openly, and

Lyle regarded Sarah as the answer to his prayers. She had indeed softened Adam's hard shell and made him more accessible. And Fran liked the way Sarah made her son happy. She was the perfect match for Adam. They were both forward-thinking people, independent and creative. No one could see any obstacles to their happiness as a couple.

In fact, the only faults Adam found in Sarah were that she was often late for their interior-design meetings and dates, she hadn't ordered all the furniture for his new office in an efficient way, and she didn't take on the kitchen duties as his mother had always done. But these were minor things, and so he and Sarah soon married.

Adam Takes a Diamond Wife—and the Family Style Differences Escalate
With Sarah as Adam's partner, the issues of his remoteness from the family subsided because Sarah maintained the contact for him. Sarah and Lyle were famous for sharing family stories over the phone, and Fran and Adam would join in for a while and round out the foursome. The young couple did not attend church as Adam's parents had hoped, but Lyle and Fran thought that perhaps when Adam and Sara had children, they would not only become churchgoers, but also would become more responsible. In general, Fran and Lyle simply assumed that Adam and Sarah hadn't grown into the stage of life that required them to settle down and attend to family duties. But year after year, the grandchildren never came. Adam and Sarah remained focused on their work and their dynamic lifestyle. They Jeeped across Mexico; skied several times a year; bought a new two-bedroom condominium. Fran and Lyle gasped, "Only two bedrooms! And the second bedroom is to be Sarah's studio?" Fran and Lyle had been waiting for them to plan a nursery.

To Adam's parents, this was a rupture in family values that brought Sarah's responsibility into question. It wasn't that Adam and Sarah couldn't have children; rather, they didn't want to change their lives. To Adam's parents, and especially to Fran, such ideas were strange. Having children is what married people do, if they can. That was the traditional reason for two people deciding to marry. Lyle's perspective was that he wanted Adam and Sarah to experience the joys he had known as a parent, notwithstanding his struggles with Adam.

Now, during the phone calls and home visits, the seemingly innocent hints about grandchildren Lyle and Fran would drop to Sarah and Adam, began to build. The hints were humorous at first, but before long Fran and Lyle grew more insistent.

Soon the younger couple became aware of the pronounced differences in values between Adam's parents and themselves. Sarah noticed this first, for several reasons. Since she was an outsider to the family, she was more perceptive of the messages that didn't ring true with her own diamond attitudes. To Adam, his parents' pleadings for him to behave a certain way were what he had lived with forever. He had always assumed that everyone grew up with the same kind of parents. Their nagging was so much a part of his family history that he paid little attention to it. Often Adam's dismissive responses to his parents' persistent arguments didn't even register in his conscious awareness. He dealt with his parents as if he were on automatic pilot. He heard their criticisms of him and Sarah, but he tuned them out and instead focused on the problems of his daily life that interested him—his work. And to a spade, after all, relationship issues can have less standing than technological problems, competitive solutions, and business operations.

Thus, Adam's parents' comments annoyed Sarah, but with Adam they went in one ear and out the other. Moreover, Sarah's diamond nature was offended by her mother-in-law's suggestions about what she should do with her life. The next time Sarah and Adam were at Fran and Lyle's house on holiday, Sarah became increasingly aware of the conflict between herself and her mother-in-law. Fran, she realized, was always telling her what to do—no, she was telling everyone what to do! Or so it appeared to Sarah. In the kitchen, Fran told Sarah how to prepare Fran's favorite recipes and what Adam had always liked. Fran said that she always heated the plates before dinner, and folded the napkin under the silverware, and on and on. As Sarah became more bothered by these procedures, most of which ran counter to her own creativity in the kitchen, she began to challenge Fran, saying that she did things differently. She defied Fran's wishes by proceeding to do things her own way—such as leaving the napkins unfolded. Sarah's attitude became increasingly hostile to Fran, who didn't understand why her daughter-in-law was so defiant.

It was in Fran's kitchen, of course, where such a scuffle between styles would likely occur, because this was Fran's domain, her place for doing things as she wanted. Her methods, shortcuts, cooking procedures, etc., were all matters of style for her, and she had grown accustomed to them. This was one of the principal places where she expressed her club approach to life. It was her workshop, much as the assembly plant was for Adam.

When Adam was in the kitchen, he wasn't phased in the least by his mother's comments, nor was Lyle. They accepted her remarks to Sarah as being natural for Fran. Indeed, everyone in their family knew that Fran was the family administrator—the one who established the family's routines. Fran didn't mean to be controlling, rather she provided the guiding structure for the family, because doing so came naturally to her.

But "controlling" was the word that Sarah used to describe her mother-in-law in a later conversation with Adam. Sarah recounted, "And when your mother said, 'Don't you think its time you start having children,' I exploded! I mean, I just can't take all her advice on what I should do. It's none of her damn business what I do with my life. It's not that I don't ever want to have children, but right now, I like my freedom. Do you know what I mean, Adam?" Adam nodded that he did, but he didn't fully grasp Sarah's issue with his mother. "I mean, Adam, I'm not going in that kitchen with her again. I can't handle all the pressure she puts on me. 'Do this, do that.' You know—no, you don't know, do you? You don't see what she's doing." Actually, he didn't. For Adam, his mother's way was just the way a mother is. He couldn't figure out what was so appalling to Sarah.

True to her word, during the remainder of that holiday visit Sarah did not reenter the kitchen. Lyle helped out, however, as did Amy and her husband, Brad. Fran confided to Amy that she thought Sarah was being a prima donna, staying with the men while they worked in the kitchen. Fran had no idea that her own comments about kitchen methods, which sounded like instructions, had prompted Sarah to keep her distance.

Of course, Fran's main issue—that Adam and Sarah ought to be having grandchildren—was much more upsetting to Sarah than all of the dictatorial dinner procedures. But without the kitchen incident, Sarah might not have recognized that the *should do*'s were characteristic of Fran's style, which also accounted for her belief in traditional values, such as a married couple's obligation to have children. Sarah approached her new married life from an opposite perspective. She was exploring what she *could be* before motherhood.

Much of the anger and frustration that both Sarah and Fran felt leads back to their ignorance of the differences between their own personal styles. Both women assumed, as in a true/false test, that there is only one right answer to the way people should think and behave. Therefore, each woman was sure she had the answer and that the other did not: "I am right, so you must be wrong"; and, "I know the truth, so apparently you don't." To prevent their relationship from turning into a running feud, Sarah and Fran must replace their true/false model with a different one. They need to think in terms of a multiple-choice test with all four answers being right. Four versions of the truth, with each version a part of the whole truth. With this kind of "right-right-right-right" model, people defer to each other for the portion of the truth that is each person's specialty.

Had Fran and Sarah understood each other better, they might have made allowances for their natural variations in behavioral styles. Sarah could have given Fran more slack when they worked together in the kitchen and let Fran's instructions roll off her back.

And Fran could have checked her kitchen comments somewhat, and let Sarah do things her own way. They could have used the kitchen time to talk about something other than the preparation of the meal or having grandchildren. For example, they might have shifted to the heart mode and talked about Adam, swapped stories about their experiences of him, and found some common ground in sharing tales of their own fascinations and frustrations with him. Or they might even have shifted to the spade mode and attempted to analyze their differences, by telling each other what they had been feeling when they worked together, and then trying to identify what caused their undercurrent of hostility. However, neither Fran nor Sarah was aware of the style-oriented strategies, and so they held grudges against each other instead.

The Clash Between Adam and His Heart Sister, Amy

Another simmering conflict in evidence every time the family gathered, was the clash between Adam and his sister, Amy. Typically, their differences didn't result in harsh words, because they simply didn't see each other very often. They lived in different regions of the country—Amy near her parents, and Adam far away—so the infrequency of their visits kept them from coming to blows.

That is, until one Thanksgiving when the entire family converged at Fran and Lyle's. The day after the big meal, the family lunched on turkey sandwiches, and Adam said he was going off to play tennis at the community center with an old high-school friend who was back in town. Just ten minutes after Adam left for his match, Lyle slipped in the garden, fell, and cracked a rib. As the emergency squad took Lyle off to the hospital, Amy called the community center and left a message for her brother. She briefly described what had happened to their dad, that it wasn't life-threatening, and that the family was going to the hospital to be with him. About dinnertime, Adam came home to an empty house, fixed himself another turkey sandwich, and watched a football game until the others returned late that evening.

When Adam didn't appear at the hospital, Amy called the community center again to see if he had received the message, which indeed he had. So why hadn't he gone to the hospital? When Amy walked into the house, her first words to him were, "Where the hell were you?"

"Tennis. You know, with Bob. After the match we had a few brews," all of which was true. "Hey, too bad about Dad."

"'Too bad'?" Amy was taken aback. "'Too bad'! Is that all you have to say? Didn't you want to visit him in the hospital? Don't you care about him at all?"

"Yeah, I'll probably go tomorrow," Adam said, with his eyes glued to an exciting play on the tube. "I figured there wasn't anything I could do for him. But I'll go tomorrow."

Adam's attitude was incomprehensible to Amy. "That's just so like you, Adam. You don't care about anyone but yourself, your work, or your stupid games. You never have. You have never cared about being there for any of us! Never!"

"Whaddayamean? I'm here this—" Adam paused to watch a field goal attempt. "—Thanksgiving. I hooked up a new printer for Mom at the office. Whaddayawant from me?"

"A little compassion. A little caring about other people. A little being there when your family needs you at the hospital!"

"But you didn't need me, did you? What could I have done? Ask the doctor what was wrong with him? You knew all that. There wasn't anything I could have done that you weren't doing. So why go?"

Amy could not believe what she was hearing. For her, it was just a natural response to go to the hospital with her father, if for no other reason than to be a caring daughter. She always shared in his joys and in his pains, as well. There didn't need to be a reason or some problem that required her solution. Rather, she wanted to be there to support her father through his ordeal.

"Did it ever occur to you, Adam, to go just because Dad would feel comforted by you?"

"Aw, you're such a Goody Two-shoes, Amy. That's not what guys do."

"Dad would have gone for you, Adam. He would have been there at the hospital for you if you had broken a rib playing tennis. Don't give me your B.S. that guys don't care. Brad went. He didn't stay home to watch some game. And Dad isn't even Brad's father!"

"Okay, Okay, I'll go tomorrow. Now let me watch the game."

Adam didn't want to hear any more of Amy's heart-styled message, because it ran counter to his favored spade style. Of course, if a similar situation were to arise, Adam might draw upon spade-club judgment to go to the hospital, because even if he doesn't think it's necessary, he's learned that's what he should do. But at this period of his life, he was developing a more free and independent attitude from his relationship with Sarah. She was promoting what he could be and overturning much of the heart-club programming of his parents. So Adam wasn't considering his *should*s. Eventually, Adam may reconcile these two opposites (his mother's club and his wife's diamond) into a mature spade style.

While by most standards of human compassion or decency Adam's actions fell short of the normal and acceptable range, they are understandable—if we take into account the way Adam typically deals with the world: by looking for problems that need his solution. Since his particular expertise can't be applied to relationships with other people, he doesn't see any reason for doing things like going to the hospital to show that he cares for his father. He can't use the heart skills, as Amy does. When Amy challenged Adam's thinking as she did, she frustrated him to the point where he shut down and returned to his game.

The next day, Sarah and Fran figured out how to "get through" to Adam and accomplish what Amy hadn't. First, Fran checked the TV listings for major games. Then, during an interim time, Sarah said to Adam, "We need some space. Get your coat on and come with me."

"Where are we going?" Adam asked, "And how long?"

"Out of the house," Sarah said, "and not long." In the playfulness of a quest on some mysterious adventure, Adam opened up. When Sarah drove them into the hospital lot, Adam knew he'd been tricked into visiting his dad. But when they entered the hospital room and Lyle's TV was tuned to the start of the next game, Adam relaxed and stayed quite a while.

DEALING WITH THE DIFFERENCES
IN YOUR OWN FAMILY

In order to get to the root of your own family issues, you'll need to clarify the differences between you and other family members. It will be beneficial if all concerned agree to take the self-test in the chapter 1, share your profile results with each other, read about your own styles in chapter 2, and discuss your differences.

If a family member is not available for such personal interaction, you will have to guess their style. Once you have a sense of the kinds of differences between you and your closest relatives, you can relax some of the tension you feel in dealing with them and begin to try some of the strategies offered in this chapter.

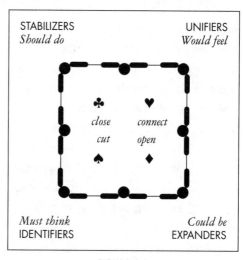

FIGURE 9.1

When you have completed the profile results, chart the key players in your family on a style table diagram. Jot down the names of your own family cast of characters on figure 9.1 in the corners or sides that most closely represent their styles.

Next, take an evening or two to write down your own family story—about yourself, your parents, spouse, in-laws, brothers, sisters, and any other significant relatives. Try to include in your story instances in which you've seen family members clash, or in which you yourself have clashed with others. Just write down the story as you experienced it, without trying to explain why things happened. Save that for later. For now, write about the issues, arguments, and differences of opinions as well as the feuding, name-calling, and feelings—of yourself and others. After you've finished writing your story, put it aside for a day or so.

When you return to your story, this time try to identify the deeper divisions among your family's various styles. Refer to your diagram of those styles (figure 9.1) and look for the underlying patterns of opposition in your family saga. See if you don't find one or more examples of the types of differences that have been described throughout this book.

Once you have identified style differences and spotted the arguments they cause within your family, you will be in a position to come up with appropriate solutions. You can help family members understand their differences. Point out the gaps in motivations and interests, and explain the barriers to smooth communication. Guide them in the strategy of shifting styles to reach each other on common ground. Or give them this book.

The most worthwhile investment you can make in reducing family conflict is to get to know yourself and your family better. As you learn about your family members' positions at the card table, you will come to accept your own characteristics, including those that others in your family may have termed flaws or weaknesses. You can also learn to shift to a perspective that allows you to appreciate, rather than get annoyed by, the traits of a particular relative. Then the next time a family member comes at you with an infuriating thought or behavior, you will not feel stifled. Rather, you'll be able to handle the situation rationally—by using the tools you have discovered in this chapter. Identify your style differences, define how they tend to create problems, and determine which alternative style offers an opportunity for finding common ground. If the other family member is entrenched in their views, they may not be able to shift out of their prevailing style. Accept that. There is nothing wrong with that person, so don't hold their natural style against them.

While you may not see things from the same perspective, you and your family can achieve greater peace and understanding by learning to shift your thinking to a more mutually agreeable style.

CHAPTER TEN

COPING WITH CHILDREN'S EVOLVING STYLES

Balancing Your Child's Interests with Your Own

As we noted in the last chapter, parents like Lyle and Fran can be baffled by a child who displays a style opposite to their own. It doesn't require an opposition in styles, however, for children to be at odds with their parents. As all of us know, kids go through stages in which they are simply difficult to get along with. A young person can be easy to live with one year and a holy terror the next. Such changes are normal, for children evolve through stages of development that bring out different styles of thinking. In this chapter, we'll review the development process that a child ordinarily undergoes so that you might better understand what your son or daughter is coping with each step of the way. You'll see how a child's conflicts with the style of their parents, or the educational program, may lead to behavior problems.

You'll also recognize how important it is to nurture a child so that he or she can develop his own strengths and be true to his nature, even though such ways of thinking may be different from your own. A child also needs to be well-rounded and capable of performing all four types of thinking, and in this chapter we'll show that all four styles of parental guidance are required for a child to mature into a fully functional, adaptable, and self-sufficient adult.

These needs may seem contradictory. Isn't being "well-rounded" almost the opposite of having a particular style, or developing one's "true nature"? We'll find that it's all a matter of striking the right balance between these different needs, which can be tricky for any parent. Up to a point, every child requires some level of proficiency in all four types of thinking. And the normal combination of parental guidance, schooling, and other cultural influences usually does a good job of producing such basic well-roundedness. However, the prevailing thinking style of the parents or of the educational system—or perhaps both—can counterpose the natural aptitudes of a child's budding personal style, which may squelch the development of the child's natural skills. When an adult—parent or teacher—attempts to mold a differently-styled child into a carbon copy of the adult, the child can lose confidence in being himself and expressing his own style.

How does a parent know when their own style of guidance will help the rounding process or work against the child's unique self-development? In this chapter, we'll offer some guidelines about putting the interests of your child's maturation first and foremost, and assessing when it is beneficial to challenge your son's or daughter's natural inclinations. In order to do so, however, you'll need a clear knowledge of your own parental style, and how your personal interests give rise to a particular kind of guidance that you tend to convey to your child.

UNDERSTANDING YOUR OWN PARENTAL STYLE

The guidance that we as parents offer a child is typically rooted in the primary and secondary modes of thinking that we favor. While we have the capacity for all four modes, and each is equally necessary for the child's development, we are inclined to emphasize our strongest suit and slight the interests of our weakest suit.

Now recall your own self-test profile. In all likelihood, the higher your score in any suit, the more you will uphold that suit's parental style, all four of which are summarized below. Keep in mind that people are not all one type or another. Rather, you'll probably recognize that you favor some combination of these various parental interests.

Stabilizers: Clubs emphasize what children should do to become orderly, moral, and productive members of society who are well-prepared for life's challenges and adversities. They want children to be good, mannerly, properly dressed, responsible, and dependable. Club parents often are task-oriented and urge children to stay busy doing chores, projects, crafts, or learning how to do things. They may prompt children to join youth organizations, form early career interests, and manage their money. Clubs tend to go by the book and discipline a child for rule-breaking behavior. They want a child to measure up to high standards.

Expanders: Diamonds inspire children to be all they can be, to develop their talents of imagination, creative expression, intuition, and perception, and to live life with a sense of adventure. They want children to be open to new experiences and optimistic. Diamond parents seek delight and encourage children to engage in free play, explore artistic interests, enjoy the outdoors, and have fun. They cultivate art, music, drama, as well as unorthodox activities that set a child apart from the crowd. Diamonds are accessible as parents, though they're inclined to let children be free, rather than set down detailed procedures for them.

Identifiers: Spades focus children on how they must think to become self-sufficient adults who can solve their own problems, identify goals, and make mature choices in life. They want children to be independent, rational, smart, and on top—the best. Spade parents tend to be achievement-oriented and prompt their children to participate in competitive sports, learn the latest technology, take the tough road and the hard courses, get into the best schools, and succeed at whatever they do. They urge children to apply themselves to serious endeavors and be assertive. Spades can be exacting taskmasters and highly critical of any failure.

Unifiers: Hearts sensitize children to how other people would feel about their actions and encourage them to live in peaceful harmony with others and with nature. They want children to be friendly, good-natured, caring, sociable, and happy. Heart parents foster interpersonal interaction and promote group or team activities. They also tend to support interests in music, dance, poetry, and the arts. Hearts are highly sensitive to a child's emotional changes and place a high priority on family needs over other demands on their time. They are inclined to foster a continuation of family ties versus a child's need for independence.

If you are a parent, you probably have some regard for all four of the above sets of parental values and interests. And you'd like to think that your own child is benefiting from all four kinds of guidance. However, you most likely favor one or two of these sets of varied interests, which are a reflection of your own parental style. Moreover, you may find that your spouse tends to uphold the parental interests that you do not. In fact, you and your partner may have very different ideas of how children should think and behave.

CLASHES BETWEEN A PARENTAL STYLE
AND A CHILD'S TRUE NATURE

Because two parents and other family members can be of different styles, there often are inevitable clashes between varying sets of interests. All of them are valid to a degree. But it actually can be dangerous to push a child too hard into any of these value sets, especially when a parental style is inconsistent with the child's own style.

For example, sixteen-year-old Ryan was a quiet young man and a B student in a college-prep program. He was reluctant to bring his friends home when his dad, Ray, was there. Ray, a top executive, held high expectations for Ryan. In fact, he once had illusions of Ryan following in his footsteps—attending Harvard and becoming a business leader. But Ryan's grades were not up to Harvard standards. To make matters worse, Ryan had begun to talk about going to a state school to study photography!

One reason Ryan rarely brought his friends home was that Ray would later make snide comments about their long hair, disheveled clothes, and lackadaisical attitudes. His wife thought that Ryan's friends were nice-enough kids, but Ray saw them as a far cry from the rugged, crewcut pals he had known in high school. After the friends left, he would say things to Ryan like, "Nice earring," or "Were you weirdoes in there studying your artsy-fartsy magazines?" To Ray, his son's looks, behavior, friends, and interests were strange. He regarded photography as a capricious fancy. He couldn't accept the idea that his son would consider such an occupation that did not offer the prestige and secure income of his business career.

Ray's snide comments were his way of challenging his son to an argument. Of course, Ray debated everyone. It was a lifelong game of his. But Ryan had long since learned that he could never win a debate with his father, who was always one step ahead and made forceful points that often were hurtful. He discovered that the way to avoid feeling wounded was to stay out of his dad's sight. Fortunately, his heart-styled mom helped Ryan cope with his father, and even supported his career plans. She saw photography as a good application of Ryan's imaginative talents. She sustained Ryan throughout the sniping war that lasted from the time he decided on a career until he left for college.

Ray's cutting, spade attitude had been reinforced by his education and executive career. He had advanced up the corporate ladder by making good decisions and likewise wanted his son to make rational choices about his own life. But cool evaluation was not Ryan's strength—creativity was. Luckily Ryan had an ally in his mother who helped him avoid being stifled by his father's abrasive attitudes. Ironically, some of the independence and toughness that Ray had hammered into his son over the years enabled Ryan to defy him and follow his own calling. Ryan stuck to his guns and entered a profession that satisfied his diamond nature.

As is the case here, friction can occur even when a parent and child are not actually opposites in style. Unfortunately, Ray and his son shared little in common. While Ryan had learned from his father about defending his interests and making hard choices, Ray's belittling attitude kept his son at a distance and limited Ryan's chances to truly learn at his father's side. Had Ray accepted Ryan's personal style as different from his own, they might have had a much better father-son relationship, which would have enabled Ryan to learn more useful thinking skills from his father.

Not only do children exhibit a natural style, as do adults, they also cycle through development stages in which they seem immersed in different thinking processes at different times. These changing stages can challenge a parent's sensibilities, because the young person can be in alignment with the parent's attitudes one year but not the next. To see how this works, let's review a typical childhood—from birth to age eighteen—in terms of the child's evolving thinking skills.

EARLY-CHILDHOOD DEVELOPMENT

From the moment of birth, a baby needs care and support. During the first months, the parents' soft language, smiling faces, cuddles, and cooing foster a deep attachment that lets the new arrival know that he is loved and accepted. The infant quickly is able to mirror these expressions and wordlessly involve his parents in the most important relationships of the child's life. This occurs automatically, without conscious guidance by either party. The parents and the child simply find themselves in the harmony of connection.

Then, as the infant learns to move about, he begins to explore the environment, attempting to understand it. He crawls around investigating teddy bears or electrical sockets, playing with any object in his path. At about the age of one, the child starts to walk and scout the world at a faster pace—encountering fascinating yet potentially dangerous environments and objects. During this stage, the parents are constantly attending to the toddler's safety, redirecting, cautioning, and saying "no." But the lessons are most powerful when the child encounters the consequences of his own actions, such as falling, tasting something bad, or sticking a spoon handle into an uncovered electrical socket. Exploration leads the child to identify the sources of unpleasantness and danger.

Language allows the child to further identify, name, and categorize various parts of the environment. In conjunction with learning to speak a language, the child distinguishes himself from others, and forms an "I" identity, which is applied toward getting what he wants during a period called the "terrible twos." This emergence of the willful side usually produces cantankerous behavior on the part of the child, which must be shaped by equally strong parental guidance. This period can seem like a war between parents and the child's "I want" attitude. It is a challenging game of chicken, which the parents must win for the child to attain proper balance. Parents learn to be firm with the otherwise lovable, irrepressible child. Often the child's instruction during this stage follows three steps: First, denying the child's unreasonable wants; then telling him what he may have or should do; and lastly, showing him affection so that the child realizes that he is still loved in spite of the parent's cross words or restrictive response. In time the child develops valuable boundaries which last a lifetime.

With willfulness starting to settle down and rules for good behavior accepted, the child increasingly becomes a solid little member of the family. He intently watches what his parents do. He carries on discussions and questions "why" at every puzzling new situation. "Why is the sky blue?" "Why do you put salt in cookies?" He hereby expands his big-picture understanding of the world and figures out fundamental reasons why things happen and how to go about various operations. The child settles into the family's routine, following repetitive steps such as those of bath and bedtime. More and more, he is expected to independently proceed through these routines on his own. Eventually he may become so adept at going by the family's rules and procedures that he begins to tell his mom or dad, "I'm bored. What should I do?" Then the parent is called upon to inspire creative ideas that foster the child's playtime learning— to kindle and reopen the child's own imagination which, just a few years before, had carried him into unbounded exploration and investigation. Joining a play group, nursery school, and then kindergarten class further stimulates the child's mind by exposing him to the wonders and challenges of a broader world and inter-acting with other children.

In the space of a few years before elementary school, the child moves through a series of learning stages, each one serving a critical role in developing all four types of thought. When the child then begins to spend more time away from home, this ongoing learning process spirals up to higher and higher levels of mental growth, each preparing him to interact capably with the ever-larger world he encounters.

Before proceeding to the next developmental level, let's consider the kind of guidance that this early period of childhood requires.

PARENTAL RESPONSIBILITIES
REQUIRE ALL FOUR STYLES

Each developmental phase places new demands on parents to adapt to their child's needs and supply the necessary love and guidance. Early on, the parent must give basic caring affection, touching, and sensitive support to the infant. Later, the parent must be open to a toddler's exploration, but also watchful to maintain the toddler's safety. Interestingly, the parental guidance during these vital early periods fits the combined traits of the heart style, which includes both diamond and club as secondaries—consistent with the tradi-tional stereotype for women.

Later, in the terrible twos, the child's "I want" attitude requires a parent to firmly set limits and acceptable rules of behavior—all in conjunction with identifying things and teaching the child to speak.

Then the child's "why"s lead to the formation of a broader under-standing of the world, which incorporates procedures for how to live in it, along with learning to follow the family routine. These latter stages of guidance tend to utilize the combined traits of the spade style, which includes both diamond and club as secondaries—con-sistent with the traditional stereotype for men. With such balanced guidance being so essential for a child's development in these early years, this also may explain why women are generally more adept at shifting among all four types of thinking than men are.[1] While two parents may take on opposing roles in guiding the child, a mother often has more capability to undertake the entire responsibility.

During this crucial early period, the child depends on parents or others in the family to supply all four types of thinking. Such a balanced approach optimally supports a child's safety and growth. And the child's development calls for parents who can shift their thinking among the various modes in response to the child's growth. This flexibility in thinking patterns must exist either within the parent, the combination of both parents, or elsewhere in the family for the child to make optimal progress. Indeed, here are the advantages that marriage partners of different parental styles can offer in rounding-out their own offspring. All of this fits our com-monsense understanding that two mature parents are beneficial for child-rearing. Nevertheless, it is also true that a well-rounded, well-balanced, well-educated single parent can handle the full job alone, if they are able to shift back and forth among all four modes in response to the child's fluctuating needs.

In some cases, one well-rounded parent can be better than an imbalanced couple. For example, an insensitive couple in which both parents are independent spades may not satisfy the infant's needs for affection, acceptance, and connection that are so vital in the first months. Or a caring, non-confrontational set of heart-styled partners may not find the boldness to match wits with their child's strong demands during the terrible twos. Two club-styled partners may limit the child's exploration, or—when the child becomes bored and in need of imaginative inspiration—may instead give them chores to do. Two diamonds may not provide the routine structure necessary to develop good manners and polite behavior. These same conditions, of course, can apply if a single parent is limited to one or two of these styles. On the other hand, an extended family with the active involvement of older siblings, grandparents, or other relatives of differing styles can mitigate such imbalances. It would appear that the more elders who are available to a child, the better off that child may be.

It is natural that any individual parent will feel tested in meeting the diverse needs of the child's early development, especially at those times when such needs go against the grain of the parent's own style and strengths. It may be comforting to know, however, that most of us have weaknesses in one or two modes, and these may be areas in which our mate or family can help guide the child.

MID-CHILDHOOD DEVELOPMENT

The child's development continues in preschool. In nursery school or kindergarten, the first order of business is to teach him or her to get along with others and tame cases of unruly behavior left over from the earlier, home-trained phase. The child gains from such experiences as playing with classmates, going on field trips, and working as a group in the classroom. In addition, the child is given new opportunities for creative exploration and expression that they may not have had at home. Dress-up play, skits, musicmaking, and painting are a few of the ways that the child's imagination may be exercised. Indeed, to some parents the preschool classroom might seem chaotic with its multitude of activities available for the child's investigation. The child's early efforts are rewarded by the teacher with symbols of encouragement such as drawings of happy faces and lively stickers. There are also blocks of time devoted to teaching basic language, science, and math concepts to the assembled class. Thus, the child not only gains information about the world, but also learns the important rules of behavior that will be necessary to make the transition into the more-ordered classrooms of elementary school and beyond. Nursery schools and kindergartens usually develop all four types of thinking processes and prepare the young person for the transition to a more-structured school.

When the child reaches elementary school, the teaching emphasis shifts to reading, writing, language(s), math, science, and social studies. These subjects are taught in a setting that requires children to follow a step-by-step regimen in group learning. Children must settle down, take their place at a desk, listen carefully to the teacher's instructions, follow orders, and perform tasks. For many children still bursting with spontaneity, to be contained for hours at a time in such a setting is very difficult. Recess is one way to release their built-up tension. Art, music, drama, gym, and sports are usually a part of the curriculum, but many people treat these subjects as extraneous to the fundamentally important "three Rs." In addition, the child is now graded. They are measured against objective standards for performance and expected to excel. "Grade school" begins the emphasis on spade-club training, which is deemed to be most important for preparing people to succeed in our competitive world—to get good jobs and live comfortable lives in a stable society.

Problems in School

Not so surprisingly, some children do not measure up to others when it comes to either their academic skills or their classroom behavior, and they may be labeled as "problem" children. Typically, such children are non-conforming or overly dominant, and unable to exhibit the expected well-rounded balance. They are considered to be outside the circle of the normal, solid, steady achievers. What may be happening here, however, is that such problem children are actually "diamonds in the rough"—who have a hard time fitting into a non-diamond atmosphere. School curricula are skewed toward spade-club training. Elementary-school instruction involves step-by-step procedures, rules, and structure (club), and the initial push to compete, achieve, and succeed (spade). But exploration, creativity, and freedom of expression (diamond) are often given short shrift in most schools, so diamond-styled students have limited opportunities for developing their talents.

Students other than diamonds may also face problems when their individual style clashes with that of their teachers. For example, if Mary is a spade-styled tomboy, she may find it frustrating to have to cope with a heart-styled teacher who wants her to get along peacefully with the other students, and fit in like the rest of the girls. Consequently, Mary might rebel and challenge the teacher at every turn. If Mary were moved to another class with a teacher of another style, then the opposition would not exist, and Mary might be more accepting of that teacher. However, by remaining with the heart-styled teacher, Mary would gain valuable lessons in dealing with people who do not operate the way she does.

Students and their teachers are often at odds with regard to style. Thus, parents can receive alarming evaluations of their child's weaknesses, which—although quite true from the teacher's perspective—could be less worrisome to anyone who lives with the child and takes a longer view of their development. Indeed, Mary may be an absolute terror in grade school, yet go on to become an entrepreneur and president of her own business. The traits that allow a child to conform in school are not necessarily those that will lead to adult success. Life is full of examples of great people who had difficulties in school.

This is not meant to discredit teachers or school rules. Indeed, a child's low grades or behavioral mishaps in school can be serious in nature and warrant resolution. However, it is worth considering the possibility that a child's problems in school could be attributable to style conflicts between the child's style and that of the school or teacher. While children are still developing their own thinking patterns, and can often shift from one style to another depending on the circumstances, you know your child. You have a sense of what they like to do, how friendly they are, how imaginative, disciplined, or how sharp they are. If you have a child who is creative, dramatic, and a class clown, be prepared to get notes from teachers, such as, "Johnny has been out of step lately. He will not abide by classroom rules, nor will he follow instructions for how assignments ought to be done. . . ."

An opposition in styles between a child and a teacher can be an excellent learning experience for the child if his teacher and his parents help him to understand what is at issue. While a child's own style should be nurtured and appreciated, the youngster must also understand the importance of adjusting his behavior to fit in with the classroom rules and standards. Again, it's a question of balance. Even if a diamond child eventually becomes a TV comic, he will still have to be on time for rehearsals, meet shooting schedules, and pay his bills. So it's worthwhile for Johnny to learn in elementary school to balance his inventiveness with the school routine.

Since school generally emphasizes a spade-club education, the child's time outside the classroom is vital for their social and creative development. Informal, after-school playtime, summer freedom, family vacations, camp experiences—all of these fill a critical need to activate the diamond-heart processes. Restrict such activities and you've got an unhappy child on your hands.

LATE-CHILDHOOD DEVELOPMENT

In the upper grades, the school system turns to preparing young people for work and adult responsibilities in a serious way. The elementary-school classes taught for an entire year by one teacher or a team (with whom a child could bond, like parents) gives way to high-school specialists who teach particular subjects. Middle school is the transition from the child's world of recess and playtime to the teen's experience of making it to classes on time, organizing breaktime to get to the restroom and to exchange books, securing possessions in lockers, doing homework, and satisfying instructors who are concerned with achievement.

Once students reach high school, they are expected to settle into a college-prep or a vocational program, and to prepare for entering real life beyond school. The student now independently negotiates the hallways to their scheduled classes. Indeed, even the child's meaning of the word class changes from a group of students (that is something like a family) to a course of instruction. The teacher's role also narrows, primarily to that of imparting information and methods. Subjects like art and music, which are usually part of an elementary-student's education, typically are electives in high school, and only the students interested in these subjects need take them. But all students must complete the required subjects such as math, science, English, history, etc. During classtime, humor may be used by the teacher to interest the students in the subject matter, but sugar-coating subjects to make them palatable to students is not done. It is time to get down to business.

In high school there is a substantial (although not complete) abandonment of matters outside the spade-club orientation toward work and adult responsibility. In a steady, gradual progression that has been going on since preschool, the student is taught to put aside family dependency, classroom kinship, spontaneity, playful creative expression, and childhood fun. This is superseded by independence, conforming to standards, striving for goals, specialization, academic excellence, competition, meeting expectations, grade pressures, accumulating credentials for college acceptance, orderly behavior, being on time, acting responsibly, and staying focused on important priorities.

The carefree child does not readily yield to this agenda. Several years are spent transitioning through wild and gawky adolescence before the youthful spirit gives way to the steady comportment associated with adulthood. It is no wonder that many kids do not have the internal balance to make the required metamorphosis, and may resort to drugs or alcohol to prevent themselves from feeling the loss of their earlier freedom. Even many of those youngsters who do successfully adjust seem strangely unnatural and inauthentic. Most of us look back on our own high-school yearbook picture as if it were not really us, but some weird, imitation version of the person we have become.

Imitation is the operative word, because teenagers try to act like adults, but they haven't yet got the methods down pat. They think being adult is about getting their way and controlling things as their parents seem able to do, and they identify themselves with their own burgeoning independence. Suddenly they're in another big-time confrontation with their parents, strangely reminiscent of the terrible twos. It's the "I want" attitude again. ("I want to stay out late. I want to get a tattoo. I want to do my own thing.") Naturally. Doing their own thing is what the entire system is now prompting them to do. Except they haven't yet mastered the technique of doing their own thing responsibly. They haven't fully put away the whims of their free, childlike selves and adopted the orderly, well-organized behavior that will be expected of them in a job or in college. So in the final years before they leave home, parents challenge their teenagers in order to make sure that they take on the club responsibilities, and engage in the club procedures, that will prepare them to both venture off on their own and to stay out of trouble.

Your child's ability to cope with this transformation depends on many factors beyond his or her own intelligence or ability to get along with others. Your child's own personal style plays a key role. As we've said, school tends to ground students in logic and procedural skills. This enhances the natural strengths of spade- and club-styled students, making them somewhat more expert and one-sided in their thinking. As a result, spade and club individuals become specialists who are less apt to struggle with their own identity or have to sort out who they are later in life. However, eventually they may suffer from not having their conceptual and relational skills nurtured. (Hence, the problems that some couples bear from partners not being aware of their diamond or heart side.)

But for diamond- and heart-styled people, the normal spade-club educational program rounds out and balances their thinking, albeit at the risk of downplaying their interests and underutilizing their natural strengths. The diversity of both their schooling and their natural skills produces generalists who may be more adept at tapping a wider range of their own mental capacities. While undergoing their primary- and secondary-school training, it is the diamonds and hearts who are most obliged to stretch beyond their favored ways of thinking and being, which to them can feel frustrating and even defeating. Later in life, they may experience some kind of catharsis that spurs them to individuate their own diamond or heart nature from the spade-club ways they were taught.

THE IMPORTANCE OF YOUR PARENTAL STYLE

The ease with which a child can adapt to such conflicting pressures in her youth is influenced by whether or not the parental style employed by her parents contains a balance of club, spade, heart, and diamond approaches. As the child goes through each stage of development, the degree to which her parents can shift their own parental styles to appropriately guide her can affect whether as a young person she will be fully fit for adult life or handicapped by the lack of some traits needed for individual success.

For example, in Ted and Alice's family, their lack of parental skills associated with two of the four suits—namely club and spade—resulted in serious problems for their daughters. Ted and Alice (both of the heart style) have two teenage daughters (both diamonds). During their early childhood, the girls experienced exceptionally warm, congenial family unity. The parents are non-confrontational. They happily spent time together as a family. The children are loved dearly and continually reminded of that fact. It wasn't until the girls entered high school that Ted began to question his daughters' performance in school. Their grades were not up to Ted's expectations, and he chided them about their flippant attitudes. Despite their father's remarks, the girls weren't able to focus on schoolwork, particularly the required subjects. Their interests lay, instead, with band, cheerleading, chasing boys, and having fun. Whatever money they were given, they spent—often irresponsibly. When they got into trouble, their caring mom left it for their father to discipline them. But attempts on Ted's part to challenge his daughters' behavior were always halfhearted, because he didn't like to be tough on anyone. Since the girls did not have good grades, their parents realized that they would not go on to college. Ted and Alice rationalized their daughters' fate, stating that the girls could take jobs nearby, which would allow them to remain a close family.

The combined effect of the girls' diamond styles, the parents' predominant heart styles, and the parents' inability to shift out of their own favored thinking processes, produced a situation in which the girls never truly adapted to the spade-club school environment. During the emotional eruptions of their teens, their parents were unable to challenge the girls' wants and to shape their behavior. Indeed, only rarely did either parent ever create enough disciplined, club structure for their daughters, or find the spade toughness and fortitude to rein in their daughters' irresponsible tendencies. Given this lack of spade-club parental guidance, the girls were not adequately prepared to be self-reliant and to handle problems on their own.

This is not to say that all families with this combination of styles will have the same dynamic, for our lives depend on many other factors. But Ted and Alice's story points out the potential dangers of raising children without all of the necessary parental skills at your disposal. In their case, they lacked the skills associated with the club and spade styles. But perhaps you can detect deficiencies in certain kinds of thinking in your own family.

While it may be easy to recognize such imbalances in another family, we may have a blind spot when it comes to our own. That is because, no matter what our style and skills, our traits seem to meet our own needs. We are smart enough, responsible enough, warm enough, tough enough to get through life. So we don't truly grasp how our own characteristics may be deficient in comparison with a full range of thinking skills. The upshot is that we may criticize our children for some deficiency—for not being perfectly well-rounded—even though their deficiency may well have been influenced by our own deficiencies. In the above example of the heart-styled parents, Ted spotted his daughters' inability to set goals, engage in challenging pursuits, and discipline themselves, but most likely he didn't see his own weaknesses in making decisions, operating independently, and challenging his family members to think for themselves.

To avoid this all-too-common family malady of "the pot calling the kettle black," parents must recognize and accept their own strengths and weaknesses. Your self-test profile can indicate possible gaps in the guidance you are giving your children. Even when you combine your profile and that of your spouse, you may realize there are still voids in one or more styles and, thus, areas where well-rounded guidance is not getting through to your children. If so, you may need to become more attuned to your children's weak spots and consciously shift out of your own favored style to address various guidance requirements. This may work best as a team approach with your spouse, or even with other family members who can help fill the gaps in your parental style.

ACCEPTING A CHILD'S TRUE NATURE—AND ADJUSTING YOUR PARENTAL STYLE

Most parents' frustrations with their teenagers boil down to, "Why can't they be accomplished, well-behaved, and perfectly well-rounded?" Some parents might add, "Why can't they be like me?" With an understanding of the four styles and what it takes to achieve balance, you can see the impossibility in such aspirations. Although people think of themselves as perfectly well-rounded, most of us are actually skewed in our thinking toward one or more of the four styles. In guiding our children, we may want them to be both (a) well-rounded, and (b) similar to our own style. Such expectations are not only unrealistic, but unfair to the child—particularly so if two parents are working on the child from opposite ends of the spectrum.

Looking back on the story earlier in this chapter about Ray's dissatisfaction with his son's choice of photography, note that Ryan met the first set of conditions rather well. He was a good student and exhibited no serious behavior problems. As a diamond-styled child who had successfully adapted to the spade-club school program, Ryan was well-rounded. But Ryan didn't meet Ray's expectations that his son would be like himself. That's what gave rise to the snide remarks and discontent between them. Because Ryan didn't measure up to Ray's own standards for rational, analytical thinking, Ray wasted opportunities to engage his son in such a way that Ryan could learn from his father's strengths.

For Ray and Ryan to find a zone of positive interaction, they would need to accept their differences. They both would have to acknowledge the other's skills in areas outside their own expertise. Ray, however, might not easily come to such acceptance, because as a spade he is prone to narrow down anything to a singularity—even ways to think and behave. In making evaluations, one choice stands out above all the rest. Applying this process at home, Ray deduced that he himself had attained the best way to think and behave; thus, his son's style was flawed. Ray's insistence on how Ryan must think kept him from accepting Ryan's true nature.

Although Ray did not respect his son's career choice, Ryan actually was well-prepared to deal with life on his own. That was not the case with Ted and Alice, however, who neglected to take their daughters' diamond natures fully into account and to realize that the girls needed some spade-club parental guidance if they were to succeed in school and in life. With an awareness of their own personal styles, Ted and Alice might have realized that they had to go beyond their heart-styled inclinations in order to give their daughters the kind of parenting they required. Accepting a child's true nature doesn't mean simply letting kids do their own thing. Sometimes it means recognizing who your child truly is and then adjusting your parental guidance (i.e., shifting your parental styles) accordingly.

But how can you recognize whether the weaknesses perceived in a child's behavior are due to some lack of balanced guidance—as in Ted and Alice's case—or to a failure to match parental expectations—as in Ray's case? Indeed, Ray considered his son to be ill-prepared for an independent, responsible life, even though Ryan did well in school and went on to prepare for a satisfying photography career. Ray had not thought of Ryan as being well-rounded at all.

The difference in these two cases is that Ray expected his son to be more spade-club, like Ray himself, while Ted and Alice's daughters needed spade-club guidance that was unlike the parents' own styles. So if, like Ted and Alice, you believe that your child needs a type of instruction that is outside the characteristics of your own style, then chances are you're right—the child most likely would benefit from your shifting into another style and offering a type of guidance that differs from your normal way of thinking. However, if you believe that your child needs more instruction in the rigors of your own style, as Ray did, then consider the possibility that your own parental expectations may be driving your perception of your child's needs. If you are dealing with your child in a manner of identifying her needs, setting goals, and holding her to procedures that you've formulated, then your parental expectations may be intruding on the development of your child's own style. Moreover, if you get stuck forcing your expectations on your child, you are setting the stage for family conflict, as discussed in chapter 8.

You can help guide the balanced development of your child's true nature by learning to employ all four styles of parental guidance yourself. If Ray had applied this understanding, he would have recognized that Ryan was a good son and a good student, and switched off his demands that his son meet all of his expectations. Ray might have employed his own diamond openness to accept and appreciate Ryan's different talents and inspire his son to put them to best use. And Ray, perhaps with some help from his wife, might have learned to engage his heart side to be sensitive to Ryan's feelings and share in a non-judging relationship with his son, without the criticism that often hindered their friendship.

Ted and Alice both might have accepted their daughters' diamond natures and at the same time stepped out of their own heart styles to give the girls some club-spade discipline and focus. They might have reasoned with their daughters to help them identify problems with their own behavior and to spell out the life consequences if the girls didn't make some adjustments. Perhaps they might even have encouraged the girls to set their own personal goals, which the parents could then help them accomplish.

SOME GUIDELINES ON LETTING YOUR CHILD DEVELOP HIS OR HER OWN STYLE

Because of the many combinations of styles that exist within families as well as various levels of maturity, it's difficult to define precisely when it's (a) useful to challenge a child's thinking and behavior to help round out his capabilities, or (b) best to let him follow the natural inclinations of his own style; but here are a few broad guidelines that might help you determine an appropriate, balanced course of action.

Round Out Early—Ease Up Later On

Well-rounded guidance is crucial to a child's early years of development. The more you can use three or four parenting styles, the better-adjusted the child is likely to be. Since an infant and a toddler's needs are basic, you'll know almost automatically what to do: give them love, provide for their safety, allow them to explore and satisfy their curiosity, and help develop their speech and language skills.

Through preschool and elementary school, the child continues to receive a generally well-rounded education. Your parental guidance is melded with what the child learns at school, and your efforts most likely will benefit her development and maturation. Since the child is still learning fundamental lessons in thinking and behavior, your own instincts about offering balanced parental guidance are likely to be exactly what the child needs. The greatest dangers at this stage are overscheduling your child's time with too much instruction or too eagerly pushing your child to master skills for some future career that you envision for her. For example, if a child has a real interest in music, then encourage her to take lessons and practice all she wants—but if that is not her interest, don't try to make the child into a concert musician to fulfill some dream of your own. The same goes for sports, the arts, and academic subjects as well. Offer your children support, instruction, inspiration, and structure without trying to manipulate their interests.

At around the onset of adolescence, the child begins preparing for adult life and giving more evidence of her strong suit—her own natural skills. This is normally the time when parents need to adjust their ways of dealing with their son or daughter. They must ease up on telling the child what to do, and instead, participate with the teenager in the choices that she makes. This allows the teen to become more responsible and independent in a way that reflects her own interests. Certainly she won't be able to make every decision on her own; but she should be gradually and increasingly prepared for the day when she controls her own life.

As you begin to throttle back on telling a teenager what to do, this is also a good time to make an assessment of your child's style, taking into account her strengths and interests that may be different from yours. While discussing her choices of school subjects, leisure interests, and future plans, offer your input, but do not call all the shots. After several years of this kind of participation in your teenager's life, you'll come to recognize and respect her style, and the two of you can begin to develop a constructive adult relationship.

Acknowledge Each Other's Personal Styles
Before you read this book, you may have been very confused about the differences in the ways that people think or behave, because such

differences might have seemed to fit no recognizable pattern—yet your teenager is probably even more puzzled than you are by such variations. From his inexperienced perspective, he is trying to grasp why people argue and oppose each other, why they wage political battles or challenge the people they love. You can expand your child's awareness and also improve your mutual understanding of your differences by explaining that various styles of thinking do exist and that they are useful to human society. Let him know about the values and interests of your own style of thinking. But also give him a conception of how all styles are equally valid and necessary. That way your teen may eventually come to accept why you offer your own particular kind of guidance and advice. Rather than be angry about what you say, he may see where you're coming from and accede to your experienced input.

Put Your Child's Interests First

Naturally, you have high hopes for your child to live a happy and bountiful life. Based on your lifelong experience, you may realize that people in certain occupations or graduates from certain schools seem more successful. They have higher incomes and live more comfortable lives. So, logically, you want your children to apply themselves in school so that they can receive the very best education, engage in a promising career, and enjoy the subsequent benefits. Or you may want your child to attend your alma mater or follow you into the same business or career. However, your child is not necessarily going to have the same interests as you. Indeed, the odds are that your children's strong suits in thinking skills are different from yours; thus, their aptitudes for various careers are different as well. The thinking skills required to be a policy analyst are not the same as those needed to be a poet.

If your own parental expectations overshadow your child's interests, both of you are in for trouble. The child will be unhappy and resent you forcing her to accept your plans. She may do poorly in the school subjects required for your target career. And even if she does apply herself and enter the career of your choice, she may not do as well as someone whose aptitude is better-suited for that career. At each step of the way, she'll know that she is living out your ambitions, not her own, so your relationship will suffer. What started out as a career goal that you set with the best intentions for your child's happiness, can turn into a nightmare in which your child doesn't enjoy her occupation, can't succeed, and holds you responsible for her unhappiness.

You both will be far better off if you let the career and education interests flow from your daughter's or son's own natural way of thinking. Put your child's personal interests first and foremost, above your own goals and ambitions. Help them evaluate their own aptitude for the occupations they have in mind. Seek the advice of a school guidance counselor or vocational testing service to assist them in selecting a college and career. Let them develop their own goals for their adult life that make the most of their talents, interests, and personal styles.

For a clear-cut illustration of how dangerous overzealous parental expectations can be, watch the classic movie *Dead Poets Society*, starring Robin Williams. In the film, a teenage boy, a solid achiever at a private academy, has a compelling desire to act in a play. His domineering father, however, forbids his participation in the play, insisting that he give up his acting interests and stick to a rigorous course of study, in preparation for entering a prestigious college and pursuing a safe career chosen by the father. The father thinks of his son as immature and irresponsible in following his desire to act. But the son defies his father and earns a starring role in the play. When the father sees his son's performance in the play, he does not acknowledge his son's obvious excellence in the role, but robs him of acclaim, strips him of his independence in front of his peers, and takes him home, like a little child, for punishment. In a family discussion that includes the silent, Milquetoast mother, the father prohibits his son from ever again pursuing his desire to act. After the family goes to bed, the son uses his father's gun to kill himself.

Here is a clear example of a well-rounded teenager subjected to a parent's single-minded and headstrong expectations. When the father insists on how his son must think and what he should do, he offers his son no hope of what he could be. Nor does the father consider how his son would feel about having his interests squelched. Because the father can't accept any way of thinking other than his own, and because the mother is too stifled to offer her son any support, they completely crush their son's spirit. The story is a poignant reminder of the dangers in failing to accept a child's true nature.

SHIFTING GEARS WITH KIDS

Every child requires parental guidance that includes a blend of all four suit styles.

Parental Style	Thinking-style specialty	Perspective
♥ Unifiers	Relating, caring, harmonizing, supporting	would feel
♠ Identifiers	Analyzing, naming, reasoning, deciding	must think
♣ Stabilizers	Setting order, rules, procedures, safety	should do
♦ Expanders	Conceiving, exploring, imagining, inspiring	could be

In dealing with a child with whom you have a difficult time relating, take another look at chapter 8, on shifting gears. The solutions to communications problems commonly experienced by couples also apply to problems between parents and children. For example, a diamond-oriented teenager is likely to put up a fuss if he is told to follow specific rules; club procedures, rules, and routines are antagonistic to his style. But you may be able to reach him via either a spade or heart approach. Reason with him on how his style of behavior may lead to future problems that he will later have to solve. Or relate to him how others feel and are impacted by his actions. Indeed, these two different kinds of messages could require a team approach on the part of both parents, each supplying the specialty of their own style. Working with these two components, the teen may piece together an understanding for himself as to what changes he needs to make.

This same strategy can also work with a teenager of any style who is going through a particularly rebellious period. At a time when teens want to experiment with life and be both free and independent from adults, the *should*s of standards and rules have little effect. The way to get through to them involves both reasoning and relating.

A heart-oriented teen may want to spend all of his time with friends and avoid serious schoolwork. He may feel that certain academic courses will not be useful for furthering his own interests. The crux of the problem may be that he hasn't recognized his own "people skills" and figured out a way to make use of his talents. In such a case, you may want to inspire your teenager by suggesting that he consider various careers that involve the social skills he enjoys. Then follow this up by contacting friends or others in your community who are engaged in such careers. And have your son or daughter get together with some of these people. Suggest to your teenager that he find out what training and education these people needed to get where they are now. Most likely it will involve some of the schoolwork the teen has been avoiding; but once the teen sees why his education is necessary for what he eventually wants to do, he'll be much more motivated to do well. Such a strategy is more likely to be effective than a parent simply insisting that a teenager follow the rules—especially when that teen is a non-club type.

All of us have a tendency to become stuck in our own ways of thinking and communicating—which might not mesh with the thinking patterns of another person. If you are having problems getting through to your child, try shifting the style of your appeal. The simple act of switching to one of your secondary styles can work wonders.

If you think about the ways that your own children have challenged you to adapt and grow, to provide them with balanced guidance, to stay attuned to their evolving needs, and to develop new parental skills, you'll realize that the personal development has not been all one-sided. You, too, have been learning and growing right along with them.

PART 4

DEALING WITH STYLE DIFFERENCES IN THE WORKPLACE

CHAPTER ELEVEN

"DO IT MY WAY"

Understanding Workplace Styles

Varied opinions are as beneficial to work groups as they are to families, and differences in thinking styles affect relationships at work just as they do at home. Unlike families, however, organizations usually assign specific styles of thinking to particular departments, and to individual positions within a department. That way there is some assurance that the correct balance of important thinking functions is in place.

DEPARTMENTAL STYLES IN THE WORKPLACE

To see how this works, let's explore such functional roles in an imaginary corporation called the Doxus Group. This company produces widgets. It has a headquarters complex plus a plant where the widgets are made. The headquarters building, diagrammed in figure 11.1, houses several departments. In its west wing is the Management staff, which conducts evaluations, sets goals, and makes decisions. Also on the west is a Controller's department that administers financial and legal issues, such as compliance with tax codes. In the east wing are two other departments. The Design team surveys the market and invents new widgets. The Sales group

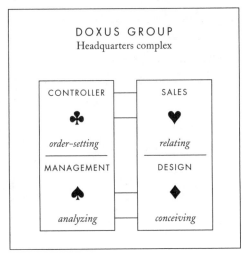

DOXUS GROUP
Headquarters complex

CONTROLLER	SALES
♣	♥
order-setting	*relating*
MANAGEMENT	DESIGN
♠	♦
analyzing	*conceiving*

FIGURE 11.1

deals with customers, handles advertising, and contains a public-relations team that also assists in some personnel matters.

This arrangement of staff by functions works well for the Doxus Group. The people who serve in its four departments tend to have certain skills or training that allow them to perform their assigned functions. The salespeople have a knack for relating to customers and for working with other company personnel. The designers are inventive folks who create new products and improve the line of widgets. The controllers handle money matters and are responsible for other procedures for keeping order throughout the company. The managers are the company's analysts, who make the choices that keep the company competitive and profitable. Although people with various kinds of talents are found in each of the departments, they are expected to perform the functions assigned to their department in order for the company to maintain its dynamic balance. The entire staff is integral to the company's ongoing success.

Management usually speaks for the company, but sometimes the sales–public-relations team also serves that function, depending on the type of communication involved. If an authoritative, hard-line stance is needed, a top manager often speaks. If a softer delivery is desired for bonding the company with others, the sales–public-relations team handles the assignment. Interestingly, both of these departments are perplexed by the other's way of handling people. Nevertheless, each accepts the fact that the other makes substantial contributions to the company's success. In a similar divergence of views, the controller's department and the design team also see things differently. The creative designers prefer to work whenever the spirit moves them. They are indifferent to the eight-to-five routine imposed by the controllers, and even neglect budget limits. The controllers are frustrated by the designers' disregard for limits and order, sometimes engaging them in squabbles that the managers must resolve. In a continual game of give-and-take, these departments cope with their differences, and the Doxus Group goes about its business.

As you can imagine, there is a unique esprit de corps in each wing of the Doxus headquarters. The west wing's managers and controllers are proper and businesslike. Everyone wears suits. To people on the other side, it appears that these west-wingers convey a privileged attitude that says, top manager walking about. But the managers and controllers think of the people in the east as a real trip. The salespeople spend an amazing amount of time engaging in small talk, while the designers come to work in jeans. You might find the latter in the office at midnight dreaming up some new idea that wouldn't come to them during "work" hours. Such differences in style are immediately felt when anyone walks from wing to wing. Yet it seems so natural that, after a while, folks cease to notice that these two wings are as different as day and night. Nonetheless, occasional visitors are confused by the fact that the managers and controllers in the west wing (on the left) are so conservative—anything but "left-wing" in the political sense—while the "right-wingers" (in the east wing) are so liberal.

Now, if the Doxus Group were organized in such a way that only people of a particular personal style were assigned to a corresponding department—spades to Management, clubs to Controllers, diamonds to Design, and hearts to Sales—then the company would be a boring place to work, and the departments might actually have a difficult time getting along with each other. For instance, the designers benefit by having a manager type within their department who will wear a suit, put on a businesslike front, and represent them by using respected spade language in meetings with management.

Thus, a smattering of different styles is found throughout all four departments. By and large, however, there is a tendency for the departments to be composed primarily of people with characteristic sets of talents and capabilities. The sharpest managers are typically spades, the most visionary designers are usually diamonds, etc.

Some discord in companies can be attributable to pronounced style differences between the departments. For example, there are variances in perspectives between the ways that managers (concerned with finances) and designers (concerned also with customer acceptance) read the market and assess what widgets to produce. In most cases, however, it is the personal style differences between individuals, and not their departmental positions, that cause conflict.

PERSONAL STYLE DIFFERENCES AND POTENTIAL WORKPLACE CLASHES

You can readily notice how people at work deal with situations in ways that favor one or another of the four types of thinking. Their special traits are identified as skills and matched to jobs, so that the company maximizes its benefits from such skills. All four styles also display their own characteristic weaknesses, slighting the type of thinking that is the opposite of their favored one. (Such opposites have been diagrammed as being diagonally across the card table, or at opposite corners of the Doxus headquarters.) However, fellow members of any particular style probably will not perceive serious weaknesses in their own ranks as they would in the three other styles. For example, a team of heart-styled salespeople may not recognize why coworkers frown on them spending much of their day chatting among themselves, perhaps about a new sales campaign or a personnel policy. And spade-styled analysts may not see why their coworkers are so enraged by their steely directives, affecting the lives of others, which are dispatched without even discussing the issues among the staff involved. Such blind spots of style can lead to some interesting skirmishes in the business world.

Recapped in table 11.1 are typical work traits of the four personal styles, including both strengths and weaknesses. (For more complete descriptions, see the summaries of each style at the end of chapter 2.) Because each of us uses all four kinds of thinking processes, typically you'll recognize all of these traits within yourself at times. But as you think of different individuals, or of yourself, one or more of these sets of traits will probably stand out as most characteristic of any particular person. As you read through these descriptions, match them up with people you know at work, such as your boss, people in your own department, or coworkers with whom you may have difficult relationships.

Traits of the Four Styles at Work

TABLE 11.1

♣ CLUB STYLE

order-setting

Steady, thorough in handling details, skilled in procedural thinking, methodical, precise, plans ahead, likes things scheduled, wants a program to follow, driven to finish agenda, emphasizes rules and laws, high priority of safety, security-oriented, loyal, conscientious, sticks with program to the end, fosters a chain of command, may be stickler on details, favors the tried and true, avoids change, may be scornful of irresponsibility and disorganization, may seem overly proper or judgmental

♥ HEART STYLE

relating

Interdependent, thoughtful, sensitive to people's needs and emotions, trusting, supportive, team-builder, cooperative, easy-going, people-oriented, skilled in sales and working with customers, likes to coordinate and communicate with others, listens to all sides, believes in group values, trusts in committees and collective ideas, is generally caring, instructs by means of stories, avoids conflict, may not stand firm in convictions, may give credence to hearsay rather than make their own analysis, may seem indecisive or submissive

♠ SPADE STYLE

analyzing

Independent, decisive, quick to find solutions to a problem, willing to challenge and debate, high self-confidence, competitive, hard-driving, likes to take charge, focuses on goals and decisions, forward-thinking, takes risks, cool evaluator, stands firm once analysis is made, may engage in one-upmanship, may have a talent for use of tools, may treat people as instruments, may not suffer fools lightly, can be insensitive to people's feelings, may seem arrogant or demanding

♦ DIAMOND STYLE

conceiving

Inventive, open to new ideas, hopeful, inspiring, interested in the big picture, trusts hunches and intuition, creates broad-reaching programs tapping many dimensions, keeps projects open for refinement, "can-do" spirit, light-hearted and humorous, will go "out on a limb," theoretical, explores new ground, looks into possibilities, freethinking and irreverent, disdains hierarchy, dislikes routine, may downplay obstacles or be loose on procedures, frustated by details, leaves things undone, may have an itch to move on, may seem impatient or unpredictable

In reading through the descriptions of the four styles in table 11.1 and comparing them to your coworkers, you may notice that the deck is stacked in favor of certain styles for particular jobs. Indeed, this is exactly the case. You would not expect a diamond to be a controller or a club to be a design whiz. You would expect a heart to be a strong candidate for sales or a spade to be considered for management. In such ways, organizations target people's strengths to specific functional applications in order to get the best out of all four kinds of thinking. However, if an employee's weakness, even if natural to their style, overshadows their strengths so as to become a detriment to the success of the unit, then this person stands a good chance of being replaced by a better-balanced coworker. For example, if a spade department manager is totally inept at communicating and relating effectively with his subordinates, they might scheme to depose the demanding, arrogant bastard—regardless of his vaunted expertise or superior decision-making ability. Thus, while dynamic organizations encourage differences of opinion and specialization in thinking, they also require a degree of balance, especially as one moves up the ladder to higher-level positions.

Still, differences in the ways that people think and operate at work are bound to produce occasional friction between coworkers, and clashes in attitudes. For example, a boss with a spade style, who is goal-oriented, hard-driving, and demanding of subordinates, can be irritated by a family-centered heart who is eager to go home rather than stay to work on important projects after hours. Even if the heart is superb at working with customers and carrying out the company's objectives, the spade reads the heart's other priorities as a lack of commitment and thus devalues his overall performance. On the other hand, the heart is anguished by the spade's insensitivity to personal needs and family interests. While this boss may criticize all non-spade members of the staff who are not as driven, the censure will fall harshest on the hearts whose traits are farthest afield from those of the boss.

In another instance, a club-styled manager with a long agenda of projects for the staff may clash with the diamond-natured designer who wants to continue working on a new product to improve its design. The manager is satisfied by the product design long before the designer is; thus, the designer's contrary interests in keeping the project open for possible redesign frustrate the manager's urge to check items off the list. When the subordinate is told to quit working on this design and move on to other things, such as preparing the department's budget and participating in meetings to set a company dress code, the designer balks—"I'm outta here!"

Each of the four styles has its own way of doing things. Thus, bosses in all departments often have characteristic methods and attitudes, which they impose on subordinates. Such traits of the boss, and their instructions as well, often communicate the message, "Do it my way." If the boss and a subordinate are of the same style, then it is relatively easy for the latter to communicate and perform work in the manner that the boss expects. If they are of neighboring styles, usually the subordinate can adjust to the boss's style and adequately perform the work. But if they are of opposite styles, then the subordinate's preferred way of doing things runs counter to the boss's, and all sorts of unfortunate consequences can result. They may have bitter arguments, and the boss may judge the underling as flawed or at fault, which can affect performance evaluations, pay increases, and chances for advancement. A person can be a solid, respected employee under one boss, and have all manner of difficulties with a new boss of a different style.

When a boss expects subordinates to operate strictly in accord with his or her own style, those who favor other styles are bound to feel frustrated or uncomfortable. Even if an opposite-styled subordinate is able to adapt to the boss's style without arguments and tempers flaring, nevertheless, the subordinate is likely to suffer some internal anguish or annoyance at having to squelch his or her own natural inclinations in order to satisfy the boss. In the next chapter, we'll discuss ways to alleviate such pressures and deal with many types of style conflicts between bosses and subordinates as well as between coworkers.

PREDOMINANT STYLES IN THE WORKPLACE

A company or work group often has a *predominant style*—a particular combination of thinking traits and skills that are deemed most valuable to achieve success. The predominant style depends on the nature of services that a work group performs, the kind of products it produces, and the style of its ownership or management. For example, a beauty shop usually exhibits a heart-diamond style because of the way beauticians chat and relate to their customers while creating new hairdos. A computer-software developer might have a spade-diamond style because of the constant need to invent and analyze logical sequences of computer code while striving to push their products to the cutting edge of technology. A church or synagogue office might have a heart-club style suited to the personal style of the minister, priest, or rabbi. Such a predominant style also conforms to the needs of the congregation and follows religious tradition. A military unit might have a club-spade style, because orders and hierarchy are of preeminent importance, and the commander is a sharp, tough leader. Such variations in the styles of workplaces can cause individuals to feel comfortable in one job but out-of-sorts in another. A person who is well-suited to a military career is not likely to be at ease as a beautician. A preacher is not apt to enjoy working for a competitive-software firm. When a person switches professions or employers, they often sense a change in the way they feel while adjusting to the new organization's predominant style.

Moreover, the predominant style of an organization can change over time, particularly in response to new ownership or management. Consider how a typical business evolves. An entrepreneur (often a person skilled in spade-diamond thinking) intuitively "sees" how to make a better widget. He or she takes the risk of putting forth effort and capital to develop the idea, sells others on investing additional funds, and organizes a company to produce and sell the widget. If all goes well and continued expansion of the company is warranted, then the entrepreneur and original investors may sell shares of ownership to the public in order to generate additional capital. The stockholders, who typically focus on protecting the safety of, and a good return on, their investment, are represented by a board of directors. Now the character of the organization begins to shift. The entrepreneur who developed the original idea was willing to take a far-flung chance on an idea that may have a distant payout; however, the stockholders and directors are interested in regular, ongoing profits. Thus, public ownership tends to convert the spade-diamond venture into a spade-club organization. Often the company's management changes if the entrepreneur isn't temperamentally suited to shift to the more structured organization required by the board.

The corporate directors work to satisfy profit-minded stockholders with regular profits so that stock values increase. In order to do this, the directors select top executives with superior skills in making keen business decisions, developing new products, and who demonstrate a track record of leading and organizing large groups of people to accomplish results. In addition, the directors regularly evaluate the performance of both the company and the executives. In turn, the executives impose a well-ordered, hierarchical system of organization to assure responsible decision-making and maintain control of information flowing through them to the board.

Within the Doxus Group, for example, it is the managers and controllers who communicate with the directors about funding the company's financial needs, evaluating the staff, deciding on key personnel actions, acting on legal matters, and so on. Such important spade-club matters are discussed with the board via the company's spade managers and club controllers—in spade-club language style. And let's face it, unless these guys satisfy the owners, the company won't be funded and employees lose jobs. So the expertise within the company to handle such serious communications with the owners is of great import to the entire staff.

In the Doxus Group, the loyal analysts who make sound, responsible decisions to protect profitability are best able to deal with the directors and other top managers. Thus, it is perhaps not surprising that they are also the ones best rewarded and promoted. Their spade-club thinking style is the dominant attitude of the company's culture, and the ranks swell with more security-minded analysts. The staff who occupy the west wing of the headquarters building even begin to consider the company's plant operations and the activities of the design and customer-relations staffs as being less essential than their own activities. While creativity and inter-personal skills are factors considered in promotability, the decision-reward ladder gets skewed toward analyzing and order-setting. Efficiency becomes valued more than harmony. Security and loyalty are respected over imagination.

With a spade-club predominant style, the Doxus employees who are of other personal styles find themselves in a bind. The company's incentive program allocates the greatest rewards and prestige to management positions. To advance within the company, employees attempt to package themselves into the predominant spade-club style, since management is where the company's million-dollar salaries, executive perks, and stock bonuses are to be found. The pay for the company's top salesperson or most creative designer is not even close to that of its president. But while the heart and diamond types feel they should have as good a chance as anyone for a top spot, their way of thinking tends to keep them out of the executive wing.

In fact, people who do not match a top manager's style may be subtly or even mercilessly derided. For instance, the Doxus top manager is a spade. When he and the company's other sharp managers gather among themselves for meetings, for golf, or to play cards, they belittle the styles of others. The salespeople and PR per-sonnel are mocked as being weak and empty-headed. The creative designers are ridiculed as "weird." The controller's staff members are insulted as bean counters who don't have the courage to take tough stands. Such cutting attitudes insulate top management and keep them from facing their own weaknesses—in this case, a spade's lack of sensitivity and appreciation for others.

This creates a condition within the company in which many Doxus employees feel out-of-sync with the west-wingers at head-quarters. The hearts and diamonds face opposition not only from individuals in the management wing over differences in personal styles, but also from the management culture, which reflects the company's predominant style. There's no way hearts and diamonds can break into the executive suite unless they put on a spade or club persona.

Not all organizations, however, display the Doxus Group's classic pattern of a spade-club management culture. For example, the needs of an entertainment firm might require many of its managers to be highly imaginative and capable of scouting out inno-vative movie ideas or new pop musicians. This firm's management culture could be skewed toward spade-diamond, causing hearts and clubs to experience limited opportunities for growth. Or, in a social-service agency, hearts might prevail as top managers and preclude spades in their ranks.

But an organization's management culture doesn't necessarily match the company's predominant style. For example, if the Doxus Group were sued over management's continual insensitivity to its employees, then, in order to heal the rift with the staff, the board of directors might fire some top spades and replace them with heart-styled managers. Such action could shift the company's prevailing management culture to heart-club, even though the new heart-styled managers would have to meet the board's basic spade-club needs. Or, for another example, the board of directors could change; and, under the new directors' prevailing attitudes, the board might simply dislike the company's spade leaders and shift the organization into another management style.

Management favoritism to certain styles can afflict any organ-ization, any level within an organization, and any management style, because people tend to believe that their own way of thinking is the best. On the other hand, if managers are enlightened about the benefits of empowering all four styles and strengths, then the organization can have a predominant style that meets its most important needs and also motivates the involvement of employees of all styles—even people whose styles might clash with the group's prevailing style. Indeed, the problem in many companies or departments is not actually the particular style of the manager in charge, but that the manager—whichever style he or she may be—does not understand and inspire those people whose styles are different from his own. In the case of the Doxus Group, its predominant spade-club style is generally useful to the company; it is a detriment only when this orientation by management represses the interests and involvement of employees with other styles.

ATTAINING QUALITY REQUIRES INTEGRATING THE FOUR STYLES

All three layers of varied thinking styles—individual personal styles, departmental styles, and an organization's predominant style—affect relationships among coworkers. Yet out of the swirling mix of opinions and power plays that result from such differences in thinking, a workplace staff must find a way to cooperatively combine their efforts in order to produce the product or service that addresses a need in the marketplace. Not only must they organize themselves and cooperate to get the job done, they also must continually strive to improve and position their product ahead of the competition. This calls upon the joint skills of the group, working as a unit, to invent better ways of doing things, to maximize customer satisfaction and service, to conform to all laws and lenders' requirements, and to maintain a highly efficient operation. All four kinds of thinking must be integrated into the common cause for the group to produce a work of quality. Quality is the essence of a product or service that is well-designed, reliable, a good value, continually improved, and pleases the customer.

When the entire staff is committed to the principle of quality, the product will most likely remain marketable and profitable. But because of the way that varying concerns often oppose each other— such as efficiency versus personnel interests, or design features versus competitive pricing—the interplay among the staff requires constant give-and-take. All of the company's coworkers must find a way of balancing their contributions. None of the different thinking styles or varied departmental interests can win all the time. Rather, as the old saying goes, You win some, you lose some. That's it precisely: Balance is fundamental to achieving quality! Unless each of the thinking styles allows its opposing style to be incorporated into the process of achieving quality, the company can't evolve and advance.

Because of the predominant spade-club management style of many publicly-owned corporations, business has a tendency to lose sight of overall quality, and to focus instead on its bottom-line efficiency. Then, every so often—typically, when economic downturns or competitive forces rattle their complacency—businesspeople must search for new ways to break out of the box in which they have trapped themselves.

The American automobile industry is a case in point. After World War II, Americans taught scientific management practices to the defeated Japanese in order to aid in the reconstruction of their economy. For several decades one such teacher, statistician Dr. Edward Deming, went to Japan to educate its business leaders in the "statistical control of quality" and other organization practices of Western-style companies. All the while, Deming became knowledgeable in the Japanese way of thinking that included Confucianism and Zen. Eventually, Japanese businesses learned to combine the Occidental scientific analysis and organization practices with their Oriental, socially-oriented, holistic style of thinking to become powerful rivals in a number of major industries, most notably the automobile industry. When American companies ran scared at this foreign competition, Deming stepped forward to teach Americans the secrets of Japanese business success. Ford Motor Company was among the first to ask for Deming's help in the 1970s, and he boldly challenged their executives' hardened attitudes. He codified principles, which he insisted that Ford and his additional corporate clients must apply. He talked about businesses as systems; the value of "profound knowledge"[1]; the idea that change is ongoing; and that quality requires continual refinement. "If you go for quality in everything you do," he said, "other problems will take care of themselves."[2] Deming was seen as a visionary for conveying the holism of the Japanese approach, which he espoused with missionary zeal.

In America, Deming's program became known as Total Quality Management. His system expressed a broad, holistic attitude, which encourages scientifically-trained businesspeople to think beyond the detailed, micromanagment of decisions, policies, financial factors, and legalities—and to additionally address the needs of the customer, the best ways to develop and improve the most innovative product or service, and to make work enjoyable for employees.

In essence, Total Quality Management attempts to integrate all four styles of thinking so that the organization functions as a dynamic system, without any particular style dominating.[3] Such team effort means that all coworkers are motivated to contribute their unique skills so that the product or service is one of quality.

Visualize an organization that encourages such team effort as a perfectly balanced, pyramid-shaped mobile, in which all four thinking processes have equal weight. This is actually similar to the initial descriptions of the Doxus Group early in this chapter—that is, before we found that a dominant spade-club management style bred some unfortunate consequences for diamond and heart employees. Nevertheless, quality requires management. The spade's ability to identify the best course for the organization and to lead it to achieve its goals is fundamental to the group's success. Nor can the club's control be relinquished, for it, too, is necessary in the mix.

To abandon either of these two grounding forces leaves an organization groping for purpose and stability. In a dynamic organization, there is an equalization of input and interests from all sectors. Every sector contributes to the decision-making process, and the group as a whole stays focused on the quality that is the goal of their combined efforts.

WHEN ONE WORKPLACE STYLE
OVERPOWERS THE OTHERS

What happens when an organization is weighted too heavily by one particular style? Here are some typical problems that can arise.

♠ An organization heavily weighted in spades loses soul. If the Doxus managers didn't listen to the sales staff, thereby ignoring customers' concerns, they might focus solely on manufacturing the least-costly widget in an effort to produce the greatest profits. Then, a few years down the road, a new competitor might start selling a higher-priced, yet more colorful line of widgets with flair, and Doxus sales would plummet. What might Doxus management do? Cut staff to make the operation more efficient; cut costs; be a lean, mean machine; outsource design, sales, legal, and accounting to consultants; close down the plant and outsource production. The company would thus become a mere shadow of its once dynamic organization.

♣ An organization overloaded in clubs loses the spirit that produces growth. If Doxus devotes itself to finding the best ways of getting things done, it may hone its production techniques to perfection and avoid the expense of developing new widgets. Indeed, any new product change requires both abandoning time-tested ways of doing things and a leap of faith that the new widget will sell and earn a profit. If the corporate culture rests on making safe decisions, however, the tried-and-true is always the preferred choice. Non-risk and non-failure allegedly equal job continuity and protection of retirement benefits. But what happens when innovative competitors threaten to undermine the company's viability? The club managers sell off whatever assets exist and put the proceeds into investments in profitable ventures of others. Play it safe and you're history.

♥ A group teeming with hearts loses focus. With a culture that places too great an emphasis on sensitivity and people's needs, Doxus managers would invest heavily in team training, employee education, and company social events. The organization would shift to a participatory style of management in which committees are formed for making virtually all decisions. With safety in numbers, no one would have to make hard choices. Committees would be formed to suggest new ideas, foremost of which would be to have more social functions to improve morale and camaraderie among the staff. Departments would be abandoned in favor of teams for all projects. Job assignments would give way to collective responsibilities. When decisions are needed, people would look around the table and then put matters to a vote. Soon bloated by non-productive staff, the inefficient company's balance sheet would go into the red. Management would have to look for an outside suitor—another company to buy the corpulent company and salvage its worthy widgets.

♦ A flighty flock of diamonds has no staying power. This condition is most likely to affect companies in their start-up phase. If diamonds outweighed everyone else, Doxus staff members would experience the chaos of disorganization. People would do whatever they enjoy doing and decision-making would become catch-as-catch-can. Remarkably good ideas might result from this diamond-heavy environment, but no organization would be in place to carry them out. Tax matters, legal concerns, financing, and capital-investment requirements would seem to be wearying wastes of time, sapping the staff's creative interests. The administration of productive operations would strain any team member who stepped into the breach to manage all the things needing to be done. Indeed, the sheer volume of procedures that must be handled by the growing business would overwhelm the innovation-seeking staff, who in due course would lose interest in the business and move on to explore other ventures.

Of all four kinds of organizational malaise, it is the spade and club deaths that we most often hear about, because big companies must contend with stockholder ownership and board management, both of which tend to emphasize spade and club styles. But no matter which style overpowers the others, a severe imbalance results in the death of the organization. All life goes out of the enterprise, and no one's talents are employed. Thus, there is a danger whenever any one style dominates and pressures the group to "do it my way." The most successful companies and organizations make certain that they maintain a healthy balance of all four thinking styles.

WHAT DOES A BALANCE OF STYLES MEAN TO YOUR WORK TEAM?

Many conflicts between coworkers stem from the lack of a broad vision of the work team's mission. If the company operates solely on the basis of Management By Objectives, or by lists of things for staff to do, it can lose sight of innovation as well as the needs of its employees to enjoy their work. But with the understanding that all types of thinking are vital to the company's achievement of total quality, the work team can make adjustments in departmental organization, job assignments, and methods of operation that will allow its members to feel comfortable, both performing their jobs and upholding their own styles as needed for the group's success.

Without an understanding of the optimum interaction of thinking styles, any staff member is likely to feel irritated when a coworker of a different style expresses his ideas or values. Such exchanges are too often entered into with the attitude that "my way of thinking is right, so you must be wrong." Hard feelings, conflicts, and feuds result when coworkers do not understand the importance of different personal styles, all of which might benefit the organization. But by learning about the different ways that people think and behave, a work team can begin to listen to all points of view with a new attitude of acceptance. Differences of opinion will continue; however, with knowledge of the four styles, workers are apt to treat each other with mutual respect.

There is another dimension to the validation of people's personal styles that has strong implications for both the organization and its employees—the importance of matching jobs to people's interests and skills. Consider, for example, an employee who has been muddling along for years through a variety of assignments, ranging from product development to financial planning to the supervision of an operation within the plant. This individual has never really excelled in any of these roles. With the awareness of the four personal styles and his own heart style, however, he finally understands why he seemed ill-suited to previous jobs. He longs to relate to people, and now realizes that he belongs in a sales-related position.

Another employee has served three years in a customer-relations position of an auto-insurance claims division. Management has continually received complaints from customers that she was surly to deal with and treated them brusquely. However, this employee had always been accurate in her processing work and amazingly sharp in identifying fraudulent claims. Naturally, this spade employee does not enjoy handling phone calls that require her to talk with people all day long. She is much better suited to a job involving, say, the legal resolution of fraud cases.

Often people are routed through different jobs to prepare them for management. While this approach makes for a better-rounded, more broadly-informed staff, it does not necessarily make for a more productive team. Also, some people are less suited to higher-level management positions than they are to other kinds of jobs they might experience on the way up the ladder. Hearts and diamonds, especially, can have struggles coping with the expectations of spade and club bosses and boards of directors. Indeed, a person of any style can be outstanding in one or more of the company's departments, yet exhibit little aptitude in the executive wing.

What's more, the move up the ladder does not necessarily equate with greater job satisfaction or long-term potential for income. All too often people are promoted without an understanding of the true nature of their skills. The result is dissatisfaction, job burnout, failure, and ultimately the loss of many highly skilled and valued personnel. Indeed, a company's ability to grow over time as a dynamic enterprise can actually be eroded by its own job-and-pay ladder, particularly if it favors rewards to a single, dominant side of the card table.

If you have been trying to cope with workplace policies that favor styles other than your own, managers who don't appreciate your way of doing things, and coworkers who carry on feuds because they don't accept one another's ideas and values, it may be comforting to know that you are not alone. Many employees in every type of business silently wrestle with such issues and strain to appear competent in the eyes of the bosses who hold the keys to job security. In such an environment, a knowledge of personal styles can relieve a pressure cooker of accumulated steam. Those who put workplace problems into the context of style differences remark, "Now I see why I have so many conflicts with my boss"; or, "So that's why that department does things so differently"; or, "Maybe I really can get along with that difficult team member now that I understand the way he sees things." Even so, change does not occur overnight. Once people become aware of their own personal styles, it takes time for them to figure out how to apply their thinking specialties toward the optimization of group performance. And most certainly it is not easy to redirect an organization's focus toward long term interests of quality that go beyond short-term returns and self-centered rewards.

Unfortunately, the typical reaction to problems in the workplace is to complain and pass them off as someone else's responsibility—the boss, the owner, the current administration. Yet if you are truly sincere about making positive changes in any organization, you can. No matter what your position, or how entrenched the power structure may be, you have the capacity to shape your working environment, to make improvements, and to enhance the quality of your own working experience. Specific strategies for dealing with typical workplace conflicts are found in the next chapter.

CHAPTER TWELVE

IMPROVING WORK RELATIONSHIPS WITH STYLE

How You Can Shift to Other Styles to Resolve Problems with Bosses and Coworkers

In the previous chapter, you saw how the *group* style of your organization, department, or management team can affect your job attitudes. But you experience such group patterns through daily interactions with *individuals*—your bosses and coworkers—each of whom prefers to use his or her own thinking specialty in dealing with the company's needs. A spade wants to solve problems. A heart likes to relate with people. A club attends to detailed procedures. A diamond searches to create something new. As you'll see in this chapter, such personal preferences often overshadow department or company goals and can cause all kinds of difficulties for people who must get along with each other in order to accomplish those goals.

We'll study specific relationship problems in the workplace by further exploring the imaginary Doxus Group. This time we'll examine the personal styles of its key staff members. We'll see how anyone—even a top leader—can be "blinded" to the vital interests of their weak suit and to important aspects of an organization's needs, as well. In the following story about Victor, the Doxus Group's president, note how his spade management style causes his disinterest in people-oriented heart concerns, and even threatens certain staff members' jobs. And notice how Victor attributes style differences to gender, which touches off discord between the sexes.

After this story, we'll suggest ways to resolve style-related problems with bosses and coworkers in your own organization. We'll use Doxus personnel to illustrate techniques that you can use to improve your workplace relationships.

Victor's Spade Management Style: Pitting the Men Against the Women
Members of the Doxus Group staff had a ritual they performed to prepare for meeting with Victor. Before entering his office they briefly stopped to talk with his secretary, Lydia, for a forecast of Victor's mood. Lydia was so skilled in her "Victorcast" that she could even give it wordlessly. Just a look from her was all anyone needed to gird themselves to meet with him. However, if Lydia had her onslaught-signaling "tiger tail" hanging discreetly from her desk, the staff need not even ask his mood. Because this orange and black striped, toy tiger tail indicated that Victor had devoured the last person who had met with him.

Victor had held the tiger reputation for some time, and even thought of himself as one. He expected the best from his staff and did not tolerate weaknesses, mistakes, or hasty schemes. Taking a proposal to Victor required thorough preparation, background studies of economic variables, complete analysis of potential problems, and a concise summary. Indeed, he would look only at reports that could be condensed into a single page. For the staff members, this amounted to a task similar to reducing a Melville novel to one page of *Cliff Notes*.

Carol, the controller, could usually deal with Victor's "bottom-line" style, especially since she had been well-schooled in preparing financial summaries for the company's board of directors. From her reports on the company's economic health, Victor could decide how to keep their investments in balance with income. Carol could perform this evaluation just as well as Victor, but she had a tendency to distrust forecasts and estimates, and often cautioned Victor against taking risks. Victor thought Carol was somewhat spineless for her hesitance to bet on any project that might fail. He attributed this characteristic to the fact that she was a woman.

Actually, Victor held similar opinions of Marie, the human-resources manager, and June, their public-relations agent. With three women in prominent positions, and the company's workforce split evenly between men and women, Doxus was certainly an equal-opportunity employer. Nonetheless, Victor did not think that any of the women on his executive team were in the same decision-making league as their male counterparts.

When Victor wanted new strategies for developing the business, he typically turned to either Frank, the plant-operations manager; Lee, the product-design manager; or Ian, the sales-and-marketing director. Of these three, Victor favored Frank, who was truly "frank" with his views. He was a no-nonsense, shoot-from-the-hip guy who lacked Victor's own sophistication and depth. But the president liked the way that Frank could entertain him with bizarre stories about what went on in the plant, and they became friendly allies.

Lee, an engineer by training, was often called in to discuss production issues with Victor and Frank. He was more reserved and calculating than Frank, yet very sharp. And Victor was continually impressed by the widget refinements that Lee's design department produced. These three men—Victor, Lee, and Frank—formed the nucleus of the company's power structure, and also the core members of Victor's golf foursome. It usually was easy for them to quickly enlist a fourth player. They often tapped Marshall, the assistant plant manager, or occasionally Doris, the research director who worked for Lee.

With a winning and outgoing personality, Ian was well-suited to working with customers. His advertising campaigns were creative and effective. He easily got along with his salespeople, and with most of the staff as well. Ian and Lydia had close ties to both the company's center of power and to many employees who entrusted them with their complaints and feelings of dissatisfaction. Ian could relate to the needs and sensitivities of the staff, seeing both management's and the staff's sides of issues. But he was not in Victor's inner circle, as Ian was not cool and tactical like his boss. Though the president respected the sales director's progressive marketing campaigns and his ability to motivate the sales team, they were not close friends.

Let's pause here to recap the key staff members and their respective styles:

♣ Clubs

Carol (controller)
Lydia (executive secretary)

♠ Spades

Victor (president)
Frank (plant-operations manager)
Marshall (assistant plant manager)
Lee (product-design manager)
Doris (research director)

♥ Hearts

Marie (human-resources manager)
June (public-relations agent)

♦ Diamonds

Ian (sales-and-marketing director)

Under this set of conditions, a distaff power structure also formed within the organization. It was composed of Carol, Lydia, Marie, and June. They occasionally lunched together and hashed out their beefs about the men. During one such gathering, Lydia observed that the women got the tiger-tail treatment from Victor more often than the male managers did. In fact, Marie and June were often distressed by

Victor's lack of regard for their work on important personnel matters and public-relations programs. Though Carol and Lydia were somewhat luckier in Victor's treatment of them, the four women concluded that their boss both distrusted women and disliked anything to do with people, job satisfaction, employee morale, and staff needs that extended beyond work. They saw this as a typical male attitude, and battle lines were drawn within the company, between the male dominators and the females, who thought of themselves as unappreciated servants.

It may be obvious, here, that the way these women and men interpreted their discord—as gender-related—was due to a lack of any other means by which they could understand and describe their differences. In this instance, it just so happened that the Doxus Group's key women were hearts and clubs, while the key men were spades and diamonds. This chance division of the staff easily pitted women against men. But this "us against them" condition was all the more divisive because Victor saw the women as more interested in gossiping about people than in solving business matters that were important to him. To Victor, the women's concerns seemed irrelevant and indicated lazy thinking, which he needed to correct. Without knowledge of the four styles, both sexes used each other's gender to characterize their opposition.

Victor believed that the women didn't have the moxie that he expected from his managers. Nor did they provide the kinds of business ideas he sought to fight their widget-making rivals, which had reduced Doxus' market share. Victor was interested in technological solutions and innovation, not company picnics or even tax matters. It seemed to him that the women were keeping the company from moving forward. He was so convinced of this—that the female staff were flawed in their thinking—that he openly challenged the entire staff, and especially the women, to be more pioneering and aggressive. He criticized those who questioned his objective of refocusing the business. In one session, he lashed out at a particular set of his managers and said, "Look people, I don't want to hear why we can't move forward. If you have issues with federal regs, tax codes, state laws, personnel practices, or some other goddamn PMS problem, work them out before meeting with me. Because I've had it with all your excuses why this company can't advance. Frank says he needs to change the production line. Yet Marie says our union policies prevent us from doing so. This kind of quibbling must stop. You people have got to solve these problems yourselves. Bring me opportunities, not obstacles. Are we clear?"

Victor's Solution: Rob the Hearts and Clubs of their Power
The nature of their problem was clear to Victor. He had too many naysaying women among his management team who were limiting the company's progress. Thus, he set in motion a reshaping of the organization to better-suit his own style. For several weeks he spoke about making shifts in personnel to gear up the company for greater success. After the quarterly results were released, showing that the costs of benefits and labor had risen faster than sales for the second time that year, Victor announced the formation of a new department that would combine accounting and legal functions with human resources. He called the new group Management Services, to be led by Marshall, the former assistant plant manager. Marshall had an accounting background and was certainly competent to run the new department. But, under the new regime, Carol lost two-thirds of her accounting staff while still retaining her title as controller, with responsibilities for evaluating new business proposals and reporting the company's overall financial results to management and the board. Marie would now report to Marshall on personnel issues, and rarely would be involved in meetings with Victor. Thus, in one move, the president modified the organization so that he was surrounded by men of his own kind of thinking, and would hear less opposition from women. Of course, an additional benefit was that Victor had filled out his golf foursome: Victor, Frank, Lee, and Marshall. This way they could take in a round of golf and discuss nearly all of the company's vital operations. All, that is, except for sales and marketing.

Now, Marshall was no more interested in dealing with personnel matters than Victor was. And Marie, by her demotion, had even less credibility with her new boss than before. Marshall treated her as someone who was on her way out. So, to no one's surprise, two months after the reorganization, Marie resigned. Victor's reaction to her leaving was like that of the winner of a chess game. He had never liked Marie's soft style and her departure made him more confident than ever that he had made the right choice in Marshall, who had the right stuff to rid the organization of deadweight. With Victor's approval, Marshall decided not to replace Marie. He believed that they didn't need someone on staff just to deal with people's needs. Whatever personnel matters there were, Marshall assigned them to the attorney in his department, as well as to his own assistant to administer job descriptions and performance evaluations. Lydia was given Marie's former duties of handling social events, such as holiday parties and company picnics.

Ian Provides Victor with a Diamond Corporate Vision

While the reorganization improved Victor's grasp on what was happening in the company's various departments and made him better able to communicate directly with his top executives, there was no subsequent improvement in the company's economic performance. Sales continued to trail expenses. Since Marshall was cutting expenses everywhere he could, Victor thought their problem had to lie in sales and marketing. He became agitated by sales director Ian's optimism. Maybe Carol was right to distrust the sales forecasts. Ian's promises began to sound hollow. Victor had already thought of moving Doris from product research to manage sales and marketing if he needed to get rid of Ian. Yet Victor knew that the loss of another well-liked key employee so soon after Marie's departure could hurt staff morale. Victor called Ian into his office for a closed-door discussion. After some pleasantries, the president got around to the topic of lackluster sales and explained that things would have to change. He detailed Marshall's program to cut costs, then asked Ian what the problem was in sales.

"The problem is not in sales," Ian answered. "The problem is that our widgets are not competitive, either in features or price. We can sell until we're blue in the face, but that can't alter the fact that people prefer the competitors' widgets. It's a matter of design."

"C'mon, Ian, don't pass the buck."

"Do you want to hear me out, or shall I leave?"

After a long pause, Victor said, "Go on."

"I believe our problem is that we are superb at reengineering an existing product, but we are not good at inventing new product ideas."

"But we have a research unit," Victor countered.

"Yes, and Doris is a talented engineer. The research group has developed many changes to our products that make them better, mostly to lower our production costs. Though there are many creative people in the design department, Lee has them focused on modifying what we already do, not on what we could do."

"Have you talked with Lee about this?"

"Yes, but we don't really see eye-to-eye. He's happy with the research that's been done. As well he should be. But face it, we can't evaluate new ideas into being. We can't get to where we could be, and enjoy the success we could have, by finessing our existing line. We need to think beyond the page. Color outside the lines. The research engineers, talented as they are, tend not to think that way. Victor, there is no solution to this problem without broadening our scope," Ian added.

"If you're right, how do we identify what we need to invent?"

"That's just it. We can't. It requires faith that we can come up with whatever we need. Perhaps we could assemble a new product team to generate some ideas. Do consumer research as well as product research. We might bring in a consultant who is not wedded to our way of doing things. We need to be as pioneering as when old man Doxus invented the first widget."

"We could try it," Victor judged, "but the study would lower profits for another year."

"Yes, but without a change in our product line, we're dead ducks."

Victor listened to Ian, and ultimately implemented his vision for the company to be more entrepreneurial and inventive. Thus, Victor exhibited the mature range of his personal style. From his cornerstone spade analysis, he involved both the club's procedures, which are basic to organizing and operating the business, as well the diamond's vision and openness to exploring untested, new ideas. Like a two-armed boxer, he alternated from one of these secondary processes to the other, all the while evaluating options with his primary, problem-solving capabilities.

WHY DEVALUING ONE OR MORE SUITS IS UNHEALTHY FOR ANY COMPANY

While Victor stayed sharp and focused—in the analytical strengths of the spade—and during his conversation with Ian realized that he had to incorporate his secondary diamond and club perspectives in order to save the company, he continued to neglect the heart aspect of management, and this had negative repercussions. He had rid the company of Marie and her human-resources interests that ran counter to his own. He had demoralized the women he judged as weak for sympathizing with the staff or deferring to group concerns. And he had fortified his spade management clique, which bred a "follow-the-leader" atmosphere.

You might wonder what difference this makes. Certainly, the collective fallout caused by an overbearing spade regimen is difficult to measure, particularly in the short term. But Victor's blindness to heart matters did eventually damage the Doxus Group and affect everyone in the company, for it caused the organization to be too narrowly focused and insensitive to human concerns. Victor's commanding attitude, which often caused people to cower in his presence, inhibited employees from creating and expressing new ideas. His demeanor not only thwarted heart-styled employees like June, the company's PR agent, but it also deterred many other staff members from performing optimally. Moreover, Victor did not inspire his employees' confidence and self-esteem. As a result, the company lost good people like Marie, who felt that management did not care about them. Again and again, the unique contributions that various people brought to the team went unappreciated, and the company lost its balance.

For example, one program that Marie, the former human-resources manager, had instituted was "Donut Day." At mid-morning on Fridays, Marie had donuts delivered and set out for the staff. Soon the gathering for donuts became a weekly ritual for employees to take a ten-minute break, chat with each other, and enjoy fellowship with their coworkers. Like recess for schoolchildren, the donut break allowed the Doxus staff to relieve the pressures of their constant problem-solving routine and to feel good about being with the company. But Victor held no esteem for the time-wasting Donut Day, and after Marie resigned, no one would risk carrying on her custom. After a while, these seemingly unimportant, people-oriented activities were culled from the company's protocol, and in time the employees showed less and less concern for each other.

Victor's demoralization of the women was especially harmful, because it dashed the motivations of many of them to be fully com-mitted to accomplishing the company's goals. As some women complained about their mistreatment, productivity suffered. Management time was increasingly spent on mending spreading rifts, rather than solving problems—a condition that was the dark shadow of Victor's good intentions.

If Victor could have stepped outside of his preconception that women were to blame for keeping the company from making progress, he might have noticed that he didn't actually distrust all the women on staff. He golfed with and approved of Doris, whom he considered for head of sales and marketing. He relied on Carol to represent the company with the board of directors. He also valued Lydia for all the duties she performed. And if he were equally observant, Victor would have recognized that he didn't get along with Ian, the diamond, as well as he did the other men who were spades, even though he was swayed by Ian's vision. Victor's gender bias was a false explanation for the real opposition that resulted from the staff's style differences, which he did not recognize and could not articulate.

Whenever an organization disregards one or more of the four styles of thinking—as Victor quashed heart concerns—there eventually may be unfortunate consequences, as we discussed in the last chapter. Indeed, Victor's reorganization, which further increased the supremacy of spade managers at the expense of hearts and clubs, foreshadowed a cutting "death by efficiency" for the Doxus Group. Yet when any thinking style gains too much of an upper hand, the consequences can be dire.

Many companies that have a management style like Victor's face similar challenges to those of the Doxus Group. The spade leader is well-suited to management by strengths in analysis, evaluation, and logic. CEOs like Victor succeed by narrowing the field of options to singularities, selecting goals, and making decisions. Their blind spot is relating and inclusive thinking. They may not value what the hearts offer, and even have trouble admitting that the diamonds and clubs are useful. Such leaders think of their staff as working under them. They hold a hierarchical view, looking down from atop the ladder. Corporate leaders like Victor figure they have made it to the top by utilizing keen analytical skills, so how can other ways of thinking be valuable? But how successful can any enterprise be without diamond vision, club precision, and heart connection? In fact, the staff of every organization should be viewed as a blending of all four working styles that together create a dynamic, vital team.

Wisely, in most organizations, major decisions are shared among several managers who tend to compensate for any leader's "blindness." And good managers continually ask their associates' advice to consider all sides of a business matter. Thus, it is valuable for a work group to have managers of different personal styles among its executive team. You most likely know whether or not a balance of thinking styles exists within your workplace. Either it has an active, lively dynamic that, for the good of the group, generally allows people to disagree, or it seems one-sided and flat, with people afraid to challenge the leader's thinking. If you work with a dynamically balanced group, then you already may feel empowered to contribute your best thinking to your work team. But if your workplace is more like the latter, then you and many of your coworkers may similarly feel unable to lend your full talents to the cause. In that case, you may need to share your concerns with your coworkers and the manager of your own work unit. You might suggest that the organization undertake some kind of educational or team training program in order to develop support for different thinking styles. Encourage your coworkers to learn about their own personal styles. Once enough staff members understand the principles of balancing the four styles of thinking, you might be amazed how a group can shift toward the greater acceptance of different styles, even though a particular style may still predominate.

DEALING WITH A BOSS WHOSE STYLE CLASHES WITH YOURS

Conflicts attributable to differences in style can happen between employees and managers of any style and are not limited to problems with the president of the organization. You might experience a clash of styles with the manager of your department, the supervisor of your work team, or the ranking officer of your military unit. The fact is, in any organization the boss's own style of thinking does hold sway, and its staff members inevitably must make adjustments to that reality.

The method for getting along with bosses of differing styles consists of two steps.

1. Identify and accept your boss's personal style.

2. Bridge the communication gap and attain common ground by shifting into your secondary styles.

Let's consider how June could use these steps to resolve her conflict with Victor. June, the company's heart-styled public-relations agent, had been laying low to avoid Victor's wrath. She gets along well with Ian, in whose department she works. His creativity and understanding of higher management allow her to be more effective in her job. Their conversations about PR ideas and advertising campaigns are fun for both of them. Indeed, she had often arranged for Ian to speak at public presentations instead of Victor, because she finds Ian's speeches to be more compelling than the sharp-edged words of their president.

But Victor is the company's leader and its most important spokesman, especially with the directors and stockholders. June must find a way of reconciling their differences and overcoming the fear she feels when meeting with him. She also must come to terms with her feeling that she is unappreciated for the skills and services she brings to her job. Indeed, when she mentioned this feeling to Ian, a few days later Victor issued a blunt memo stating to the entire staff that he was not about to go around telling people individually how well they were doing. He went on to say that he respected the work of the entire staff, and all of them should get accustomed to the fact that they would not get any special strokes from him. June took this as a personal blow to her self-esteem, and it reinforced her dislike for Victor. She never would have had the audacity to issue such a memo to the people with whom she worked.

If June could have approached her difficulties with Victor with an understanding of the four styles and the techniques in this book, she would have been able to deal with him in a more relaxed manner. First of all, by reviewing the characteristics of the styles (summarized at the end of chapter 2), she might have found that her need to feel appreciated is more of an issue to those of the heart style than it is to others. Because she favors relating, she almost can't get enough of it—just as Victor needs to solve problems, Ian relishes the challenge of creativity, and Carol gains a sense of self-worth from accurately preparing financial data. June's relationships with the other types are never what they could be, at least in her eyes, since she believes that connections between people can always be strengthened. Such dissatisfaction is the blind spot of June's style. If she can accept the fact that non-heart types do not feel quite the same way as she does—that they can get by perfectly well on fewer expressions of personal support, and need less intimacy and friendship than she does, then she can put her discomfort with someone like Victor into its proper perspective.

To address her problem of incurring Victor's angry response during meetings, June may want to apply the knowledge of communication gaps and the technique of shifting gears, described in chapter 8. June's struggle with Victor has many similarities to that of Jane (heart) and Tom (spade), the married couple described in that chapter. The communication gap is virtually the same in both cases. With Jane and Tom, the gap existed because Jane desired togetherness and relationship, while Tom sought independent problem-solving, and neither could fully enter into their partner's world. A similar situation exists at work between June and Victor. Neither can fully understand the other's way of thinking, nor can they speak the other's language. In a perfect world, Victor would at least attempt to meet June partway by shifting out of his rigid spade pattern. Victor, however, is not so accommodating. The full burden falls on June to find a way of communicating with Victor that doesn't upset him.

By shifting out of her favored, heart language style, June can avoid provoking Victor's opposition. She may need to couch issues in terms other than social considerations, or how others would feel, since these are not priorities for Victor. June may be able to accomplish her objectives by communicating with Victor via both diamond and club styles in a two-pronged strategy, represented in figure 12.1. For instance, she might begin by having Ian set up a brainstorming session with Victor to discuss a particular PR campaign, to learn his thoughts on the matter. In this meeting, Ian would expand Victor's thinking, help communicate what the

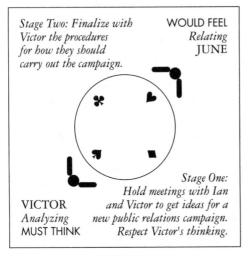

Stage Two: Finalize with Victor the procedures for how they should carry out the campaign.

WOULD FEEL
Relating
JUNE

*Stage One:
Hold meetings with Ian and Victor to get ideas for a new public relations campaign.
Respect Victor's thinking.*

VICTOR
Analyzing
MUST THINK

FIGURE 12.1

campaign could be, and at the same time act as a go-between for June. In later meetings with Victor, she could follow up with ideas of her own until the broad scope of the campaign gelled. After this, she would discuss with Victor final procedures on what they should do to carry out the agreed-upon program. By this strategy, she avoids second-guessing how Victor thinks. And she does not discuss with Victor her efforts to be sensitive to others in their campaign—because as long as the campaign produces good results, Victor won't care about how she relates with people in doing her job. If June expects Victor to care about what concerns her, she will be disappointed. In fact, entering into a discussion with him about people's feelings may spark antagonism despite a job well-done. So it is best that June respects the gap between them and administers the interpersonal aspects of the campaign on her own, using her own good sense. Afterward, she will receive more kudos from Ian than she will from Victor, but so be it.

If she doesn't have Ian to help expand Victor's vision of the campaign, June might enlist someone else with a diamond's creative gift. Or she herself would need to engage Victor in a one-to-one brainstorming meeting. She might prepare for it by imagining herself "taking the tiger by the tail," and by not letting Victor's words break her confidence, priming herself to be less sensitive, and purposely shifting out of her favored heart mode into her secondary diamond mode. She must switch it on and stay in that frame of mind throughout such meetings with Victor.

The worst thing June could do, however, would be to misrepresent herself as a spade and attempt to speak in the language of Victor's own favored style. Such a guise would seem phony to him, and she would not be likely to win a challenging debate with him—not only because of his analytical strengths, but also because he is the boss and is used to getting his own way by one means or another. If the tables were turned and June were the spade president with Victor the heart-styled PR agent, then Victor would be the one who might avoid confrontation, for then June would have the capacity to devour him. Such matters have much more to do with thinking style, and less with gender, than we commonly believe.

This may seem to be a rather chilling scenario for June. But realistically, with executive power at the Doxus Group so heavily weighted to a spade management style, the deck is stacked against a heart's receiving equal treatment—or diamonds or clubs either, though they are likely to fare better than hearts. It is the way things are in this, and many, companies. If hearts want to exercise more of their own favored way of thinking, then they might consider non-business or non-military careers. One of the greatest triumphs of the heart style is their ability to unify people, as can be seen in the success of heart-styled leaders such as Pope John Paul II, Bill Clinton, and England's prime minister, Tony Blair. And certainly the heart style is ideally suited to such professions as teaching, counseling, and social work.

In the above example, June faced major problems in dealing with Victor because their styles—heart and spade (located diagonally across the card table)—opposed each other. However, if their styles were adjacent to each other in the card-table diagram, such as diamond and spade, or club and spade, then the subordinate could relate with the boss using a combination of their individual primary styles, because each party's primary style is the other party's secondary style. Indeed, that's what took place earlier in this chapter in the discussion between Ian and Victor about the company's need to be more inventive. Since Victor's spade style was a secondary to Ian's diamond, Ian was easily able to shift to spade as they began their talk and could analyze why the company's design engineers were not creating competitive widgets. Then he got Victor to shift to diamond to involve him in Ian's vision of how the Doxus Group could become more inventive. Ian and Victor were able to relate effectively by combining their individual strong suits. Moreover, because Ian could alternate between his secondary suits of both spades and hearts, he served as a go-between for June's dealings with Victor.

Even when bosses and subordinates are of the same style, they can disagree. But their disagreements are likely to occur less often and be less divisive than if the two individuals are of different styles. In fact, spades do regularly challenge each other, but their debates actually serve to strengthen the bond between them, because they tend to analyze most matters they encounter. They disagree when they come up with different solutions, just as we all tend to do.

TIPS ON RESOLVING CONFLICTS WITH YOUR BOSS

If your relationship with your boss has deteriorated well beyond disagreement and taken on the characteristics of an ongoing feud, we suggest that you reread chapter 8, especially the first few pages that describe the "mind-stuck" nature of conflicts. If you and your boss are "stuck" in some misunderstanding of each other, it is likely that your styles of thinking are different and your boss does not understand the perspective of your style. To resolve this problem, you'll need to initiate a change in thinking that allows each of you to see the other in a new light—to open your minds to mutual acceptance. One solution might be to meet with your boss to discuss your differences. Lend this book to your boss so that he or she can develop a better appreciation of your individual styles. After your boss has done some reading, point out that your strong suit helps round out the strengths of your work team, and that your goal, like your boss's, is the success of the unit.

Not all relationship problems, however, are due to some fault of the boss. You play an equal part, so examine your own behavior for signs that might distress the boss. For example, if your personal styles are different, you may well feel unappreciated or hold some resentment that you are being forced to use a type of thinking that is not your specialty. In that case, you may seem remote and not fully interested in your work. To your boss you may give the appearance of having a "chip on your shoulder." Thus, your boss may think of you as being a marginal employee who does not contribute his full effort. In this case, you will need to recognize the nature of the "chip" that you carry, and do something about it. Perhaps you might request a transfer to a different job that better utilizes your strengths. Or ask to be involved in the kind of projects or work that interest you. Any of these changes might improve your disposition and make you a more willing participant. But don't let your dissatisfaction fester. After all, it's your own responsibility to find the kind of work that you enjoy.

In any event, don't forget that the key to a better relationship with your boss is, as we outlined earlier, to *(1)* identify and accept your boss's personal style, and *(2)* bridge the communication gap and attain common ground by shifting into your secondary styles.

DEALING WITH DIFFERENT-STYLED COWORKERS

This two-step method for getting along with your boss works with coworkers, too—usually better, in fact, because there is more equality in the relationship. That is, neither of you is expected to always be right, or to maintain the upper hand, as a boss often is. Thus, coworkers are more inclined to give a bit in order to meet each other halfway.

Let's listen to Carol (club) and Ian (diamond), who know how to apply this method. They are aware of each other's styles, and they know how to shift into a secondary style in order to find common ground. In this instance, Carol and Ian are discussing the sales and marketing forecasts that are needed for her to evaluate the financial return on a new line of widgets. She had given him a due date for his numbers, which are now two days late. Carol stops by Ian's office and asks him, "Do you have a couple minutes to talk about those forecasts?"

"Sure," Ian says, "But just a few. I'm meeting the advertising agency in about half an hour to go over the new TV commercials. . . . Oh, and to get their estimated costs on an ad campaign for the new widget line. I haven't forgotten. I've just been busy."

"With all the things you're working on, I know these forecasts are not a high priority," Carol noted, "but your numbers are the only incomplete item that keeps us from taking the proposal to the board next week. And Victor doesn't want to hold it off another month."

"Okay, I see the urgency," Ian answered. "Well, I should have the ad costs within an hour. And I've already projected all the other costs of sales personnel, promotional events, et cetera." Ian sees her relax a bit. "But actually I'm at a loss as to how to do an estimate of sales volume. That is, one that you and Victor will trust. The last time you two discussed one of my proposals, it got reduced by 25 percent, which killed the whole thing."

"Yes, well, I understand your reluctance to commit to a number."

"Put yourself in my position, Carol. Whatever forecasts I give you, I'm going to be expected to produce those sales. So I come up with a figure that I think we can reach. Then you chop it down to give yourself a safety margin, so you won't lose credibility in the future. I mean, how do we ever get a new line off the ground if we don't trust each other?"

"I trust you, Ian," Carol answered. "But I need to know the reasons for your optimism. I have to justify these proposals before the board, and they ask hard questions. They will not place any stock in my work if I answer, 'That's Ian's best guess.'"

"Okay. Okay. This proposal is really important to all of us, to the entire staff, because we are losing sales to the competition. If we don't get the board to support this line, our revenue stream will continue to suffer and we will be laying off staff. Probably within a year."

"Yes, I agree on that," Carol said.

"And we don't want to lose any of our people. That would be really sad."

"Yes, and we would both be among the first to go. Only we wouldn't be laid off."

"Right, we'd be fired," Ian agreed. "Okay. So why don't we try something new on this proposal? Since it's so important, let's clear our schedules this afternoon and develop a forecast that we both trust. We can do the analysis together. We'll look at the research and evaluate our market share for the new product line. That way you'll be comfortable with the numbers."

"That's a good idea, Ian. This afternoon's fine. We really need to do this today. But your suggestion has me thinking about something else. If you will agree, I'd like to ask Victor to invite you to this board meeting, because neither he nor I can communicate the confidence in your forecast that you can. And after our market pie-charts and forecasts, it may come down to you putting yourself on the line with the board to convince them that we can make those sales that you project. Are you willing to do that?"

"Of course."

"Good," Carol says. "I think this can work. I'll leave so you can get to your ad meeting. Can we meet at, say, one-thirty?" Ian agrees. "Good. Would you want to give me those other estimates you've worked up, so I can put them into the economic model?"

In this example both Carol and Ian honored each other's styles. Carol started this by putting Ian at ease from the start of the conversation, recognizing that her numbers were not a high priority for him. Ian also voiced a respect for Carol's needs by mentioning that he had produced most of the estimates she required. He was stuck, however, at bridging the central issue between them, her lack of trust in his sales projections (club versus diamond). Then he followed a line of conversation that placed them in a relating (heart)

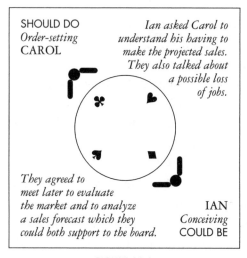

SHOULD DO
Order-setting
CAROL

Ian asked Carol to understand his having to make the projected sales. They also talked about a possible loss of jobs.

They agreed to meet later to evaluate the market and to analyze a sales forecast which they could both support to the board.

IAN
Conceiving
COULD BE

FIGURE 12.2

mode: Ian asked Carol to put herself in his position of having to deliver the sales that he forecast. He also acknowledged her basic need to have realistic figures. They then noted that if they failed, jobs could be lost, including their own (a heart issue). They recognized the vital importance of their estimating the projected sales with total agreement (with the interests of all suits balanced to equality). Ian suggested the joint (heart) effort of running through the analysis (spade), which they did later. Their shifts to secondary modes—the heart's relating, and the spade's analysis—are diagrammed in figure 12.2.

Then a beautiful thing happened. Carol recognized that Ian's optimism at being able to deliver his projected sales would be useful in selling the proposal to the board. His style might help convince the directors of how successful they could be. Ian, in turn, then placed his faith in Carol's judgment of what they should do, and he followed her advice on taking a stand with the board. She proceeded to schedule their afternoon meeting and to obtain the information he had already completed, thus checking items off her own list.

ACCEPTING PEOPLE'S STYLE DIFFERENCES
AND NEEDS MAXIMIZES TEAM SUCCESS

In their brief conversation, Carol and Ian each openly acknowledged the other's expertise, thereby fostering their mutual trust and advancing their respect for each other. Had they focused on finding fault in the other's style and accusing each other of past and present wrongs, they would have accomplished nothing. Instead, they acknowledged each other's needs and accepted their differences. They also managed to admit their own weaknesses in terms of the other's point of view. Their mutual openness and acceptance allowed Ian and Carol to maximize their individual strengths in preparing for the board meeting. By calling on each other's expertise in a team approach, they immeasurably increased their likelihood of success.

Unless we acknowledge another person's capabilities, we can't see the contributions they make. Naturally, we may find it difficult to understand how a coworker whose thinking style opposes our own can benefit us. How can anyone who differs with us so completely also serve our interests? It's a paradox. But people of varied thinking skills balance each other for the greater good of the group. For this balance to occur, all members of the organizational team must shift beyond the narrow focus of "right versus wrong." To make your work group more dynamic, you must learn to appreciate others who round out the "blind spots" of your own style.

Learning to cooperate with those in your workplace can be boiled down to just two words: accept and shift. Accept that there are differences between people that can frustrate you and cause friction, but which are ultimately vital to the success of the group. Once you identify and accept those differences, then you must recognize that at times you will need to shift your thinking to a style that can bridge whatever communication gaps exist between you and others. If you can shift with dexterity among all four styles, or at least three of them, you become even more valued and respected by your coworkers, and you reduce the likelihood of feuds and bitter arguments.

IMPROVING RELATIONSHIPS IN
A DYNAMIC ORGANIZATION

Throughout this book, you have learned many techniques for improving relationships with people whose thinking styles are different from yours. You can apply those methods to the workplace as well. In the first chapters, you discovered the telltale signs of behavior that indicate a person's style of thinking. Then in chapters 4 and 5, you learned about language styles and how to listen for clues about a person's style in the words they use. You can apply this knowledge in your relationships with your bosses and coworkers to identify their individual styles by their behavior and speech, and recognize how your thinking style may differ from theirs.

In the chapters on couples and families, you read many examples of typical relationship problems in a variety of different combinations of styles. You saw that people's differences in thinking styles are more fundamental than their differences in religion, politics, or other surface issues that we often think we're arguing about. And in chapter 8, you learned techniques for resolving conflicts and shifting to your own secondary styles of thinking to find common ground with others. This understanding will be helpful as you put your new skills to work to find ways for reaching agreement. By knowing your boss's or coworker's style, you'll have a good sense of what interests them. Using your knowledge of language styles, you'll be able to address those interests and phrase your messages toward their style of thinking. For example:

- ♣ Enlist a club to back your idea as a traditional method; reasonable procedure; a program that meets all codes and detailed policy requirements; a matter that preserves the safety or stability of the organization; or a process that maximizes financial security.

- ♠ Reason with a spade to agree with your idea as a decisive action; a clever or efficient solution to the problem; a means to the individual's or group's success; an answer that outstrips the competition; or a way to address all goals and objectives.

- ♥ Involve a heart to support your idea as a team effort; a morale booster; a betterment for all concerned; an improvement for employees or customers; a resolution to a long-standing discord; or a way to bring people together.

♦ Spark a diamond to champion your idea as a new and creative answer; a means for growth; an opportunity for freedom or change; an expansion of existing capabilities; an improvement that opens the door to unknown possibilities; or a way for people to enjoy what they do.

When you frame a presentation around one of the above sets of messages appropriate for the style of your audience, you are less likely to have resistance to your ideas. If a conflict with a boss or coworker has already arisen, then work toward satisfying the interests of that individual's style. By doing so, you will validate the other person's different style of thinking and enhance the potential for your good relationship built on mutual respect.

You may also choose to share this book with your coworkers and then get together to discuss how its principles can be applied to your place of work. In this way, members of your group can learn about each other's strengths and weaknesses and consider new strategies for working more effectively as a team. The "four styles" model we've been discussing in this book differs from "personality-typing" techniques commonly used by companies to teach managers and employees about their own individual traits. The "four styles" model encourages group members to appreciate the particular assets of every employee and to consider these varied strengths as valuable parts of the whole. When every employee acknowledges both their own and each other's unique talents as indispensable to the group's overall success, everyone is better able to work out interpersonal conflicts and help the organization flourish.

CHAPTER THIRTEEN

VALUING OUR DIFFERENCES

The Four-Way Division of Styles in Other Cultures

Long before Europeans settled North America, many of the Native American tribes had traditional symbols to depict different kinds of people. The medicine wheel is a circle that is divided into four quadrants by two strips of animal hide. The four ordinal points around this compasslike figure represent four basic and different perspectives on the circle of life. These are symbolized by the Buffalo (north), standing for cool wisdom; the Mouse (south), evoking innocent trust; the Bear (west), characterized by staying in place; and the Eagle (east), standing for illumination and vision. With the Buffalo opposite the Mouse, and the Bear opposite the Eagle, this model is like the personal-suit styles, only with the spadelike Buffalo diagrammed on top.

Interestingly, the medicine wheel and other four-way systems for acknowledging different kinds of human behavior may have had their origins in mankind's adaptation to the climatic shifts of the four seasons. Every year human society routinely cycles through spring's new growth and venturing out; summer's independence and management of crops; fall's harvest and preparation for cold weather; and winter's sheltered togetherness. Thus, life evolved different styles of thinking and behavior for adjusting to each new season and attending to survival. By now, our culture even signals such seasonal changes with holidays that commemorate a needed shift in attitude, as represented in table 13.1. This understanding of the four styles of thinking as nature's way of adapting us to the four seasons lends even more credence to the idea that all four suit styles are equally necessary to human society.

The medicine wheel and the other four-way systems which are summarized in appendix 3 indicate that down through the ages, and in many cultures, people have come to similar conclusions about human nature. What's new in the interpretation of personal styles in this book is the use of the card suits to represent the four "thinking" perspectives on the circle of life, and the survey of language styles associated with each of them. These two devices enable us to form new understandings of human relationships and ourselves as well. Since the card suits symbolize the four styles as equals, without any style superior to any other, we are reminded that any of the styles is a potentially winning hand, no matter the sex, race, or nationality of its owner. When we listen to language styles, we realize that most people utilize each of the four ways of thinking to some degree or other. Though we may favor some combination of processes, we are not limited to that set. Indeed, each person's style blends natural preferences with the thinking patterns of their upbringing and development, and may change somewhat over time. As we mature and gain mastery of the opposing thoughts in our own minds, we grow in our capacity to shift among different kinds of thinking. We become wiser. We take on new dimensions of our personality. Thus, a person is much more than any one style implies.

This means that while Victor, the Doxus president in the last chapter, can be a tough spade taskmaster when at work, he may well reveal a softer, friendlier side on the golf course or at home. This utilization of minor traits is typical of all styles. It also means that anyone, man or woman, can access any of the four dimensions within themselves if they choose to do so. Unfortunately, our society still tends to reinforce the ancient stereotypes that a man behaves one way, and a woman another. Messages in the media—and even in

The Four Styles and the Four Seasons

TABLE 13.1

♦ SPRING—CONCEIVING ANEW
Signal holidays: Easter, Passover, May Day
A time of rebirth, renewal, and resurrection. Spring is a vibrant season for plowing fields, planting crops, exploring new interests, and celebrating life—from conception through adulthood. A time for imagining how things could be.

Transition holidays: Mother's Day, Father's Day, Graduation
Honor parents who aided your development, then separate from the family. After the period of growth, shift into summer's independence mode.

♠ SUMMER—SEPARATING AND MAKING CHOICES
Signal holiday: Independence Day
A time for breaking away and deciding things on your own. Summer is a season for managing crops, taking a vacation, and evaluating your life. A time for realizing that you must think about your own needs.

Transition holiday: start of school
When the independent time is over, shift to fall's preparation mode.

♣ FALL—SETTING THINGS IN ORDER
Signal holiday: Labor Day
A time for taking stock and making preparations. Fall is a season to get ready for a season of cold weather (harvesting, securing storm windows, battening down the hatches), and studying in school to prepare for life ahead. A time for traditions and doing what you should do.

Transition holiday: Thanksgiving
When the preparations are done, shift into winter's relating mode.

♥ WINTER—RELATING AND GIVING
Signal holidays: Christmas, Hanukkah
A time of connection and togetherness. Winter is a season of being hunkered down inside, and sharing relationships with family and friends, giving expressions of love and caring to one another, and peacefully coexisting. A time for considering how others would feel.

Transition holidays: Valentine's Day, St. Patrick's Day
With cabin fever after all that relating, shift into the open spontaneity of spring's exploration mode, even new romance.

---

religious myths about what our proper role should be—often block the full expression of our individuality. And they deter many people from enjoying the full range of their own faculties.

CONQUERING GENDER STEREOTYPES

Any thinking person will inevitably conclude that they are neither Mars nor Venus alone. In fact, in many cases, neither of the types of behavior that these gender myths symbolize is the predominant feature of a person's character. While the four styles increase our richness of understanding beyond what is offered in just two gender stereotypes, even the four-way model is only the tip of the iceberg of the full complexity of human temperament. Nonetheless, four style orientations on the circle of life offer up a rich diversity which frees us from the belief that men are one way, and women are another. This book is, at least in part, an attempt to go beyond narrow stereotypes so that we can reach a wider understanding of the thinking styles that are possible for each of us, and indeed are necessary for human society to survive and grow.

What purposes have gender stereotypes served? Certainly they have fostered a fundamental, two-way diversity of thought that has prompted people to begin to consider their differences. And as we noticed in reviewing the kinds of guidance needed for early childhood, a diversity of thinking experiences provided by parents or family members is vital for a young child's optimal development. Toward that end, the traditional male and female roles do promote a balance of thought within families. But these conventional gender roles too often are laid on us almost as job assignments that we are expected to perform, regardless of our own personal nature. Such traditional gender roles work for some better than for others, and certain people who don't fit the mold are often robbed of the opportunity to develop the unique talents they otherwise could have contributed to society. In addition, the inability to express one's own nature can destroy self-confidence and spawn negativity.

Throughout our exploration of the four styles in groups of all kinds, we've learned that we need not rely on gender stereotypes to achieve a balanced society. Indeed, all we have to do is recognize how different personal styles benefit the group, then let people be themselves.

So if a woman wants to be an attorney or a corporate manager to apply her analytical strengths, why not? Or if a man prefers a more domestic life over a government or business career, what can be wrong with that? To each their own. One must do and be what comes naturally. A person's career may not fit the stereotype for their gender, but then again, following societal standards is only one way of dealing with life.

In recent years public opinion has actually swung so far in favor of women entering careers once reserved for men only, that this "politically correct" attitude can itself be debilitating. Some women—in proud, spade fashion—expect all women to strive for top careers and professions, seek high-level positions, and challenge men, with a total disregard for the many women who are splendidly happy and perfectly suited to being full-time mothers and housewives, caring for their families, and enhancing neighborhood relationships. Those who insist on how women must think often ignore the women who are well-satisfied in traditional roles. A balanced society would encourage and empower women of all types according to their own nature.

Because people often tend to view their own style as the one and only way to be, we hear a lot of name-calling and belittling of others who do not follow suit. One of the greatest goods that could come from recognizing different ways of thinking is that the energy now devoted to deriding one another might instead be applied toward constructive aims. Imagine if Republicans and Democrats did not waste their time undercutting each other, but instead applied that effort toward our mutual betterment!

The same can be said for couples and families. What if neither family member is wrong, but just sees things differently? There is a good possibility that some of your spouse's traits that frustrate you are the very ones that balance out your own style. In families, the best solutions to problems are not his solutions or her solutions, but somewhere in between. What if there was no proper way or improper way, but only the better way that you both work out? And what if you have just as much right to your own views as your spouse does to theirs? Indeed, this is democracy for the family. You may not have looked at things in quite this way, but you have every right to. Think of it as your own declaration of independence.

DEALING WITH OUR STRESSFUL CULTURAL STYLE

Of course, if you applied such independence at work, it probably would get you fired. In our places of employment, a lesser state of democracy is the price we pay for attaining economic goals in a competitive world. Since we require that managers be prudent and resourceful with the money we invest in their ventures, we would not want them to be too carefree with spending nor lose the ability to make tough business decisions. Surely the club organization and the spade control that we experience in the typical workplace serve a valuable purpose; they mobilize us into powerful units to achieve objectives. Likewise, the pursuit of a free-spirited attitude in the military could get us court-martialed. To forge an unruly bunch of individuals into a strong, coordinated military force requires organization, training in routine procedures, chains of command, and following orders. With the nation's military and business success depending on our ability to outthink the competition and to organize people to carry out objectives, it is no wonder that our educational system also is skewed toward spade and club training.

Since the business, military, and educational systems of the country are in tacit collusion to maintain analytical/orderly thinking, we could rightly consider this one-sided pattern as the nation's predominant cultural style. This may not be obvious, because we are so enmeshed in this way of thinking during our normal, everyday life that we generally take it for granted. It is only when we get away from this style—in weekend leisure activities, perhaps during worship, or in experiences in other lands or other cultures—that we briefly relax from the predominant spade-club style of our own culture. Interestingly, the lifestyles and languages of Native Americans offer an example of styles that differ from the more "European" thinking that now characterizes America. With Native Americans, we sense a more holistic attitude and a more harmonious connection with nature than in our nation's prevailing way of thinking. We may wistfully revere the cohesiveness and vibrant spirit of traditional tribal cultures. We may wonder what it would be like to be less driven and not so tied to a job—or even a fixed location. Then we snap out of it, go back to work, and put aside such glimmerings of other ways of living, which seem impractical to our modern minds.

We often can't see our own culture's predominant style. However, people of other cultures and other lands see us from the perspectives of their own styles. Some of them consider us as insular as we might regard Victor, the president of the Doxus Group in the last chapter. They might hold some contempt for a dominant, independent nation that tends to maintain the upper hand by its spade-club expertise. Like Victor, we may not recognize that, to people of other cultures, Americans seem heavy-handed; we believe that we are working for everyone's best interests—but others might perceive that our way of thinking values winning and succeeding above all else, regardless of the cost to the environment or the well-being of other cultures.

Moreover, as all of us know, living and working in a spade-club culture can be stressful. Indeed, one wonders whether America's high rates of heart attacks, suicide, and violence are not linked to our predominant spade-club style. Certainly, we are the most litigious nation on the face of the earth. We sue each other at the drop of a coffee cup. We tend to seek retribution for any insult, or when someone does not meet our standards for behavior. We hold a critical opinion of attorneys, yet we employ them constantly to wage war for us. Court TV is now a form of evening entertainment, and courtroom dramas are a favorite film genre. In addition to attorneys, journalists also get in on the attack. TV news shows capitalize on wrongdoings and inequities. We're all familiar with the hostile tone of such investigative programs: What went wrong? Who is at fault? What are we going to do about this? How can the government let this happen? Who's going to pay?

And then there's the physical violence to which we are subjected daily, as entertainment in network programming, and on local news shows, and in the newspaper. Even kids' cartoons involve violence to capture their young audience. In such a sea of violence and wrongdoing, how can we feel safe? What can we do about such threatening problems? Should we wall ourselves in? Like a dog chasing its tail, our culture is caught up in a circular game of analyzing, problem-solving, judging, criticizing, suing, publicizing, competing, winning, getting, stealing, prosecuting, analyzing, problem-solving, and around and around.

Now, in all probability, just reading the last two paragraphs made you feel a bit stressed. Ceaseless investigating and problem-solving keep us stressed out much of the time. But it is not only wrongdoing that brings on angst. Anytime we become ensnared in spade-club thinking without a break, we feel tension building up. Therefore, stress can happen at work if we take it too earnestly. We are a society of people with stressful jobs in a stressful society, longing for relief from our incessant problem-solving routines. We take vacations to escape, like kids bursting out for recess. But before we know it, we're back on the job and in the thick of it all over again. Working harder and longer doesn't solve our problems. We just seem to have less and less time, solving more and more problems. Even skilled problem-solvers reach a point of saying, "Enough!"

It's interesting to consider that the mental relaxation we seek when we take a vacation is inherent in the more balanced, everyday existence of early Native American cultures. They understood the importance of incorporating all four perspectives into daily life.

From our review of the four types of thinking, you have also seen that joy comes from exploring the heart and diamond processes. You can apply this understanding to deal with stress and enhance your sense of joy. In order to shift out of the stressful modes of problems and worries, shift into the opposite mental processes. You might leave the problems at the office, and go out with friends or a loved one. Turn off the worrisome news, and put on some music. Get away from the routine, and do something you've never done before. Put aside the report that's got you stumped, and go to the beach. Forgo reading the morning newspaper, and hike to the top of a mountain. In each case, the second part of the prescription is as necessary as the first. Thus, solutions for stress not only include leaving the office, turning off the news, getting away from the routine, putting aside the report, or forgoing the morning news—they also include the heart and diamond joys of going out with friends and loved ones, putting on music, doing something new, going to the beach, or hiking a mountain.

Shift your style of thinking to relieve stress. This may seem so simple as to sound dumb. But if you know which way to shift, it really works! Integrating relaxing, spiritual, creative, adventurous, or social experiences into your daily life is better than medicine. Prince Charles paints watercolors, as did Winston Churchill. Truman played the piano. JFK sailed. Jimmy Carter turned to spiritual matters. Bill Clinton jogs, golfs, and plays the saxophone. Janet Reno canoes. Oprah holds slumber parties with her women friends. Each of these people found ways to balance their lives with interests that relieved their stressful routine.

APPLYING THE FOUR STYLES TO
RESOLVING BIG ISSUES

In addition to its predominant spade-club style, America also has divisions something like the departments of the Doxus Group. Different regions of the country display different traits rooted in how they were settled. The pioneering far West is more free-wheeling than the established East, because the explorers among us have always looked for ways to break away from settled society, to open new territory. Thus, the diamonds flocked to the West where they could prevail. While repetitive manufacturing occupied the settled East, the innovative entertainment, computer, and software industries sprang into being in the free-spirited West. Indeed, it is difficult to picture any other region of the country giving rise to the imaginative fantasies of Walt Disney. Differences between "Western versus Eastern" ways of thinking thus place Hollywood in contrast with Washington, D.C. Similar divisions of style have tended to exist between the industrious North and the more genteel, agricultural South. More than once have people faced off against each other over differences in regional style.

One interesting thing about the card suits is that they can be applied to all sorts of domestic issues. For instance, let's look into the recent Southern Baptist boycott of Disney Company movies, products, and theme parks. This is a protest against the company's accepting policies toward homosexuality. The club-minded Baptist leadership wants to protect moral standards based upon their traditional interpretation of the Bible, while Disney's diamond-styled leadership accepts people's rights to live and work as they freely choose to do, and as granted by laws handed down from the Constitution's Bill of Rights. Both sides—traditional moral standards and individual freedoms—are valuable to our society, and neither approach is totally right nor totally wrong. Nevertheless, the leaders of both the Baptist Church and the Disney Company believe that their opponent in this controversy has a very odd way of thinking. This is the same "club versus diamond" split that led the conservative Republican members of the House of Representatives' Judiciary Committee to impeach President Clinton, and to insist that the rule of law must apply to everyone—while a majority of Americans wanted to forgive the President's indiscretions and forgo the legal hair-splitting of a long impeachment trial. This "club versus diamond" division also occurs between fundamentalists such as the Christian Coalition versus the freethinking American Civil Liberties Union. Struggles over such differences in thinking are taking place all over the world in many other serious political and religious conflicts.

We're faced with the clashing of differing attitudes every day. Turn on any TV roundtable debate and apply your knowledge of the language styles. Soon you will see an exchange of ideas bouncing back and forth in something like a four-way volleyball game. Picture two nets crossing each other, and four teams, one in each quadrant of the court. The ball, which is the subject for debate, is batted from one team to another, each giving its own unique spin on the issue. For instance, the game might go as follows:

♠ "I think it's very important to determine how we're going to deal with immigrants before we let them into this country."

♦ "But we have always been an open society. How can we close our borders if people need a refuge from oppression?"

♥ "I agree. We can't be heartless and shut people out. We have always welcomed people in need. Someone has to care."

♣ "But think what it costs in government services. We should not be the dumping ground for all the world's irresponsible societies that won't establish some order of their own."

♦ "What? Despotic societies have way too much order. What people need is freedom."

♠ "It's beside the point whether other societies are orderly or free. The problem is how does this nation resolve the pressures to accept more people? We can't take care of everyone."

Around and around, the issues bounce, from one style to another. It is amazing that we ever settle anything. Over time and after many interactions with people of other styles, we begin to understand how we, as well as others, look at life differently. We may argue with friends or family when we discuss such controversial issues as abortion, gun control, affirmative action, or protection of the environment. On a variety of such causes people speak their minds and define their own styles.

This process of coming to grips with one's own style is a more difficult task for some people, because they may wrestle with patterns formed in childhood, through education, by workplace policies, or by our culture in general. Some people go to extraordinary ends to define their styles. In the process of learning to express his or her own nature, a person can be driven to an extreme corner of the boxing ring. Most people eventually come in from the corners and grow into a well-rounded maturity. But some, unfortunately, get stuck in a place where they have no compassion for others, and lack the sense of self-worth or confidence to use their talents for positive, constructive ends.

From the world stage down to the garden-variety arguments experienced in our daily lives at work and at home, the four-way model of personal styles offers us a useful tool for grappling with many levels of interpersonal interaction and conflict. Because the card suits are simply a shorthand for describing different ways of thinking, and since virtually all conflict is attributable to people's differing thoughts, you are likely to find many useful applications of this system of resolving style differences which go beyond the ideas touched on here.

PLAYING AT THE TABLE

To represent the ways that different styles interact with each other, two kinds of diagrams have been used in this book—the card table and the boxing ring. Let's now bring them together (see figure 13.1). The circular card table is a symbol for people who are actively engaged in an interactive game in which all styles are beneficial for rounding out and balancing a group's thinking. The square boxing ring portrays those who tend to battle for their own style, who have

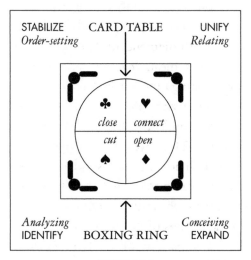

FIGURE 13.1

gone to their own corner, if you will, to gather support for the next round. As illustrated in figure 13.1, you could think of the card table as located within the boxing ring. In this composite view you can see that those who are out in their own corner seem to be struggling in more strenuous competition. The people playing cards around the table have an easier, more enjoyable time than the boxers duking it out. Thus, the art of the game is to be involved at the table, because mental discussion takes much less energy than physically battling each other. And it is less costly and painful to resolve a matter diplomatically than to use physical force.

One might ask whether it wouldn't be better if we all were simply located at the center. Certainly, if we didn't differ and disagree, the world would be a much more relaxed and peaceful place. But imagine a society in which staying at the center was deemed to be the way people should think and behave. While it is fine for some to live this way, a whole society of people engaged in staying at the center would not express all of the rich human traits that are found around the card table. People would not be free to be themselves. Nor would such a society be most fit to evolve and survive. If the earth were about to be hit by a large asteroid, for example, would a fully "centered" society be able to avert global catastrophe? The resolution of this kind of dilemma would require each of the four thinking styles: analysis, imagination, organization, and unification. If we all were simply an equal blend of the four, no one would possess enough of any one trait to deal with such a crisis.

While becoming more centered and rounding out our culture's predominant spade-club activities with diamond-heart involvements can relieve daily stress, this does not mean that we should all be totally undifferentiated in our thinking. Indeed, being completely centered appears to be inconsistent with life's own strategy for survival and advance, for evolution evidently has favored all four styles in roughly equal proportions. Thus, we as a society may be better off when people play their individual strong suits from their respective positions around the card table than we would be if they either *(a)* stood at the table's center with no differentiation in style whatsoever, or *(b)* fought from the corners of the boxing ring.

No matter what size group we're part of, we are more effective when we have our differences. Different styles of thinking force us to look at all sides of a situation. Therefore, the best way for us to be is the way we are! As frustrating as our diverse values and attitudes may be, there are distinct advantages to having different ways of thinking and the particular skills they represent. Life has equipped humanity with a combination of talents so we can deal with the challenges we face.

The answers seem not to lie in any single way of thinking, but in the diversity of them all. Truth itself is paradoxical. Our mutual interests do not require that we all come to the center in a common viewpoint. Rather, it is most advantageous for us to have our differences and to be who we are. Each of us has the opportunity to advance our condition by finding our strong suit and putting it to good use.

SCORING THE
SELF-TEST

To develop your personal style profile you will need to score the self-test found in chapter 1. This appendix gives you the information you will need to do so. Follow these simple steps to translate your thinking traits into the vocabulary of card suits that is used throughout the book.

Step 1

Transfer your rankings on each numbered question from your Answer Form to a clean photocopy of the following Scoring Key form (which has symbols of the card suits at the top and bottom of the columns). Note that the *(a)*, *(b)*, *(c)*, *(d)* placement has been arranged on the Scoring Key so that your responses will automatically be categorized in columns by suit, by transferring them to this sheet. Just be careful that, for each question number, you transfer the value you gave *(a)* on your Answer Form to the correct space for *(a)* on your Scoring Key, and *(b)* to *(b)*, etc., through all four answer choices to each question.

Step 2

After you have transferred numbers from all twenty questions to the Scoring Key, total all the numbers on the Scoring Key by suited columns. Enter the total for each of the eight columns into the blanks on the bottom line—the one designated for TOTALS.

Step 3

Now combine the totals for part 1 with the totals for part 2 by suit. Simply add the totals for both columns designated by the ♣ symbol, and place the grand total for that suit in the divided square (figure A.1) at the bottom of the Scoring Key. Enter this grand total in the box with the ✓ mark at the ♣ symbol. Follow this same procedure, adding part 1 and part 2 totals, for each of the other suits (♥, ♦, ♠). Your scoring is completed when you have grand totals entered in all four ✓ boxes on the Scoring Key (see page 316).

Discovering Your Personal Style

Scoring Key for the Self-Test

	PART 1					PART 2			
1.	*b.* ___	*a.* ___	*d.* ___	*c.* ___	11.	*c.* ___	*a.* ___	*d.* ___	*b.* ___
2.	*b.* ___	*c.* ___	*a.* ___	*d.* ___	12.	*d.* ___	*a.* ___	*b.* ___	*c.* ___
3.	*d.* ___	*a.* ___	*c.* ___	*b.* ___	13.	*a.* ___	*b.* ___	*c.* ___	*d.* ___
4.	*a.* ___	*c.* ___	*b.* ___	*d.* ___	14.	*c.* ___	*d.* ___	*a.* ___	*b.* ___
5.	*d.* ___	*c.* ___	*b.* ___	*a.* ___	15.	*b.* ___	*c.* ___	*d.* ___	*a.* ___
6.	*c.* ___	*a.* ___	*d.* ___	*b.* ___	16.	*b.* ___	*c.* ___	*a.* ___	*d.* ___
7.	*b.* ___	*c.* ___	*d.* ___	*a.* ___	17.	*a.* ___	*c.* ___	*b.* ___	*d.* ___
8.	*b.* ___	*d.* ___	*c.* ___	*a.* ___	18.	*b.* ___	*a.* ___	*c.* ___	*d.* ___
9.	*d.* ___	*b.* ___	*c.* ___	*a.* ___	19.	*b.* ___	*c.* ___	*d.* ___	*a.* ___
10.	*b.* ___	*c.* ___	*d.* ___	*a.* ___	20.	*a.* ___	*d.* ___	*b.* ___	*c.* ___
	___	___	___	___		___	___	___	___
	♣	♥	♦	♠		♣	♥	♦	♠
	TOTALS					TOTALS			

Combine totals for both parts by suit and enter the grand totals for each suit in ✓ boxes in figure A.1

INTERPRETING YOUR PERSONAL STYLE PROFILE

You have now boiled down your responses to four scores in a square diagram that is called your Personal Style Profile. The card suit symbols represent the qualities of your thought processes and temperament, so the higher your score in a particular suit, the more you tend to use that type of thinking. Throughout this book you will be discovering more about these styles—how they oppose and interact with each other, how people with similar styles assemble into like-minded groups, how your personal style can clash with those of other styles, both at home and at work. Think of the chapters of this book as the interpretation of your own personal style profile.

For discussion purposes, an example profile diagram (figure A.2) is filled in with a set of scores. In the example, note the pattern to the scores, the way one suit has a highest score, two suits have moderate scores and one has a low score. Here, the strongest, most favored process is clubs, followed by hearts, then spades, with diamonds weakest. Regardless of your strongest suit, your scores may show a similar pattern of two secondaries on either side of your primary suit. Imagine the pattern of scores (represented by figure A.2) as a boxer standing with his back to

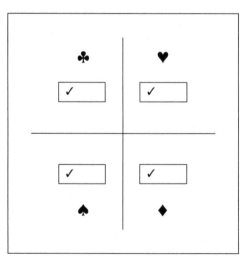

FIGURE A.1

the ♣ corner of a boxing ring. Since this person highly favors the ♣ corner, his two arms are spread out on the ropes, one to the ♥ corner and the other to the ♠ corner. In the example, the ♣♥ arm is stronger than the ♣♠ arm. This is not to say that a two-armed pattern is the right one, only that it is the most typical pattern. Some people's scores are about equal in all four suits. That's okay—it's just more rare.

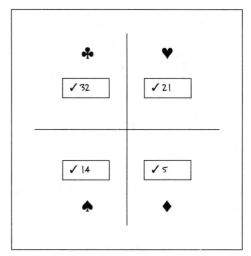

FIGURE A.2

If you have taken the test with a friend or a partner, compare your profile scores and make a mental note of the strongest and weakest suits for both you and the other person. You may find it useful to evaluate the differences between your individual scores by suit. That is, for each suit, one of you probably scored higher and the other lower, so subtract the lower score from the higher. The number difference between your individual scores by suit represents how much you differ in using a particular style of thinking. As you learn more about the four styles, such comparisons can help you define how the views and values that you each hold are similar or different.

Now proceed to chapter 2 for the meanings of the card symbols and the scores.

THE FOUR STYLES REFLECTED IN FAMOUS QUOTES

Chapter 4, "Language Styles," shows how a person's style of thinking relates to the words they use in spoken and written language. Signature words that characterize a style of thinking are founded on four key words (*open, close, cut, connect*), each of which is associated with one of the four styles.

This appendix is a compilation of quotes by well-known people that express attitudes and ideas associated with each of the four styles. As you read each block of quotes, one for each of the styles, you can see how a person's message, attitude, and tone align with the ideas and values of other people of the same personal style. There tends to be a common perspective on life that is expressed by the individual advocates of each particular style.

As you study these famous quotes, first read through them for the overall message and tone of each style. Note which of the groups is serious, humorous, hard, soft, liberal, conservative, collective, independent, etc. Then go back and try to spot their signature words.

In these examples, not every one of the spokespeople listed here is necessarily articulating their own natural style. Each statement does, nevertheless, define a truth that is emblematic of that style, and in most instances the speaker is a dyed-in-the-wool member of the listed style.

Club Language Style
♣ Stabilizing, order-setting thought

"To persevere in one's duty and be silent is the best answer to calumny."

—*George Washington*

"Law is the witness and external deposit of our moral life. Its history is the history of the moral development of the race."

—*Oliver Wendell Holmes*

"Let all things be done decently and in order."

—*Corinthians 14:40*

"When liberty destroys order, the hunger for order will destroy liberty."

—*Will Durant*

"There is no right to strike against the public safety by anybody, anywhere, anytime."

—*Calvin Coolidge*

"It's the quality of the ordinary, the straight, the square, that accounts for the great stability and success of our nation."

—*Gerald R. Ford*

"The U.S. Senate—an old scow which doesn't move very fast, but never sinks."

—*Everett Dirksen*

"America, do not abandon the great traditions that stretch to the dawn of our history, do not topple the pillars of those beliefs—God, family, honor, duty, country—that have brought us through time and time and time and time again."

—*Bob Dole*

"I really believe my greatest service is in the many unwise steps I prevent."

—*William Lyon Mackenzie King*

"The idea that people can behave naturally, without resorting to an artificial code tacitly agreed upon by their society, is as silly as the idea that they can communicate by a spoken language without commonly accepted semantic and grammatical rules."

—*Judith Martin ("Miss Manners")*

"NO to condom distribution in the schools, NO to taxpayer funding of abortion, NO to sex-education classes in the public schools that promote promiscuity (and) NO to homosexual adoptions and government-sanctioned gay marriages."

—*Christian Coalition*

Spade Language Style
♠ Identifying, analyzing thought

"Executive ability is deciding quickly and getting somebody else to do the work."

—*J. C. Pollard*

"I don't meet the competition. I crush it."

—*Charles Revson*

"Business is a combination of war and sport."

—*André Maurois*

"The heart of a statesman should be in his head."

—*Napoleon Bonaparte*

"Power is the ultimate aphrodisiac."

—*Henry Kissinger*

"Power . . . is not an end in itself, but is an instrument that must be used toward an end."

—*Jeane Kirkpatrick*

"Power can be taken, but not given. The process of the taking is empowerment in itself."

—*Gloria Steinem*

"The great question—which I have not been able to answer, despite my thirty years of research into the feminine soul—is 'What does a woman want?'"

—*Sigmund Freud*

". . . The mind is an attribute of the individual. There is no such thing as a collective brain. There is no such thing as a collective thought. An agreement reached by a group of men is only a compromise or an average drawn upon many individual thoughts."

—*Ayn Rand*

"There is no feeling in this world to be compared to self-reliance."

—*John D. Rockefeller*

"My own mind is my own church."

—*Thomas Paine*

"Reason is also choice."

—*John Milton*

Heart Language Style
♥ Unifying, relational thought

"With malice toward none, with charity for all, with firmness in the right that God gives us to see the right, let us strive on to finish the work we are in, to bind up the nation's wounds."

—*Abraham Lincoln*

"Love thy neighbor as thyself."

—*Matthew 22:39*

"Kindness is the golden chain by which society is bound together."

—*Goethe*

"All our reasoning ends in surrender to feeling."

—*Blaise Pascal*

"The poet's mind is . . . a receptacle for seizing and storing up numberless feelings, phrases, images, which remain there until all the particles which can unite to form a new compound are present together."

—*T. S. Eliot*

"For where your treasure is, there will your heart be also."

—*Matthew 6:21*

"Religion is love; in no case is it logic."

—*Beatrice Potter Webb*

"True prayer is not asking God for love; it is learning to love, and to include all mankind in one affection."

—*Mary Baker Eddy*

"There are many in the world dying for a piece of bread but many more dying for a little love."

—*Mother Teresa*

"Teach us to give and not to count the cost."

—*Ignatius Loyola*

"If you really believe in the brotherhood of man, and you want to come into its fold, you've got to let everyone else in, too."

—*Oscar Hammerstein*

"He who sees diversity and not the unity wanders on from death to death."
—*Brihad-aramyaka Upanishad*

Diamond Language Style

◆ Expanding, conceptualizing thought

"Resistance to tyrants is obedience to God."

—*Benjamin Franklin*

"Liberty is always unfinished business."

—*American Civil Liberties Union*

"I have made my world, and it is a much better world than I saw outside."

—*Louise Nevelson*

"A hunch is creativity trying to tell you something."

—*Frank Capra*

"A work of art is a corner of creation seen through a temperament."

—*Emile Zola*

"I'm not a member of any organized party, I'm a Democrat."

—*Will Rogers*

"You were once wild here. Don't let them tame you!"

—*Isadora Duncan*

"I never saw a wild thing sorry for itself."

—*D. H. Lawrence*

"We live in a rainbow of chaos."

—*Paul Cezanne*

"I've been on a calendar, but never on time."

—*Marilyn Monroe*

"One of the advantages of being disorderly is that one is constantly making exciting discoveries."

—*A. A. Milne*

"Science is an attempt to make the chaotic diversity of our sense-experience correspond to a logically uniform system of thought."

—*Albert Einstein*

"Conception, my boy, fundamental brainwork, is what makes the difference in all art."

—*Dante Gabriel Rossetti*

"No artist is ahead of his time. He is his time. It is just that others are behind the time."

—*Martha Graham*

APPENDIX 3

OTHER PERSONALITY TYPING SYSTEMS

It is said that Alexander the Great classified his generals into four categories, depending on whether they were energetic or lazy, and whether they were intelligent or stupid. He made the intelligent, energetic generals into field officers, to direct the rapidly changing events of the battlefield. The intelligent but lazy ones he made into staff officers, so they could sit back and plan future engagements. He did nothing about the lazy, stupid ones, since they tended to get themselves killed off on the battlefield anyway. But, according to this story, he had the stupid, energetic ones assassinated, so that their bumbling activities on the battlefield would not endanger the entire army!

Although the historical accuracy of Alexander the Great's behavioral-style classifications is uncertain, it does represent the earliest example of personality typing. We do know, however, that early Greek philosophers, including Alexander's own tutor, Aristotle, were aware of differences in temperaments among individuals, and reflected on how such differences come about.

HUMORS

One very old notion found its fullest expression in the writings of the Greek physician Galen, who ministered to Roman emperors in the second century A.D. This was the idea that the body was composed of four fluids—called humors, or biles—each of which was supposed to produce a particular type of temperament when it dominated over the others. The four humors included blood, black bile, yellow bile, and phlegm, and these correspond to the sanguine, melancholic, choleric, and phlegmatic temperaments. A sanguine person is cheerful and energetic, while a melancholic one tends toward depression. A choleric person is peevish and grouchy, while a phlegmatic one is passive and lethargic. The idea of these four constitutional types is related to the ancient, mythical notion that the world is made of four basic elements: earth, air, fire, and water.

The humors theory held considerable sway through the Middle Ages. In modern times the idea of these four basic personalities was favorably reviewed by Wilhelm Wundt, the "father of experimental psychology," and became the basis of a contemporary personality-model developed by the prominent British psychologist Hans Eysenck in 1953. It is also the subject of a recent book, *Galen's Prophecy: Temperament and Human Nature*, written by Harvard psychologist Jerome Kagan.

ENNEAGRAM

A currently fashionable way to categorize personality styles is the Enneagram, which is said by some to have its origins in ancient Babylon. This approach assumes nine basic types, termed the reformer, the helper, the status seeker, the artist, the thinker, the loyalist, the generalist, the leader, and the peacemaker. This system stands on its own, quite independent of other systems. Unlike most ways to categorize human temperament, it tends to emphasize each type's weaknesses over its strengths. For instance, the artist is said to be prone toward depression and self-pity, from which he or she must turn to others for help and emotional support. An artist's salvation is to move away from his intrinsic, introverted self-absorption outward into the objective world, where he can seek purposeful action. While the Enneagram accounts for both introverted and extroverted types, its does not reflect the polar opposition that is embodied in most other personality models.

MEDICINE WHEEL

Most systems for categorizing individual differences seem to have four basic "poles," or types, which combine to yield the rich variety of personal styles encountered each day. Certain Native American traditions have a medicine wheel, oriented to the ordinal points of the compass and at the same time pointing toward four perspectives on the circle of life. These are symbolized by the Buffalo (north), representing cool wisdom; the Mouse (south), portraying innocent trust; the Bear (west), characterized by staying in place; and the Eagle (east), illustrating illumination and vision.

JUNG'S TYPOLOGY

Today, the most widely discussed system of psychological types is one originally suggested by the Swiss psychiatrist Carl Jung in the 1920s. Jung postulated the existence of four basic "functions" of the mind, arranged into two pairs lying at opposite poles from each other. He termed these functions thinking, feeling, sensation, and intuition. Jung believed that while we each posses all of these functions, one of them tends to dominate, while at least one of them, its "opposite," stays undeveloped or even suppressed. The other two remain in limbo to be cultivated in some individuals but not in others. The first of these functions, thinking, is the ability to think in a rational and analytical manner. The feeling function is its opposite. It brings us into empathetic contact with other people, and plays an important role in our appreciation of music, art, and literature. Both thinking and feeling are means by which we come to understand the world around us and our relationships with others. They are opposite in that one emphasizes a clear, rational, and even logical approach, while the other relies on a more subtle, internal sense of value and quality. Though they are opposites, they share the common feature that they both represent ways in which we evaluate knowledge acquired through the senses and intuition. The latter two functions, sensation and intuition, which are themselves opposites, pertain to the ways we comprehend the world around us—whether we understand it either directly and factually through our senses, or by dint of intuition. Let us briefly consider each of the four functions separately in terms of what they mean when each dominates the personality.

A person dominated by the thinking function—a "thinking type"—tends to be logical, systematic, and to make decisions based upon some system of logic or rules worked out ahead of time. They make good theoretical thinkers, but often do not show concern for the uniqueness of other people or situations. A feeling type of person, on the other hand, cares little for logic, but is concerned with values such as beauty, truth, or love. They are likely to be involved with literature, music, or the arts, and while they are usually the most empathetic and compassionate of the four types, they also tend to have strong personal likes and dislikes which others often tire of hearing about. The person dominated by the sensory function tends to be a pleasure-lover. They prefer to live in the present and attend to concrete facts. With a practical frame of mind, these folks have little tolerance for the abstract passions of the intuitive type, who often finds the sensory world of physical interests and practical concerns uninspiring. The latter comprehends the world by their intuition, and is intrigued by opportunities and possibilities. Intuitives tend to be interested in philosophical issues rather than practical affairs.

The system of personal styles defined by the four card suits that is presented in this book owes a debt of gratitude to Jung's theory. Indeed, there are many similarities. For instance, a spade individual clearly uses the thinking function. Likewise, a heart person relies on his or her feeling function. It is less obvious, but on reflection perhaps reasonable, to think of an intuitive person as a diamond, using his or her inner resources of imagination. And club individuals tend to be fact-oriented, like sensory types, with little patience for intuitive obsessions. There are, however, important differences between the two systems. For instance, diamonds are defined by their openness and creative perception, qualities that come naturally to some intuitive types but are not always found in them. Likewise, the conservatism that defines our club type is different from the realism of a sensory, pleasure-seeking type; many sensory types are not conservative at all. And the Jungian feeling type, though very much aware of interpersonal values in the outer world and within themselves, is not necessarily a connecting, relating, heart-styled person.

For the sake of illustration, here's an example that shows how the suit-related personal styles differ from Jung's system. Imagine a man, Ken, who is the personnel director for a medium-sized company. His responsibilities include interviewing new job applicants, planning social activities for the staff, and occasionally dealing with conflicts between coworkers. He is also required to manage the health-insurance programs for the company's employees, a job he sometimes finds difficult, though he has managed to do it successfully for many years. On the weekends Ken sings in a local barbershop quartet. In Jung's system, Ken is a feeling type, as evidenced by his ability to work well with other people and his enjoyment of music. His second-most-developed function turns out to be intuition, a quality that is very helpful in creating social events and mediating personal conflicts between coworkers. Because the Jungian system keys in on his two predominant functions, Ken is defined by feeling and intuition, and his procedural skills, which are displayed in managing the complex insurance policies for the company are disregarded or downplayed. In considering his personal style, however, he would be a heart, with well-developed diamond and club qualities. Ken's competence in handling detailed, routine paperwork (a club skill) is inconsistent with his being labeled a non-sensory type in Jung's system. Our system of personal styles recognizes that Ken's opposing diamond and club secondary processes both function at various times with the primary heart process of relating. Thus, in our four-suit system, a person's style is referenced to their primary process, which by definition also includes associations with each of the secondary processes. The Jungian system correctly identified the importance of Ken's intuitive and feeling functions, which in fact characterize the way he typically experiences himself, but it did not catch the fact that he is also methodical in his approach to life. The latter trait is included in our system of personal styles, which looks at a person's overall pattern of thought and behavior.

We want to emphasize that we are not simply rewriting Jung's ideas into a different format. For example, note that all four personal-styles are unique thinking processes that occur in the brain. The Jungian label of one function as the "thinking" process implies that the others are not thought processes. The personal styles model, on the other hand, emphasizes the idea that all four of the suits are, in fact, defined by their own special cognitive, or thought, processes. Thus, all four types are defined in terms of their cognitive operation.

An essential difference between the personal styles and the Jungian view is that our system recognizes the truth in Jung's ideas, but shifts emphasis away from the internal functions of the personality, moving outward toward a broad sense of the overall style of an individual's thought and behavioral processes in the world. Indeed, though we were familiar with Jung's typology as we developed our own system, our own understanding came primarily from the observation of ourselves and other people. As we became aware of differing language styles, it was possible to identify many personal conflicts as clashes between different kinds of thinking. We could see such clashes occurring in groups of all sizes throughout human society. We noticed that most people tend to fall into one of four categories in terms of their style of thought processes and interaction with others. As we reflected on this and studied alternative systems for classifying personality, such as Jung's typology, we were drawn increasingly to the conclusion that the four personal styles symbolized by the card suits, the spade, heart, diamond, and club, represent a kind of mean, or in Jung's terms, an archetype—a universal pattern of human temperaments. Jung's typology features inner aspects of this pattern, while other systems emphasize other aspects of the pattern, such as creative thinking and problem-solving; or some exhibit a greater concern with the social and interpersonal aspects of personal styles. All seemed to us to be orbiting within the same gravitational field of these four styles, describing them in different ways with different inflections. To this extent, all appear to reflect different hues of the same color-spectrum of human nature. To our own way of thinking, however, none have the clarity and simplicity of the system presented here, which cuts to the core of differences in personal styles of thought, feeling, words, and behavior.

MYERS-BRIGGS TYPE INDICATOR

Over the past few decades the most popular personality test in the world has been the Myers-Briggs Type Indicator (MBTI), developed in the 1950s by American psychologists Isabel Myers and Katherine Briggs. It is an easy-to-use application of Jung's basic ideas concerning the personality types, and it is useful for identifying traits of personality that extend beyond the four suits of personal styles. Many serious Jungians, however, have been less than happy with the Myers-Briggs model. In addition to Jung's original double-axis of "functions" (thinking versus feeling, and sensation versus intuition), the MBTI also takes into account two other polarities, or "attitudes." These attitudes are extroversion versus introversion, and also judging versus perceiving (not part of Jung's original four-way system)—two more sets of opposites. In order to refine the personal styles, we have put aside extroversion-introversion, and focused on the differences in the way people think, which seemed to us to include the latter set of attitudes. Judging appears to be important in describing an ordered, procedural way of thinking (club qualities in our system), and perceiving is descriptive of a more open-minded view (diamond in our system). It is this "judging versus perceiving" axis (which in terms of thinking styles seems to us to parallel the "sensation versus intuition" axis) that often allows the MBTI to encompass the opposing secondary traits seen in the example of Ken. In the Myers-Briggs system, Ken's personality might be typed as a combination of feeling and intuition "functions" along with an "attitude" of judging. Thus, it embodies the mixture of heart, diamond, and club traits.

Both Jung and the MBTI treat the intuitive type as idealistic and abstract, and the sensory type as realistic and concrete. Though these are, indeed, dimensions of personality, they do not necessarily correspond to our thinking styles. For example, a "theoretical" spade might be as abstract and idealistic in the intuitive application of his or her analysis as a heart might be in intuitively developing interior harmonies into works of music. Even a "methodical" club, who is, let's say, an expert in financial reporting, can be quite intuitive about how his reports will turn out. The club's core skill is that of putting financial details in order. Their intuition points to an ability to integrate all of these matters within their mind before they are actually put to work.

The four styles of thinking embodied in our system roughly correspond to these categories in the Myers-Briggs personality typing system:

♠   Cut/*Analyzing*   Myers-Briggs category: *Thinking*   (T)

♥   Connect/*Relating*   Myers-Briggs category: *Feeling*   (F)

♣   Close/*Order-setting*   Myers-Briggs category: *Judging*   (J)

♦   Open/*Conceiving*   Myers-Briggs category: *Perceiving*   (P)

Interestingly, compilations of Myers-Briggs test results show that when rating between just "thinking" and "feeling," roughly 60 percent of men prefer thinking, while 40 percent favor feeling. The reverse is true for women. Roughly 60 percent of women favor feeling and 40 percent prefer thinking. On the other axis, there is no significant difference in the way the sexes rate "judging" and "perceiving." Men and women are equally as likely to favor either of these two modes.

The MBTI method selects from opposing sets of traits in each of the four pairs of opposites that it tests. Our four-suit system uses only two of these sets of opposites, as listed above. For comparison, a feeling/judging (or FJ) type in the Myers-Briggs roughly equates to a preference for heart and club processes; a feeling/perceiving (or FP) type corresponds to favoring heart and diamond processes, and so it goes with various combinations of two styles around all four sides of our square. Each of the Myers-Briggs personality types has traits something like those represented by a single side of our boxing ring.

When the accumulated data on MBTI test results are grouped into four categories which combine two neighboring thinking processes—TJ, TP, FP, and FJ—there is a relatively even distribution of the population around all four sides. When psychologists David Keirsey and Marilyn Bates studied married couples in the 1970s using the MBTI method, their book included data on percentages of the population per type that, when aggregated into TJs, TPs, FPs, and FJs, showed an equal 25 percent of the population on each of the four sides.

LINKING AREAS OF THE BRAIN TO
TYPES OF THINKING

Many recent approaches to personality classification—at least in the popular press—have, one way or another, relied on brain research as either a cornerstone or a justification for their validity. Indeed, since the late 1960s, advances in the study of the brain have made it an irresistible inkblot on which to project all kinds of ideas about human nature and the mind. Some of these ideas are very useful and creative, and some are not. From our point of view, the most fascinating thing about all this material is the extent to which writers have used the complex and indefinite facts of brain research to find their way back to the wide gravitational field of the basic four-part system of personality styles with which we are already familiar.

Certain general observations about the brain seem to be well established, however, and worth mentioning. These include the fact that the frontal portions of the brain—the frontal lobes—are more involved with thought, planning and organizing actions, decision-making, and the regulation of attention, than are the rear portions. The latter, speaking very generally, are involved in sensory processing, especially visual sensation and perception. Also, the left side of the brain, at least in the majority of individuals, both right- and left-handed, seems most involved with language and analytic thought in general, while the right side seems more involved with conceptual-ization, holistic thought, gesture, and expression. Beyond this, it seems clear that the cortex—the highest, and evolutionarily the most recent, portion of the brain—is the center of consciousness and thinking, while a complex set of structures in the core of the brain, termed the "limbic system," is essential to emotion—though emotion is probably experienced in the cortex and not the limbic system.

The exceptions to these generalizations are too numerous to mention, but the overall picture invites speculation as to whether different individuals use different parts of their brains more inten-sively than other parts. Indeed, the idea has a certain obvious truth to it. For example, imaginative thinking must make heavy use of the right side of the brain, and linguistic thinking must make use of the left side. Whether anything is added to this by saying that I have a bias for my right brain over my left, however, is more questionable, unless I simply mean that I prefer imaginative to analytic thinking. These reservations in mind, let us proceed to another system of styles that has received attention in recent years.

During the 1970s and 1980s, Ned Herrmann, an independent management consultant, conceived four different thinking styles based on the notion that these were related to four different regions of the brain. His model emphasized the differences between the left and right hemispheres of the cortex, and between the cortex and the limbic system. Thus, he highlighted distinctions that were under intense discussion during those years in which he was developing his theory. Herrmann, however, did not rely on speculation alone, but backed up his theory with a considerable amount of behavioral research conducted in management seminars and elsewhere. The result was a four-part organization that he calls his Whole Brain Model, which is similar to our own system, but focuses on thinking and problem-solving. His interest in problem-solving comes from his involvement with management groups working on solutions to problems in their organizations.

Because there is still much about the operation of the brain that we don't know yet, any model of temperament or personality that assigns types of thinking to specific regions of the brain—and especially with regard to the limbic system, as does Herrmann's model—remains open to question. Nonetheless, his questionnaires, collected from many people over several decades, have accumulated an impressive body of evidence concerning the distribution of thinking styles among the population. Assigning people to four broad categories, which Herrmann terms analyzers, organizers, visualizers, and personalizers based on their patterns of preference for four different kinds of thinking, he amassed thousands of test results which indicate that all four types are about equally represented. This equal representation includes both men and women. His findings suggest, however, that men are slightly more biased to the analyzing mode, while women tend toward personalizing. This corroborates the finding from the Myers-Briggs Test data and the Keirsey-Bates application of it, as mentioned earlier.

ADDITIONAL PERSONALITY TYPING SYSTEMS

In addition to Herrmann's work, there are many other four-way models in common use by management and human-development consultants. A typical example is the Learning Style Inventory, developed in the 1970s by David Kolb. It classifies people in terms of four preferred learning styles: concrete experience, reflective observation, abstract conceptualization, and active experimentation. From this, each person is assigned one of four types, including the diverger, converger, accommodator, and assimilator classifications that are reminiscent of diamonds, spades, hearts, and clubs.

Many other systems are available in popular books, with variations on the familiar basic types. It is not our purpose to review these in detail here, but we invite you to explore them as your curiosity dictates. It is our experience that the many facets of human nature that are depicted by these various typologies are a fascinating source of insight.

CITATIONS TO SYSTEMS REFERENCED ABOVE:

Hans Eysenck, *The Structure of Personality*. London: Methuen, 1953.

Ned Herrmann, *The Whole Brain Business Book*. New York: McGraw-Hill, 1996.

Carl G. Jung, *Psychological Types. Collected Works (Vol. 6)*. Princeton, NJ: Princeton University Press, 1971. (Original work published 1921.)

Jerome Kagan, *Galen's Prophecy: Temperament and Human Nature*. New York: Basic Books, 1994.

David Keirsey and Marilyn Bates, *Please Understand Me*. Del Mar, CA: Prometheus Nemesis Book Co., 1978.

Isabel Myers and Paul Myers, *Gifts Differing: Understanding Personality Type*. Palo Alto, CA: Davies-Black Publishing, 1980.

D. R. Riso, *Personality Types: Using the Enneagram for Self-Discovery*. Boston, MA: Houghton Mifflin, 1987.

NOTES AND
QUOTATION SOURCES

Chapter 2: Your Personal Style

1. From a Martha Stewart Enterprises document published in the *New York Observer,* February 6, 1995. Quoted in Jerry Oppenheimer's book, *Just Desserts* (Martha Stewart, The Unauthorized Biography). New York: William Morrow and Co., 1997, p. 362.

2. "Oprah: A Heavenly Body?" *U.S. News & World Report,* March 31, 1997, p. 18.

3. William J. Bennett, *The Death of Outrage.* New York: The Free Press div. of Simon & Schuster, 1998, p. 9.

4. See appendix 3 for the research findings that suggest the generally equal distribution of thinking styles among both sexes and between the population as a whole.

5. Note also that the card suit symbols visually oppose each other, as do the contrasting types of thinking processes. The spade is the heart shape turned upside down and opposite in color, just as the "cutting" process of analyzing opposes the "connecting" process of relating. Similarly, we might think of the "open", conceiving diamond as the "closed", order-setting club turned inside out. When the suits of the thinking processes are arranged as in figure 2.4, they can be

combined with each other from corner to corner of the square. But diagonally they are opposites and mutually exclusive. In much the same way, each symbol relates to its neighboring symbols in the diagram. The spade has a point on top (like the diamond) and a stem (like the club). So it goes around the square with each symbol's points, rounded tops, or stems embodying either the top or bottom of its adjacent symbols.

6. In the descriptions of the four styles, you'll find career specialties associated with each of them. This is not to say that people in these fields exhibit only this way of thinking, or even that the jobs listed under each personal style are the best ones for people of that style. They are included here mainly as a means of describing the styles. Indeed, in any career field it can be beneficial to include people with different styles in order to round out that group's typical pattern of thinking.

7. The four styles of thought processes—*analyzing, relating, order-setting, and conceiving*—correspond very roughly to the widely used Myers-Briggs personality types as listed below. These, in turn, were conceptually derived from the theories of psychiatrist Carl Jung, as discussed in appendix 3.

♠	Cut/*Analyzing*	Myers-Briggs category: *Thinking*	(T)
♥	Connect/*Relating*	Myers-Briggs category: *Feeling*	(F)
♣	Close/*Order-setting*	Myers-Briggs category: *Judging*	(J)
♦	Open/*Conceiving*	Myers-Briggs category: *Perceiving*	(P)

Neither the personal styles represented by the card suits, nor any pairs of suits, are simple derivations of the Myers-Briggs typology, or of Carl Jung's original four character types, for that matter. Both of the latter systems, and especially the Jungian one, are directed toward one's psychological disposition. They are rich frameworks for inner exploration, and for understanding how we differ in terms of our thoughts and emotions. The system presented in this book, however, is based on observing how people interact with each other, how they comport themselves in groups and social institutions such as businesses, churches, schools, and government, and how they address themselves to the many creations of culture such as law, literature, religion, art, and science. Historically, this approach owes much to Kurt Levine's field theory, in which each individual is understood in the living context of a "life field" defined by family, profession, and significant social groups, as well as their long range goals and aspirations. It is becoming increasingly apparent that any view of human nature which does not take into account the larger context of a person's life and ongoing exchanges with the social and cultural environment, is doomed to fail in the long run.

Keeping the above in mind, do not be too surprised if you find yourself in a different position in the system of personal styles than you might have expected based on previous use of Myers-Briggs or Jungian typology. It is most likely, however, that you will not be too far off. You might, like one of the authors, be a strong feeling/intuition type on the Myers-Briggs, but here display a diamond style, reaching out toward both spade and heart.

Chapter 3: Boxing in the Palace

1. Jonathan Dimbleby, *The Prince of Wales.* New York: William Morrow and Co., 1994, p. 297.

2. Dimbleby, p. 356.

3. Basil Boothroyd, *Prince Philip: An Informal Biography.* New York: The McCall Publishing Co., 1971, p. 203.

4. Dimbleby, p. 157, quoting Prince Charles.

5. Dimbleby, p. 266.

6. Prince Charles, in a speech in 1987. Excerpted in *The Windsors—A Royal Family, Part II: Family Affairs,* produced and directed by Annie Fienburgh, Boston, MA. A WGBH/Brook Associates Coproduction for PBS-TV, 1994.

Chapter 4: Language Styles

1. Answers for identifying words with the four language styles:

   a. Heart language (Relating)

   b. Spade language (Analyzing)

   c. Club language (Order-setting)

   d. Diamond language (Conceiving)

2. Each of the two quotation sets includes phrases from various occasions by Hillary Rodham Clinton (Quotation Set 1) and Bill Clinton (Quotation Set 2). The first set of quotes is from the book *The Unique Voice of Hillary Rodham Clinton*, edited by Claire G. Osborne. (New York: Avon Books, 1997, pp. 67, 81, and 77.) The second set of quotes, from Bill Clinton, are from *(a)* his news conference of April 18, 1995; *(b)* the book *The Seduction of Hillary Rodham*, by David Brock (New York: Free Press Paperbacks, 1996, p. 70); and *(c)* his 1993 inaugural address.

3. Bob Dole, in a campaign speech, March 19, 1996.

4. Bob Dole, interviewed by Jim Lehrer on the PBS-TV show *The News Hour*, April 19, 1996.

5. Dr. Leslie Gelb, president of the U.S. Council on Foreign Relations, speaking at the Freedom House–sponsored "Clinton Foreign Policy Mid-Term Review" held in Washington, D.C., and broadcast on C-SPAN2, October 20, 1994.

6. Sam Keen, *Fire in the Belly*. New York: Bantam Books, 1991, p. 171.

7. Joseph Campbell, interviewed in the PBS-TV series *The Power of Myth,* with Bill Moyers, Program 6. A production of Apostrophe S Productions, Inc., in association with Alvin H. Perlmutter, Inc., and Public Affairs Television, Inc., 1988.

8. The Reverend John Myers, Bishop of Peoria, on the TV program *Adam and Eve,* broadcast on the EWTN Catholic Network, October 18, 1994.

9. Donald Trump, *TRUMP—The Art of the Deal.* New York: Random House, 1987, pp. 3, 32, 33, and 35.

Chapter 5: Understanding the Language Styles of People in Your Life
1. Answers for identifying the language styles in ten examples:

1. Spade language (Analyzing). First, decide, goals, critical.

2. Heart language (Relating). We, band together, care, common, people.

3. Club language (Order-setting). Should, safe, check, sure, legitimate.

4. Diamond language (Conceiving). Idea, explore, hunch, forget costs, outside the lines.

5. Club language (Order-setting). Schedule, keep, order.

6. Diamond language (Conceiving). Spontaneous, open, spur of the moment.

7. Heart language (Relating). We, commune, talk, bond.

8. Spade language (Analyzing). Break, I want, alone, make the cut.

9. Club language (Order-setting). Won't take flyer, won't bet ranch (risk), foolish scheme.

10. Diamond language (Conceiving). Fun, follow where it goes, discover.

Chapter 6: Seeking Completion in Another Person
1. M. Scott Peck, M.D., *The Road Less Traveled*. New York: Simon &
Schuster, A Touchstone Book, 1978, p. 88.

Chapter 7: It's a Battle of Styles, Not Sexes
1. This refers to the symbolic treatment of the sexes in John Gray's
Men Are from Mars, Women Are from Venus. New York: HarperCollins,
1992.

2. David Keirsey and Marilyn Bates, *Please Understand Me*. Del Mar,
CA: Prometheus Nemesis Book Co., 1978, p. 20.

3. There are actually more than sixteen types when you include gay
and lesbian bonds among members of the same sex; relationships of
people who don't fit the normal pattern of one dominant style with
two secondary modes (which we portrayed with the two-armed
boxer image); and so on. Indeed, all of these, as well as all sixteen
types, are worthy of individual case studies in and of themselves. It
is not our intent to make less of those relationships which are
included here only by way of reference, but to delve into them all
would deter our primary goal of showing how style differences are
prevalent throughout human society.

4. Note how these issues between the diamond woman and the heart
man match those that plagued Diana and Charles. Their problems
make much more sense when you understand how neighboring
styles interact. Study Jay and Harriet and you'll find there the same
core discord that troubled Charles and Diana. In neither instance is
the problem about money, or social events, or work. It is really about
a negotiation of who claims which styles.

Chapter 8: Shifting Gears to Resolve Couple Conflicts
1. Even though our civilization has developed words to describe a
variety of behaviors and ways of thinking, this certainly does not
mean that everyone who uses the words has full familiarity with the

kinds of processes involved. We can see a TV show or read about a doctor performing an operation and not really know how to do one ourselves. Likewise, people can think that they know about spirituality, creative impulses, or deep love, but may not truly understand them until they've experienced and practiced these states of mind.

Chapter 9: Is Your Family Feud a Question of Style?
1. For a whole psychology on this matter, see the widely respected work of Erik Erikson: E. H. Erikson, *Childhood and Society*. New York: W. W. Norton & Co., 2nd Ed., 1960.

Chapter 10: Coping with Children's Evolving Styles
1. Research suggests that women have more flexible and integrated thinking patterns across many regions of their brains than do men, who show more specialized thinking patterns. For more information on this topic, see the following references.

Anne Moir and David Jessel, *Brain Sex: The Real Difference Between Men and Women*. NY: Dell Books, 1993.

Simon Levay, *The Sexual Brain*. Cambridge, MA: MIT Press, 1993.

Chapter 11: "Do It My Way"
1. In 1988, Dr. Deming defined four broad principles that summarized what he meant by the term "profound knowledge":

1. *Appreciation for a system*: See the business as a network of people working together toward a common aim.

2. *Theory of variation*: Use statistical analysis to identify the causes of deficient quality and define solutions.

3. *Theory of knowledge*: There's no true value to anything. Change the procedure and you get a new number. Knowledge is based on prediction.

4. *Psychology*: People are born with a need for relationships and have a natural inclination to be innovative. They have a right to enjoy their work. This enjoyment is eroded by rankings, ratings, personnel appraisals, etc., which set up competition.

(Summarized from Lloyd Dobyns and Clare Crawford-Mason's book *Quality or Else*. [Boston, MA: Houghton Mifflin, 1991, pp. 59–62.])

2. Dobyns and Crawford-Mason, p. 100.

3. We do not mean to imply that the existing Total Quality Management programs were specifically designed to balance the four thinking styles, because TQM certainly was not founded on knowledge of these different types of thinking. But without even knowing it, TQM seems to promote an inclusiveness of all skills and interests that corresponds to the idea of incorporating all styles.

INDEX

ABOUT THE AUTHORS

Mike Was is a writer and founder of The Paradox Group, which helps business teams and other groups benefit from the validation of people's different styles of thinking. He created a board game to teach the understanding of personal styles and is currently investigating the rates of heart disease associated with various thinking styles. His wide-ranging career has also included entrepreneurial co-ownership of a building company; an architectural practice; twelve years of planning, marketing, and corporate management for a new town in Virginia; and teaching community development at Arizona State University. Mike lives in southern California.

Allan Combs, Ph.D., is a psychologist and systems theorist at the University of North Carolina at Asheville and the Saybrook Institute in San Francisco. Author of over fifty articles, chapters, and books on the mind and the brain, he co-founded The Society for Chaos Theory in Psychology and is a member of The General Evolution Research Group. His books include *Synchronicity: Science, Myth, and the Trickster* (with Mark Holland) and *The Radiance of Being: Complexity, Chaos, and the Evolution of Consciousness*, winner of the 1995 Best Book Prize of the British Scientific and Medical Network. He has chaired several organizations, including a university department of psychology, a twelve-community mental-health-center board, and the Western North Carolina Psychological Association.

Julie Navin Combs has pursued careers in engineering, psychology, and administration. Currently she owns a consulting firm, Adaptations, Inc., which provides custom designs for adaptive equipment for severely disabled persons, as well as guidance to businesses, governmental agencies, and individuals on the Americans with Disabilities Act. She holds degrees in psychology and mechanical engineering.

WESTHILL
LIBRARY

WESTFIELD PUBLIC LIBRARY

7 8292 000155367

155.264
Was, Mike
Finding your strong suit:
how to read your spouse,
boss, partner

Discarded by
Westfield Washington
Public Library

WESTFIELD PUBLIC LIBRARY
333 West Hoover Street
Westfield, IN 46074

WESTFIELD PUBLIC LIBRARY
333 W. HOOVER ST.
WESTFIELD, IN 46074

DEMCO